Mary Barnard

2212   E.   Street

Vancouver

Washington

U.S. America

EZRA POUND
VIA MARSALA 12-5
RAPALLO
ANNO XII

W. C. WILLIAMS. M. D.
9 RIDGE ROAD
RUTHERFORD, NEW JERSEY

Bill

Assault on Mount Helicon

BY THE SAME AUTHOR:

"Cool Country," in *Five Young
    American Poets*, 1940
A Few Poems, 1952
Sappho: A New Translation, 1958
The Mythmakers, 1966
Collected Poems, 1979

Mary Barnard

Assault on Mount Helicon

A Literary Memoir

UNIVERSITY OF CALIFORNIA PRESS
Berkeley / Los Angeles / London

University of California Press
Berkeley and Los Angeles, California

University of California Press, Ltd.
London, England

Certain portions of this book were previously published in
slightly different form in *The Iowa Review* 13 (Winter 1982)
and *William Carlos Williams: Man and Poet*, ed. Carroll F.
Terrell (Orono, Me.: National Poetry Foundation, 1983).

Library of Congress Cataloging in Publication Data

Barnard, Mary.
    Assault on Mount Helicon.

    Includes index.
    1. Barnard, Mary—Biography.   2. Poets, American—
20th century—Biography.   I. Title.
PS3503.A5825Z463   1984   811'.54   83-6887
ISBN 0-520-04818-0

This book is dedicated

To my Young Friends,
    Fledglings
in the Forests of Helicon

"You hate translation???
What of it?? Expect to be
carried up Mt. Helicon
in an easy chair?"

E. P. TO M. B.

JANUARY 22, 1934

Contents

List of Illustrations

FACSIMILES IN TEXT

Acknowledgments

GRATEFUL acknowledgment is made to the following for permission to quote previously published material:

To James Laughlin and New Directions and to Faber and Faber Ltd, London, for quotations from *The Selected Letters of Ezra Pound* (Copyright 1950 by Ezra Pound); also for five lines of poetry from *Personae* (Copyright 1926 by Ezra Pound), published in Great Britain as *Collected Shorter Poems*, by Ezra Pound.

To Philip Purser for quotations from his book, *Where Is He Now? The Extraordinary Worlds of Edward James* (London: Quartet Books, 1978).

To John Murray (Publishers) Ltd. for eight lines quoted from John Betjeman's *Summoned by Bells* (London: John Murray, 1960).

To Eudora Welty for permission to quote from the Preface to her *Collected Stories* (New York: Harcourt Brace Jovanovich, 1980).

To the estate of Marion Morehouse Cummings for permission to reprint the text by E. E. Cummings accompanying the photograph of Marianne Moore by Marion Morehouse, both the text and the photograph from *Adventures in Value: Fifty Photographs by Marion Morehouse* (New York: Harcourt, Brace and World, 1962).

Acknowledgment is also made to James Laughlin, to John H. Edwards, and to Edward James for permission to quote from their personal letters, unpublished.

In addition I wish to express my thanks to Patricia and Ruth Stephens for their painstaking labor in typing the manuscript, especially the Ezra Pound letters; to Hermine Duthie Decker for copying the faded photographs; and to August Frugé for his gentle insistence on the inclusion of quite a lot of material I had omitted.

Foreword

A MEMOIR has never been on my list of Things
to Be Done or Books to Be Written. Now, at age seventy, I am
changing my mind, as the world I lived much of my life in is
disappearing, and many of the people I knew are disappearing
also, not so much into the grave, which would be only natural,
but into unwieldy tomes written by people who never knew
them.

I can still think of a number of reasons against writing such
a book as this:

First, a life singularly lacking in dramatic incident.

Second, a reluctance to set forth the dramatic details of
other, more interesting lives in order to satisfy a public (and
editorial) craving for gossip.

Third, an absence of the urge to confess, which seems to
impel so many writers of reminiscences.

Fourth, no feeling that I need to justify my actions, or my
inaction.

Fifth, a conviction that lyric poems should be able to float free of biographical anecdote or footnotes, so that the reader may appropriate them as an expression of his own experience, observation, or emotion, or at least as an extension of his own experience, not the writer's.

The affirmative reason that I weigh in the scales against all these reasons for keeping silent is the hope of writing a useful book. I do not mean a book useful to scholars who might be able to establish a date or identify a would-be poet in a walk-on part, but useful to young writers who read literary biography or autobiography much as a young explorer whose goal was the South Pole might read journals of Scott's or Shackleton's expeditions. The magnitude of the success or the fact of the failure is of less interest than the day-to-day account of what happened: the equipment, the rations, the precautions, the errors and accidents. I once read in this way myself, and I think young writers must still be doing so, judging by the questions they bring me.

With this purpose in mind I originally thought of beginning with my first letters from Ezra Pound and William Carlos Williams and my first publication, but on second thought I realized that the reader needed to know where I started from and how I got to what proved to be my taking-off point. I am therefore beginning with a bit about my grandparents, more about my parents, and still more about my education. Along the way there will be non-literary digressions, but on the whole the narrative will deal with a feminine climber's determined and sometimes partially successful assault on Mount Helicon: There be Griffons.

Chapter 1

DURING THE last years of my grandmother's life we could always quiet her restlessness by placing a book in her hands, although she had long ago lost the ability to read or even to recognize her family. She would sit in the rocker by her bedroom window, rocking contentedly and occasionally following a line of print with her forefinger. It broke my heart. Sometimes I thought that the unslaked thirst for books of my female forebears had culminated in my own passionate reading and singleminded desire to write books as well as read them.

Perhaps I exaggerate, but I know that this grandmother had had only six months of schooling in her entire life, and that the only book the school boasted was the Bible. This would have been in Indiana perhaps about 1850. By the time the Civil War broke out she was working as a hired girl on a farm, cooking for harvesters. Her parents were presumably literate, since they named her Melissa for the heroine of a popular novel of that day—*Alonzo and Melissa*. I still have their copy of the book. In her old age she read most of the time, though slowly and painfully. I doubt that she scaled any greater heights than *The Enchanted April*, which I remember giving her one Christmas.

My father fared a little better than his mother, since he went through most of eight grades in a one-room country school. I say "most" because he said not long before his death that he never did have fractions because they always did fractions in the spring, and he was always plowing—that was from age twelve. I forget what it was that he missed every fall when he was harvesting. Until recently I had his eighth-grade reader: "Snowbound," "The Great Stone Face," "Evangeline." You could do worse. As soon as he could escape from the farm he completed his education in Indianapolis by attending business college and the theater, which at that time was probably as good as it has ever been in the American provinces.

On my mother's side of the family things were a little better. *That* grandmother, who was said to be bright in her books, was teaching school at age sixteen. I believe it was called an infant school, and I know she was paid in kind. This was in Boone County, Kentucky. If she craved books, she did not crave them long, because she and her husband both died young, leaving my mother an orphan at age three. What kind of education the young husband had, I can only guess. The family lived on Mud Lick Creek in Boone County, and my great-grandmother Johnson considered them shiftless. I have two of his silk handkerchiefs, but no book. He may not have had one, though I doubt that he was illiterate.

My mother was probably the first in the family in either line to attend high school or its equivalent—not a young ladies' seminary, but a Baptist orphans' boarding school which eventually became Midway Junior College. She said one day, while writing a check for Midway, that she owed the school a great debt, because the teachers (who seem to have been excellent—a pair of sisters) saw to it that she learned shorthand, typing, and bookkeeping, and with these skills she was able to leave her grandmother's home and go to Greenfield, Indiana, to work. It was there that she met my father. That boarding school gave her a good grounding in what we now call the basics. Her grammar, whether she was speaking or writing, was irreproachable, unlike my father's, which was decidedly shaky in spots. It is

2

noteworthy that I never in my life heard her correct him. I took my cue from her, and I never corrected him, either.

There they both were, then, in Greenfield in 1905 when they met at a picnic on Blue River and shared a feast of fresh-caught frog legs.

Now Greenfield had a claim to be considered a kind of cultural center. It was the hometown of James Whitcomb Riley, and Riley was at the height of his fame. It is true that during the year 1907, when my parents were courting and marrying, Ezra Pound, who was to prove to be more my dish of tea than Riley, was undergoing a special purgatory not far away at Wabash College. His experience in that cultural wasteland (as he saw it) drove him from the country. I never thought to ask him whether he had ever read any Riley. It seems strange to mention them in the same breath, yet I think that Riley may have helped to bring me to Brunnenburg castle, where I am beginning this book with the Pound Room one floor below, and the patter of his great-grandson's feet overhead.

For one thing, I have always wondered whether the pride Greenfield took in its only famous son did not do something—perhaps not much, but *something*—to exalt the word "poet" in my parents' minds, and lead them to take more pride in their fledgling than might have been expected. Perhaps my poet friends have exaggerated, but according to their stories, their parents' attitude was always, "Why can't you cut out this nonsense and do something *practical*?" I had only encouragement, especially for the poetry.

For another thing, Riley's *Child Rhymes* were humming in my head from my earliest years. I knew "The Runaway Boy" and others by heart before I could read. Perhaps this was not the best possible influence, but I don't think it did any harm, and of course I had Stevenson, too. The Stevenson rhymes especially appealed to me because I was also a lonely child, and I knew the Land of Counterpane only too well, but Riley's were funnier, and I loved the dialect. Besides, Riley, unlike other authors of books, was a person to me. My mother had worked briefly for his brother, and her Greenfield great-uncle had gone to school with Riley. The place names in his poems were part of my family history.

Two years to the day after my parents met, they were married in Walton, Kentucky. They settled down at once in a rented house in Greenfield, with their new furniture, and their friends around them. Less than six months later they sold their furniture, purchased one-way homesteaders' tickets, and boarded a train for Portland, Oregon, where they knew nobody. They had not so much as a letter of introduction.

My family seems always to have had its fair share of the restlessness that is part of the American inheritance. My mother's people began to arrive in Virginia in the 17th century and gradually pushed westward until by about 1800 most of them were already in Kentucky. My maternal grandparents had moved on to Florida as soon as they were married, and my mother was born there. My father's people came from North Carolina to Indiana in time for my grandfather to be born a Hoosier in 1835. Earlier the Barnards may have come to North Carolina from Nantucket, but I have never tried to trace that journey. Perhaps my parents inherited a certain restlessness, but they were given a push by my father's employer, who saw fit to reduce his salary as soon as he was safely married and settled down. They chose Portland because my father wanted to work in the lumber industry, and my mother wanted to "really go some place," as she said, "not just move over into Kansas." She had no immediate family to leave, and was ready to go to the end of the world with her husband, the farther away the better. The Lewis and Clark Exposition of 1905 had helped to make Middle Westerners aware of Portland's possibilities, and may have influenced my father's choice of Portland as a destination rather than Seattle.

It was a bold move, and a rasher act than they realized it would be. As they traveled westward into the Rockies (the first mountains either of them had ever seen) the Panic of 1907 swept across the country. Banks were closing, money was short, and jobs were scarce. They arrived in Portland in November. My reader will not be surprised to learn that it was raining and continued to rain steadily. They were in one of the little rooms at the top of the old Portland Hotel, where my tall father was continually knocking his head against the sloping ceiling. Things must have looked bleak, but my parents were young and very much in love, and my father, besides, was an incurable optimist. He remained one to the end of his life.

At that time the Masons were a powerful organization, and my father was a Mason. He found that the head of the Masonic Order in Portland was Mr. Henry L. Pittock, who was among other things owner of the *Portland Oregonian* and a partner in the Pittock and Leadbetter Lumber Company. My father accordingly made an appointment to see Mr. Pittock, who recommended that he apply at the Pittock and Leadbetter mill in Vancouver, Washington, where there would soon be a vacancy in the office staff. He applied, was hired, and they moved across the river to a rooming house near Esther Short Park in Vancouver.

Greenfield, if it was not a cultural paradise, was at least a pleasant, quiet town with tree-shaded streets and substantial houses. Vancouver, in those years, was a frontier town. East of Main Street lay Vancouver Barracks, a venerable army post which had succeeded the Hudson's Bay Trading Post on the same site; and to the west, where a railroad bridge was being built across the Columbia, there stood at least one large sawmill. Main Street itself was planked. According to my mother's count there were thirteen blocks of paved sidewalk in Vancouver when they arrived, and thirty-three saloons. For her, the first months of 1908, while they were still in the rooming house, were sufficiently grim. She told me how she looked from her window one bright spring day and was astonished to see a number of women in pretty dresses emerge from a house across the street and cross the lawn to disappear into a house next door. She could not imagine where all those nice-looking women could have come from. Was it possible that they actually lived in Vancouver? But where? Later she learned that the party she had observed was an annual affair. Two ladies who lived next door to each other entertained their friends with luncheon at one house and a card party at the other. "And the *next* year," my mother said with satisfaction, "I was invited."

By that time they had moved into the house on 11th Street where I was born. Also, by that time she had a number of young women friends who called on her and each other, wearing, of course, hats and gloves, and carrying calling cards. Soon most of them were pushing prams. They took china-painting lessons, did all kinds of needle work, and made clothes for themselves and their children. They did their own laundry without benefit of any electric appliances except, perhaps, an iron. They cleaned without vacuum cleaners. They canned and they cooked and they got up picnics for the children.

After I arrived my parents built the house on E Street that was to be their home for most of the next forty-five years. However, my father's work for Pittock and Leadbetter ended when the mill burned, and we made a temporary move to Buxton, Oregon, in 1914. My own memories really begin with Buxton. I was four and a half when we moved there.

2

Vancouver was the Paris of the West compared with Buxton, which was hardly more than a clearing in the Coast Range forest. To get there we took an interurban electric train that ran through Hillsboro and Forest Grove. Somewhere (at Forest Grove or Banks or Manning) we changed to a little gasoline-powered car with curious round windows. It was known locally as the Skunk. I forget whether Buxton was at the end of the line, or whether the Skunk continued as far as Timber, which was the last outpost. I, at any rate, never went beyond Buxton.

The village consisted of a general store, a meat market, a saloon, a one-room school, and two little churches, one Protestant (I believe it was supported by Presbyterian mission funds) and one Catholic. The minister and priest were itinerant. Buxton's only doctor was a known alcoholic. The village itself was supported by two sawmills, including their logging operations, and a few farm families, mainly Swedish and German. My father was manager of one of the sawmills.

Our house stood on the brow of a hill above the railroad station and looked across a cultivated valley to wooded hills on the other side. It was a ten-room house with a large porch and a lean-to in the back. Once it had had a prime coat of paint now much worn off. The porch pillars were cracking. The last time I saw the house, it looked better than it did when we lived there. There was, of course, no gas or electricity, and the only plumbing was a faucet (instead of a pump) at the kitchen sink, the only running water in town.

The house stood on several acres of cleared land including the hill running down to the tracks. There were no trees except two or three stunted firs by the gate. The men who cleared a living space in those dense fir forests were bent on getting rid of trees, not planting them. The expanse of yard was surrounded by a wire fence to keep the straying cows out, but they learned to open the gate. Although the ground was covered with more weeds than grass, it was relatively level and served as a croquet ground. I had a swing on the porch, and a young shepherd collie for company. I had several playmates including a little English girl named Lucy and a little Swedish boy named Freddy. Freddy was ambitious. After finishing grade school at Buxton, he managed to get to high school, then to college, and eventually he became a vice president of one of Portland's largest banks. At his place we played in a quick, shallow creek, and in the flume that came down from the mill.

The mill was about one mile from the village, deeper into the hills. The farms that Lucy and Freddy lived on lay between. The logging was done with the help of a donkey engine. The logs were dumped into a log pond and pulled out as needed to enter the mill on a conveyor. The finished lumber floated down to the railroad in a V-shaped flume containing a swift flow of water. The flume extended for a mile down the hill to the loading dock, where my father had his office. When the whistle blew at quitting time, the men liked to jump on one of the last planks to leave the mill and ride it into town. That must have been a fine, smooth ride, part of it high in the air as the flume strode on stilts across the valley.

Today, of course, caterpillar tractors are usually used instead of the donkey engine, and logging trucks would do the work of the flume. Recently, hearing Gary Snyder read his poetry to a college audience, I was amused at a reference to his brief career as whistle-punk. It struck me that he and I were probably the only people there who knew what a whistle-punk was, although they are not yet a totally extinct species. Log ponds, too, are a rarity now, because heavy equipment can handle even Douglas fir and Ponderosa pine logs on the ground.

The slab wood that was first trimmed from the log was useless. There was no market for it whatever. Accordingly, the slab fires burned continually near every sawmill. (And my grandmother remembered seeing whole walnut trees piled up and burned—alive, as it were—when Indiana was being cleared for cultivation.)

On the whole, I think I enjoyed the part of my childhood that I spent at Buxton, yet it was certainly there that I first became aware of fear. I was never afraid of going to bed in the half-furnished upstairs, and being left alone there in the dark. It had not even occurred to me that there was anything to be afraid of. My mother thought it was sinful to scare children with bogey-men. When I say that I became aware of fear, I do not mean that I was afraid for myself. It was rather that I became aware of menacing forces out there beyond my parents' control.

In part this may have been contagion. I sensed my mother's fear, because she was never at ease in Buxton. She liked and respected Freddy's parents and some of the other farmers, but most mill hands and loggers then were floaters, not, in her view, to be trusted. When my father had to go to Portland, as he often did on week-ends, we went with him and stayed at the Imperial Hotel. My mother was not bold enough to stay alone with me in that big house, isolated in its big yard above the railroad tracks.

She was not only afraid for herself, she was afraid for my father. Our years in Buxton were those of World War I when the Wobblies were on the march. I am sure that there was never a strike at the Buxton mill, but there was some sabotage and a general feeling of unrest. The only time I know of when my father was threatened with physical harm was one night when a mill hand, possibly drunk and certainly on the warpath, came to the house and threatened him. I was in the living room with my mother, who was terrified; we kept very still, listening to my father's calm voice on the porch as he gradually persuaded the man to quiet down and go away.

Another time I was awakened in the middle of the night by

my parents' voices coming from one of the unfurnished rooms near mine. Alarmed to hear them up at that hour of the night, and in that room, I went to investigate and found them watching a red glow in the night sky. It was a forest fire. If I remember correctly, we had three forest fires while we lived at Buxton. A fire in a virgin growth of Douglas fir is like a fire-storm. The green tops, one hundred or more feet in the air, explode with a sound almost like a cannon shot. The boughs go up in an instant, leaving a tall, slender, completely naked snag to smoulder for perhaps weeks. The desolation afterwards is indescribable.

In this case the fire was probably arson, set by a disgruntled workman. The mill had been forced to shut down temporarily the day before. This meant that there was no crew to fight the fire. They had left for town. Somehow a crew was collected, but the cook had also left, and my mother had to leave me with another family while she went out to the mill and cooked for the firefighters. One night my father sent her home, saying that the men were so far away that they would not come back to the mill for breakfast. However, at midnight they came trooping in and rolled into their bunks. Fortunately my father was always a handy man in the kitchen. He cooked ham and eggs and coffee for about a dozen firefighters, and firefighters are hungry men.

When an attack was actually made on one of us, it was my mother who was the victim, and the attacker was not a logger or a mill hand, but a boy with whose family we had been intimate in Vancouver as well as Buxton. He struck her twice on the head with a croquet mallet while she was sitting at her sewing machine. I was playing on the porch with his sister when I heard my mother scream. I tried the front door, which was locked, and then started around the house to the back. I heard the front door open, turned, and saw her standing in the doorway with her hands to her head, and the blood streaming down over her face and her dress. We scurried for help, the doctor came and stitched up her scalp, and my father, who had gone up into the woods with the logging crew that day, was sent for. She recovered without any ill effects except extreme nervousness that lasted for a long time. The boy never denied that he struck her, but said it was an accident, which seemed impossible. At the same time, no one could imagine what his motive for a deliberate attack could have been. As far as my mother knew, they were on good terms.

I would not say that the incident was traumatic for me, but it left its mark and influenced what came after. If the attack had not occurred, I might have begun my schooling in Buxton's one-room school, where the boy who had wielded the croquet mallet was in one of the upper grades. There had been an inconclusive trial in juvenile court in Hillsboro. My parents did not press for conviction. They knew that he had already been in trouble (and, in fact, this was close to the beginning of a long criminal career), but they had no hope that a sentence to reform school would help him, and they feared that if they were influential in sending him away, he might take revenge when he came back, possibly on me. Naturally, they never discussed this possibility in front of me, but they decided that in the fall my mother and I should move to Hillsboro, to a furnished apartment, and that I should start school there. During the school year the Buxton house was let to the school teacher and his wife. My father, I believe, boarded with them during the week, or ate at the mill cookhouse, where the food was superb. On week-ends he was with us in Hillsboro, or we all took the train to Portland. I had two years of schooling in Hillsboro, but we returned to Buxton each summer until 1918, when we moved back to Vancouver.

Hillsboro, as it was when I lived there, is rather vague in my memory. Madeline De Frees, who started school in Hillsboro shortly after I did, says that it was a town of around three thousand inhabitants, and that sounds about right. It was chiefly a market town and county seat, surrounded by fertile farmland and orchards. We lived in half of a house on Main Street near the hotel. It had stained glass panels in the front door and a round turret-like projection at the corner which formed an alcove off the living room. This was my playroom. There was a sideyard that must once have been an orchard. I know that I had a swing in one of the trees. Chiefly I remember the smell of the fallen, rain-wet leaves and rotting pears in autumn, pleasurable, and yet not. I also remember a maypole dance on the courthouse lawn one spring, possibly the only one I ever saw.

I think that until I started to school I was more often lonely than not. Like most only children I learned to occupy myself with pastimes that can be enjoyed alone, but until I was able to read, the best escape from loneliness was unavailable. At that time parents were told that it was bad policy to teach children to read before they started to school, and my mother at that age usually believed what she was told. She did not teach me, but she did not take books away from me to prevent me from learning to read by myself, and I learned.

I have few memories of the first two years of school, perhaps because I was not learning much that was new, or anything that was exciting. The one textbook I remember was a beginning "language" book, not a reader, but a book intended to teach the rudiments of writing. It contained dramatic pictures *without* stories; for instance, two women or girls in medieval headdresses gazing from a castle turret at a distant horseman riding down the road towards them; a young man in the costume of a court page hesitating, key in hand, before three identical doors. The pupil was to make up a story for each picture. This was wonderful. This was better than a story book. I could hardly wait for the chance to write out the stories I was concocting. Unfortunately, before we got further than the first picture, I had left the Hillsboro schools for good, and Vancouver schools used a different text book.

By this time, however, I was reading avidly on my own. I had a few books that I read and re-read, as children do, and two of them are worth mentioning. One was a volume of short stories and poems with attractive illustrations. Intermixed with original stories about children were re-tellings of Greek myths. The other was a volume of short stories, brief biographies of famous people, and, again, re-tellings of the Greek myths. I absorbed all these stories without bothering to distinguish between those written purely for my entertainment and those designed to educate me. I had to do a little sorting out later, as between Ulysses S. Grant the general and Ulysses the Greek hero, but on the whole I think the initial confusion did me no harm, and probably made my entry into the classical world an especially easy one.

The two winters in Hillsboro coincided roughly with America's involvement in World War I. My mother was Hooverizing. My father would have had to go in the next draft. A Vancouver boy, Arthur Smith, who had been working for my father at Buxton and was engaged to a Buxton girl, was killed in action. The *Ladies Home Journal* was filled not only with spy fiction, but with the most lurid anti-German propaganda. A picture of Belgium with her hands cut off and her wrists dripping blood made a deep impression. The spiked helmet and the Kaiser William mustache were, I supposed, what every German wore. They were seldom called Germans, however, only Huns or Boches. This was the war, you remember, when Beethoven was banned.

In the other half of our Hillsboro house we had a pretty and friendly neighbor named Bertha Aiken. She had a piano on which she played the popular songs of the day while she and her friends sang. (There was, of course, still no radio.) I'm Forever Blowing Bubbles, K-K-K-Katy, Over There, Lil Liza Jones, she had them all. It was on her piano that I began my music lessons at age seven. Since I never got to first base with music, that fact would not be worth mentioning except for one indelible memory. My first piece of sheet music was a very simple tune with words—a four-line verse, I suppose. On the back were the first few bars of two or three similar compositions with the accompanying words, which broke off where the music broke off. One was about a robin, a line of verse that presented me with an uncompleted rhyme. I felt no urge to complete the tune, but the line of dangling verse that needed another line as well as a rhyme-word stimulated my imagination as the pictures without stories had stimulated it. I completed the verse, supplying the rhyme, and found that I had—almost—written a poem. This was better fun than anything I had found yet. I was off to the races.

3

We returned in 1918 to a different Vancouver from the one we had left. Prohibition had closed the saloons; wartime shipbuilding had greatly increased the population; and of course the automobile had changed life everywhere (we even had one ourselves now). That summer the Interstate Bridge across the Columbia River was opened. It not only linked Portland and Vancouver, but carried the new Highway 99, which was to extend all the way from the Mexican border to the Canadian border.

We returned to our E Street house, and my father went into the wholesale lumber business in Vancouver. The mill at Buxton, like most sawmill operations in the days before the coming of log trucks and the roads to carry them, was a temporary one. A mill was put up near the standing timber that was to be cut, and when the stand was removed, the mill was closed down and the machinery was sold or moved to a new site. During the four years we spent in Buxton, the timber near the mill was exhausted; the owners were unable to buy an adjacent stand, and the Buxton Lumber Company went out of business. I think my parents were more than ready to move back to Vancouver.

The most important thing to me about my father's new business was that he had to make frequent trips into the mountains to buy lumber. If I was not in school, I went with him. If I couldn't go, my mother went, and often we all three went. Sometimes we took a friend of mine along for the ride, but usually we were alone. The narrow, winding roads, slower cars, and frequent stops at mills meant that we sometimes had to stay overnight, perhaps at Guler, or at the Columbia Gorge Hotel when it opened, or in Eugene. In any case, we always took a lunch (thrown together in ten minutes flat after my father called and said he was going), and though time for lunch stops was limited, he was never too hurried to make a small detour to some attractive glade or gravel bar that he had spotted on a previous trip. He had the best eye for a lunch spot that I ever knew. We never, never drove on until we were famished and then had to eat in a ditch by the roadside. In bad weather we ate in the car. The whole atmosphere of these trips was completely different from the typical picnic excursion into the mountains on a summer week-end. We went in all seasons, and in all kinds of weather except snow, when the mills would be shut down for lack of logs. The trip had to be made in any case, and the pleasure given by mountains, rivers, woods, wildflowers, baby lambs, waterfalls, and the like was sheer golden bonus.

At the mill stops I usually sat in the car and read, or (later) took a sketch pad and tried to make sketches of the mills. The stops were most often long ones. It was not a matter of haggling over money, but of listening with sympathy and understanding to the troubles of the mill operators. They all had troubles, it went without saying; they had nobody to talk to except their wives or their mill crews; and since my father had operated a mill himself, he could at least listen intelligently and sometimes could offer advice. I have seen him, when I knew he was much pressed for time, sitting on a pile of lumber with his hat pulled down to shade his eyes, listening, talking, and looking as relaxed as though he had all the time in the world. Once in the car again, his foot went down on the accelerator, and we were off in a cloud of dust—literally. Mill roads are not paved.

Of course we had our adventures. We drove corduroy roads, sawdust roads, plank roads, almost perpendicular roads; we forded little brooks, rattled across bridges thrown together apparently without spikes, and could expect at any blind curve to meet a logging truck. The car got stuck in red clay and had to be pulled out by a team of horses, or we cut two tires at once on crushed rock, or we lost our way. There were never road signs pointing to mills. A new one had to be tracked down by sound, smell, and the tracks of log or lumber trucks in the mud.

Friends in Portland, other lumber wholesalers, told him he was a fool to stay on with a small-time business in Vancouver, but he persisted in dealing with the little mills, most of them operated by men who would have shied off from going into an office building in downtown Portland. They preferred to drive into Vancouver in their work clothes and climb the one flight of stairs to his office without changing their muddy boots. They not only felt awkward in Portland, they were inclined to distrust anybody who operated out of a big city, a big building, or a swank office. It is impossible to exaggerate the sketchiness of some of these sawmills. One, I remember, was powered by a Ford truck engine. Some of them would get out perhaps one car of lumber in six months. It was more or less understood that they ate more venison than beef or pork, in season and out. They had garden patches and a few chickens. They had wild blackberries and huckleberries. They survived, and most of them preferred their independence to a steady job for wages even if they could have found one.

The millmen themselves were all types. I remember one time, as we were heading east into the mountains, we saw a disreputable car parked by the roadside and a very tough-looking customer with several days' growth of black beard, a tattered jacket, and a greasy and misshapen hat, emerging from the underbrush with a can of water for his radiator. While I was thinking that he looked like a character out of some Dickensian underworld, my father threw on the brakes with a glad cry of "There's Charlie now!" We had caught our millman on the way into town. On the other hand there was Dr. Belsheim at Guler, who took us through the lava and ice caves near Mount Adams. He was a medical doctor who had given up his profession because of bad health, and was running a small sawmill in the Ponderosa pine country.

All through the Roaring Twenties (which hardly roared at all in Vancouver), the Depression, on through World War II and into the postwar period, my family lived in the house on E Street and my father continued in the same kind of business. It was during World War II that his decision to stay with his small operators paid off. At that time the owners or representatives of large mills could attend a government lumber auction for a few hours and come away with all the orders they could handle. They no longer needed the services of a broker. The men my father dealt with, however, were usually their own sawyers. If they left for the day, the mill closed down. Furthermore, most of them would have been as much at a loss at a government lumber auction as I would be at Sotheby's. When the Portland brokers were wringing their hands and crying for business, my father had all he could handle. During the last years he had another man on the road most of the time, but by then I was in the East.

The memories of these trips to White Salmon, Trout Lake, Appleton, Lyle, Klickitat, Underwood, Wind River, Cougar, Maupin, Boring, Tygh Valley, Camas Corral, Kalama, Clatskanie, Mollala, Silver Creek, Elsie, Jewel, Mist, Birkenfeld, King's Valley, Amboy, Ridgefield, Fargher Lake, or where have you, are so blended in my mind that it is impossible to impose any sort of chronological sequence. I was constantly looking, feeling, registering, and trying—*always* trying to find words that would capture something of the experience so that I could put it down and keep it. Even when my memory gives me a clue to the car we were driving, I have little clue to chronology, because we drove one car for twelve years, through all my high school and college days and for some time after. It has seemed best, therefore, to summarize this part of my life in one place, and to state, simply, that whatever else was happening these mill trips were constantly recurring, a part of my Vancouver existence, yet outside Vancouver.

Another set of memories is almost equally blended into a background that lacks chronological sequence. Again, this is part of the Vancouver experience, yet geographically removed.

North of the Columbia River estuary is a long finger of land—at least it appears to be land on the map, but it is, as it were, in fief to the ocean. It is about twenty-eight miles long, a mile wide, and fifty feet high at the summit, with the Pacific Ocean on one side, building it up, and Willapa Bay on the other, gnawing it away. I like to think that in the distant future it may become an island. It is composed more of sand than soil, but bears a healthy crop of thick-limbed wind-stunted pines. The dunes are wide. The beach is so level that when the tide is out it uncovers a stretch of glistening wet sand perhaps a quarter of a mile in width. The sandy shoreline is unbroken for twenty miles or more by any rock, fence, stream or headland. One settlement on this North Beach peninsula is Oysterville, celebrated by Willard Espy in his book of that name. Oysterville, which is on the bay side of the peninsula, is a ghost town and has been for as long as I can remember. On the ocean side of the peninsula, not far from Oysterville, a beach resort called Ocean Park came into being in the 1880's. Probably because riverboats in the early days made Ocean Park as accessible as, in later years, it became inaccessible, most Vancouver people who had beach property had a cottage at Ocean Park. By my time, we had to go to Portland by ferry and trolley, board a river boat sometime in the evening, and next morning debark at Megler on the Washington shore opposite Astoria. From here we took Mr. Espy's grandfather's narrow gauge railroad about twenty miles up the peninsula to Nahcotta, on the bay side, and from there I suppose we had a conveyance of some sort for luggage and toddlers (as I was the first time I went) across the peninsula to Ocean Park. When the automobile age came in, we drove down the Oregon side of the Columbia and ferried at Astoria.

The railroad ended at Nahcotta, and the automobile road ended at Oysterville. North of Ocean Park on one side and Oysterville on the other, there were no settlements and no roads. There were eight miles of peninsula, or dunes, some covered with pine, spruce, and alder, but at Leadbetter Point they were extinguished in salt water. There was no beyond. Until the 1930's the few settlements on the north shore of the Columbia between Kalama and the peninsula were served only by river boat. The peninsula itself, though not actually an island, was also accessible only by boat—the ferry from Astoria, the riverboats plying between Portland and Astoria, or a sea-going vessel entering Willapa Harbor (a rare occurrence). This was the way we liked it.

While we never had a cottage of our own at Ocean Park, we knew a number of families who had places that we could rent for part of the summer. We occasionally went to the more scenic Oregon beaches, which my mother loved, but we never went as often or stayed as long at any other beach. We never went to one I loved half so much. We went back at intervals through all my school years; later I went with college friends or by myself; recently I have started going again. When I returned the last time, I walked all over the village and it seemed to me that almost every cottage figured in my earliest memories. For the most part, they seem to be occupied by the same families, second, third, or fourth generation, coming from Seattle, California, or points east. The few new cottages have been built by members of these same families who have, as it were, been squeezed out of the nest. Over the years a number of older couples have retired there, and that has helped to provide continuity.

Of course progress has poked its nose in, even here. During my school days the cottages always had a pump at the sink, a privy, and a wood range to cook on. We burned bark chips (picked up in the dry sand) in the range, and larger driftwood in the fireplace. My mother contended that there never had been and never would be a good bed in Ocean Park. The pumps and privies are gone now, and the beds are a bit better. The oyster shell lanes have a more conventional surface, though they are still bordered with sandy paths instead of sidewalks. There is at last a bridge to Astoria; the ferries have gone the way of the Columbia Lightship. And there is, I regret to say, a development farther up the peninsula. However there is no bridge across the straits at the north end of the peninsula and no ferry. The road that runs now past Ocean Park and Oysterville instead of simply *to* them is still a dead-end road. As I drive down the Washington side of the Columbia and then turn inland past Deep River, Naselle, and around the end of Willapa Bay, I still feel that I am pulling a door shut behind me, on my way to a vast and private place that no one can go through to get to anywhere else. If people can't go through, they usually turn aside and go by another route. Hence, private.

These dunes are patterned with wiry grass, sand verbena, and the like. When the sun shines on them they have a rich fragrance, but they are mostly chilly and windy, often rainy even in summer. They discourage sun-bathing. The breakers are magnificent, but the water is usually bitterly cold. When you go to Ocean Park you pack your oldest clothes, only. Sweaters and windbreakers are in order. The cottages are equipped with clam shovels and crab rakes (though there is less and less use for them). There is a furious undertow. At Ocean Park we always lived by the tides. We went surf bathing despite the numbing cold of the water. Ridge after ridge of breakers made swimming impossible except for the strongest swimmers, who went out beyond the breakers. We usually jumped into a toppling breaker and rode it in towards the beach. This kind of sport was impossible when the tide was on its way out; therefore we went into the water about two hours before high tide, whenever that was, and we ate when we came out. In the early days there was a bathing bell to signal the proper time to go in. Low tides determined the times for clamming and crabbing. These are razor clams that put on a burst of speed downward and seaward when they feel the shovel strike the sand. The crabs are (I almost said "were") Dungeness.

Meals rotated through the day according to the tides and the activities they determined. On fine evenings, especially weekends when fathers came, there were enormous beach bonfires composed of, and partly sheltered by, the silvered driftwood logs that had broken loose from a log raft somewhere on the Columbia, drifted out to sea, and finally washed up on the peninsula. Beach bonfires are now illegal.

The village was almost completely hidden behind the dunes, but there was an evening ritual of watching the sunset from the dune top, one's own dunetop or a bench at the top of Main Street where it crested the dune. Or, instead of sitting, one walked up the beach as far as the *Alice*, a wrecked French wineship whose mast rose out of the surf about a mile north of the village. Through all my childhood the mast stood erect, though slanting, still bearing two spars where seagulls perched at sunset. It stood for years, and finally fell in a violent winter storm. For Ocean Park it was like a death in the family.

Usually there were other children for me to play with, but it seems to me that I liked best roaming the beach and the dunes by myself, making up lines of poetry or reciting to myself poems that seemed appropriate to the place, very likely Masefield at one time, but after I learned Greek it was Homer shouted into the noise of the breakers, or Joyce's "I Hear an Army." Only one cottage peered over a dune-top, and it was always empty. Often there was not another soul on the beach, or only a few tiny figures doubled in a mirage effect far in the distance. Nowhere else have I ever been so alone and so little lonely.

4

I have been putting off the difficult task of saying something succinct about the city where I was born, received most of my schooling, and now live. The subject seems a difficult one to take hold of, partly, I know, because Vancouver has changed so much over the years that it is hard for me to summon up the town I knew before I left it. If I had never returned, I could probably recall it more vividly. Another reason why I seem to be confronting an amorphous blob is that Vancouver, poor girl, like many of our young people, has had a hard time trying to find out who she is.

In the beginning there was no problem at all. Fort Vancouver was in her early days the only settlement in the Pacific Northwest, or the area that was ultimately divided into Oregon, Washington, Idaho, and British Columbia. Vancouver can proudly assert that she is the oldest *continuously occupied* settlement in the Northwest, but, alas, there is that awkward modifying phrase. Astoria was founded first by the Americans although the settlement was abandoned by the time the Hudson's Bay Company founded Fort Vancouver at a site on the Columbia already named by Lieutenant Broughton for his captain, Vancouver. The history of my Vancouver while it was the capital of the Northwest fur trade is fascinating. There is no disputing that, but for the last one hundred years or more its citizens have had to explain again and again and again until they are exhausted that they are *not* Canadians. Vancouver U.S.A. had the name first and is proud of it; every proposal to change the name of the city has been rejected at the polls; but our younger and more successful sister has left us only the echo of her name. That in itself is enough to create an identity problem.

To add to the difficulty, Vancouver has had to struggle hard for the light, being always in the shadow of Portland, another johnny-come-lately that overtook and outstripped her long ago. Nothing interesting has ever happened in or near Vancouver that Portland did not appropriate it. When the Russians flew their red monoplane over the North Pole and landed at Pearson Air Field in Vancouver Barracks, Pearson Air Field made a still more astonishing flight across the Columbia and became a part of Portland. Not that it mattered. If the dateline had read "Vancouver," everyone would have thought that the Russians had landed in Canada. We are still waiting to see whether Portlanders will decide that a live volcano has enough news value to make it worth claiming, or whether they will decide it is a liability as a pollutor of the atmosphere and may as well remain in Washington.

To make matters worse, Portland is across the state line.

Unable to vote in Oregon, but with concerns more closely tied in with Portland than with the Puget Sound area or Spokane and the Tri-Cities, Vancouver is in the frustrating position of being the stepchild of two states. This again makes for an underdeveloped and even slightly schizoid personality. We listen to Portland radio, watch Oregon TV, and read the *Oregonian*; even our letters are postmarked "Portland, Oregon"; but we are represented in the Senate by the Senator from Boeing. Seattle knows very well that our team is the Blazers, not the Sonics, and washes its hands of us.

Downtown Vancouver remained stunted long after it should have been a respectable small city. We shopped in Portland, went out to lunch or dinner in Portland, went to concerts or the theater or movies in Portland. We even went to Portland doctors and dentists (some people still do). Yet we were not a bedroom suburb, we were an industrial suburb. We had no class. A number of wealthy and/or socially prominent people have from time to time lived on our side of the Columbia, especially after Oregon began to collect a state income tax (Washington has only a sales tax). However, these people seldom mix with the Vancouver citizenry to give us a little tone.

To make matters worse, like many small cities across the state line from a large city, Vancouver has long served as the place Portland people go to for pleasures prohibited at home. For many years Vancouver was Oregon's Gretna Green, when Oregon's marriage laws were stricter than Washington's. Later, when Oregon prohibited the sale of liquor by the glass, Vancouver supplied a felt want. Now Vancouver is Portland's convenient "little Las Vegas" with its card rooms, pawn shops and quick loan establishments on lower Main Street. We are also, as I mentioned, a tax haven. If Portland thinks of us at all, it is only to deplore our proximity.

While Vancouver Barracks was an active army post, Vancouver had its share of the women who were known to the relief office as "Reserve Street widows." On the other hand, the officers and their wives usually kept to themselves or infiltrated Portland society. The one commanding officer who ever gave a sign that he knew Vancouver was there was General George C.

21

Marshall. He even joined Kiwanis. A poll taken in Vancouver would probably rank General Marshall next after General Washington in the ranks of our military heroes.

For all these reasons it is difficult for me to describe Vancouver. I can tell you what it is not better than I can tell you what it is. In the Twenties about 15,000 people lived and worked there, practised law and medicine, went to church and school, and held political office. It was the county seat, and the site of state schools for the deaf and the blind. It had a port where ocean-going vessels loaded grain and lumber.

Vancouver had, like Portland, its rows of Caroline Testout rosebushes by the curbs, and its residential streets lined with ricks of cordwood waiting for the woodsaw. Some time after school started, the whine of the woodsaw was heard as it moved from street to street. Ice was delivered to the back door in big blocks; a card in the window told the iceman what size block to leave. When we made lemonade, we chipped ice off the block with a pick. An Italian vegetable man also made the rounds with his truckload of garden produce. Grocery stores were small, mom-and-pop affairs; meat markets were separate establishments, and they both *delivered*.

What else should I say? I lived within easy walking distance of both my grammar school and the one high school. I always came home for lunch and so did my father. For years my grandmother lived with us, and as she became more difficult to care for we had live-in "help" to take part of the burden off my mother. Sometimes it was a girl, sometimes a middle-aged woman; whichever it was, she was usually straight off a farm and completely untrained. With one exception these girls or women ate with us, so that we usually sat down five to the table, three times a day.

When I entered Arnada school in Vancouver I had, according to the records, completed two and a half grades at Hillsboro, but I was placed with a class just beginning grade 3. The reason given was that Oregon schools were behind Washington schools. There was something that Oregon pupils did not begin to study until fourth grade, whereas Washington pupils began with the third. This was really nonsense. I could have gone straight into fourth grade with no trouble at all, but the

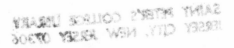

principal at Arnada was opposed to skipping anybody, any time, and I continued with my class all the way through high school.

A friend of mine who was skipped two full years feels that in her case it was a disaster, not because she could not do the work, but because she was not mature enough to move into a social group whose members were her seniors by two years. Recently, I believe, stress has been laid on the social development of the child; if he can do his work in double-quick time, he is given extra projects to keep him from getting bored or spending his time day-dreaming over the illustrations in his geography and history books as I did.

In my case, however, I think the casual decision to put me back half a grade was a mistake. In the first place, I had not started school until I was almost seven, so that I was almost a year older than many of my classmates. Furthermore, I was always extremely tall for my age, so that I was at least a head taller than other children of the same age, and with my extra year I was head and shoulders taller than my classmates. This must be difficult for a boy, but for a girl it is murder. When I entered high school at age fourteen (nearly fifteen) I was approximately the same height I am now, five feet, eight inches. During the last two years in high school my friends shot up, and by the time we graduated I could for the first time look them in the eye instead of stooping to hear what they were saying. Of course I stooped, not, I think, in a vain attempt to conceal my height as people always assume, but because I had never had a school desk high enough for me, or friends I could walk beside without stooping to talk with them. If I had been pushed ahead half a grade instead of being set back half a grade, I would still have been too tall, but not that much too tall.

At that time creative writing courses had hardly begun to appear in the college curriculum. Creative writing was not encouraged in high school, and was never even mentioned in grammar school. No one ever suggested that I write a poem or a story, but I was scribbling all the time. During recess I would find a spot on a bench in a corner of the basement and start a story (a book, even) in my pencil tablet. Before I had got very far a teacher on duty would spot me and drive me outside to play. None of the stories were ever finished, but I also wrote verses and these I finished.

All my verses could only be characterized as doggerel. I don't see anything wrong with that myself. I liked rhyme and a swinging rhythm. I was creating a pattern in sound rather than expressing my deeper emotions if I had any. I disagree whole-heartedly with an approach to creative writing for children that denies them rhyme and lilting rhythms on the grounds that if they read that kind of poetry they will turn out doggerel. A child of eight or ten is most unlikely to produce a great poem. He, or she, had better be developing an ear for the technical aspects of poetry writing. I have quarreled (mildly) with one of my friends on this issue, but another who has a little grand-daughter now just beginning to write poetry, advises me not to worry. She says: "Children will find what they want, whether it is given to them or not." The child in question uses rhyme very skillfully in the poems she writes for her own pleasure, but never for poems assigned at school. "If you use rhyme, they think you're repressed," she says. Oh God!

When I was in seventh grade I made my first friend. Until then I had only playmates, children chosen by my mother or thrust upon me by proximity, with whom I played games, or house, or paper dolls, or whatever. My first friendship, in which I shared my love of reading with someone else who also loved reading, was a great joy to me. Week after week for years we went to the library together.

The library was a small red brick Carnegie Library with one room and one corner of the one room devoted to children's books. I suppose I must have read almost everything in that corner a number of times before I outgrew it, but besides li-brary books, and a few books of my own, I had a fresh copy of *St. Nicholas* every month. At this time the magazine had a rather romantic cast, with many poems and serialized historical novels for young people. I loved it, especially a series of rather long narrative poems about the knights of the Round Table. When I was sixteen, I lost interest. The format had changed; it published more stories of the here-and-now and less poetry. In any case, I had before this moved out of the children's section of the library to read at random in the adult fiction. I was in no danger of being corrupted by salacious literature. The few "daring" books of the time, like *Grand Hotel*, were on the closed shelf behind the librarian's desk.

While I was in the eighth grade my interest in poetry was stimulated by two books, the first a newly-published reader which included poems by modern poets like Noyes and Masefield instead of relying entirely on the standard fare that had made up every eighth grade reader since my father's day: Longfellow, Bryant, Whittier, Poe, a bit of Tennyson and Scott. The second stimulus came from a book I found one dark, rainy afternoon when I was poking about in a particularly gloomy and unpromising corner of the library, brooding over shelves that I had never explored before. Most of the titles were forbidding enough, but my eye lit on one that held my attention: *The Art of Versification*. I wondered what versification was. Could it be . . . ? I looked inside and saw scansion, found the lovely words "iamb," "trochee," "dactyl" for the first time. I carried the book home in a state of high excitement and showed it to my mother. To my amazement I found that she already knew about iambs and trochees. For once, I cried out at her in anger: "But why didn't you tell me?" Whereupon she said, "But dear, I thought you learned that kind of thing in school!" *She* had, but sometime between her schooldays and mine someone had decided that having to learn about scansion put children off poetry, and the scanning of verse had been dropped along with the parsing of sentences. Even in high school, metric was hardly mentioned, but by that time I had pretty well digested everything *The Art of Versification* had to tell me.

As for art and music, up to this time you could hardly say that they existed for me. I have spoken of going to concerts in Portland, but that came later. At this time radio was still a toy. Symphonic and opera broadcasts were yet to come. A few families I knew as a child had phonographs and a few scratchy Caruso records. I had been taking music lessons, but nobody ever gave me a bit of Bach or Mozart, only "Falling Leaves" and the like, the kind of thing I was sick of long before I had mastered it. My teachers, of course, never thought of stimulating my interest by telling me that I could learn something from music that might help me to write good poetry. They only suggested that it would be most impressive if I were to become proficient in *two* arts. My interest flagged, and the lessons ceased when I entered high school.

Art was to become one of my major interests, but almost my only experience of it at this time came through full-page color reproductions in *The Ladies Home Journal*. The Caruso records were far and away better than the pictures people hung in their homes, and ours was no exception. There were no reproductions of art works in our schools or our library, unless, possibly, "Washington Crossing the Delaware." It was fortunate for me that my talents lay in the literary line. Books were much more accessible to me than art or music.

Before I continue, let me emphasize that I thought myself a lucky child, and I was, compared with most of the children I knew—perhaps even compared to the young Henry James who looked back ruefully upon his youth as a "hotel child" being dragged through the capitals of Europe or parked temporarily in French and Swiss schools. He had cultural advantages, but I had other kinds of good fortune.

In the first place I had affection in abundance. My great-grandmother, who had the care of my mother after her parents died, considered that a display of affection denoted a weakness of character. She was a great hand with the peach tree switch. My mother realized only after she was grown that her grandmother had actually loved her—in her own way—and she was determined I should never be in doubt that I was loved. Both my parents were demonstrative with me and with each other. This was before the psychologists had hung out red flags warning parents of the possible danger to the young psyche inherent in too much loving. My mother, anyway, was aware from her own experience of the opposite danger. At the same time, neither of them let me think for a moment that I came first with either of them. I was central in their combined regard, but they came first with each other. This relieved me of the terrible burden placed on only children by a parent (usually a mother) who puts the child first and the spouse second.

To continue, then, I had affection, family stability, and financial security. I had a better house to live in and better clothes to wear than most children in my school, some of whom were always in hand-me-downs. Not only that, I had traveled. By the time I entered high school I had been three times to the Midwest, and once to California. I had been several times to Vancouver Island, where we had relatives. I had been to Denver and Salt Lake City, and had crossed the Rockies on Canadian Pacific. I was at home in Pullman cars, upper and lower berths, dining cars, and hotels. Few children of my acquaintance could say as much.

Besides all this, I had Ocean Park and the excursions to the mills. It would never have occurred to me to be sorry for myself. For my time and place, a small town in Washington State in the Twenties, I was doing very well. I might have been worse off with teachers who, in encouraging my talent for writing, might have tried to shape the plant instead of just letting it grow. However, with this wave of nostalgia for the simple life of our ancestors sweeping over us, I think it is well to point out that if we had a better natural environment in those days (and in the days of my parents and grandparents) there were many desirable things that we lacked, things which increasing population and better technology have brought within reach. There are worse things in life than pumps and privies and a childhood devoid of books, even, as my grandmother's was; but when we cry out for the past and the simple life, we should remember what that life was like.

5

When I have talked with other writers about their schooling, I have been amazed to hear many of them say that high school was for them a total waste of time. My four years in high school were happy—much happier than the previous eight—and also profitable.

I think that we had a good high school. I not only had a number of excellent teachers, but the student body as a whole had a good tone. It was free of cliques, sororities (which were not allowed), and clubs with closed membership. Sports were encouraged, but never allowed to dominate the school life. The class of 1928, with which I graduated, numbered about one hundred and twenty, including the mid-year class that graduated with us. It was a good class.

At that time college entrance requirements included: four years of English, two years of math (algebra and geometry), one year of a lab science, one year of history and civics, four years of foreign language study, of which the first two must be Latin; after that we had a choice of two more years of Latin or two years of either French or Spanish. (German had been dropped during World War I and had not been reinstated.) Normally we had room for one elective each year. That wasn't much room to thrash about in. I elected art one year. Another year I took a journalism course which had a cleansing effect on my prose. The author of the journalism textbook took a sterner view of English usage than did the authors of our English grammar textbooks. My third year I began French and at the same time continued with a third year of Latin in which we read Virgil. I do not remember my other elective.

Several people I have talked with have said that high school would have been a waste of time for them except for one teacher. I cannot say that, because I had a number of excellent teachers, but one did more for me than any other. I first encountered her in a sophomore English class which I entered in flight from one of the few really deplorable, incompetent teachers I ever had. I knew that students whose first concern was grades avoided Margaret Page Johnson. I was not worried about my grades, especially in English. I only wanted to get out of an English class in which erasers were flying across the room, the teacher was screaming, and I was asked to read and report on success stories in *Red Book Magazine*.

In that one semester of sophomore English, Margaret opened doors on vistas I had not dreamed of, and when, the next year, I had to decide on my third year language course, I took two—first-year French and third-year Latin (Virgil), because she was teaching both of them. She had a good classical background, and had served as a nurse in France during World War I, so that she had a first-hand as well as a text-book knowledge of the language, the literature, the landscape and the people. Few high school language teachers in the Pacific Northwest in those days had so much to give their students. In my senior year I had still another term with her as English teacher, but the course that meant most in the long run was the Virgil, especially because Margaret steered me in the direction of the Greeks, giving me assignments for outside reading in Homer and the Greek dramatists.

Besides my studies, which were demanding more effort on my part, school activities of one kind and another kept me busy. One year I edited the school paper. I belonged to various clubs, made posters, wrote skits, went to football and basketball games, and acquired a circle of friends. These were real friends, with two of whom I am still in close touch. The new friendships, unlike the first, were not based on a shared love of reading, but they meant a great deal to me then and still do. If I suffered any adolescent agonies of the sort I understand are normal at that age, I do not remember them. I am afraid I was abnormally satisfied just as I was.

The greatest satisfaction was in my writing. The verses were no longer doggerel. I published light verse frequently in the school paper; though it was topical, I was able to do things that pleased me, for instance, a salute to the departing senior class in an attempted approximation of Virgilian hexameters. Other poems, not for the paper, were more ambitious. My teachers, especially Margaret Johnson, were taking an interest and doing more to guide my reading.

Besides my classroom work with Margaret there was one summer when she invited me and three or four of my friends to come to her house for an afternoon of reading and talk about poetry. I believe there were several of these afternoons, but I remember only one, with a fine rain falling in the shrubbery, a golden collie, a golden fire on the hearth, and—was it Rupert Brooke? Every high school girl who wrote poetry in those days had a crush on Rupert Brooke.

During the first two years of high school, reading on my own, I had gone through English lyric poetry with a hop, skip and jump, beginning chronologically with an enthusiasm for ballads, moving on to Elizabethan lyrics, and then, with a leap over the metaphysical poets and the Eighteenth Century, to the Romantic poets. By my junior year, I began to be acquainted with Harriet Monroe's anthology, *The New Poetry*. I read Amy

Lowell, Edna Millay, the Benéts, and Elinor Wylie, who was my favorite. I rejected Carl Sandburg and Edgar Lee Masters because I was looking for music and did not find it in their poems.

Emily Dickinson also swam into my ken about this time, but I think that I was more fascinated by the legend than I was by the poems. I liked conventional form, yes, but I wanted more variety, longer lines, more music.

I believe I did my first bit of verse translation in second-year French. It was an assignment: I was asked to translate a poem in *L'Illustration*, to which our class subscribed. The poem was by the Comtesse de Noailles, heaven help us. I was naturally completely baffled. Nothing resembling French symbolism had yet come my way. I translated it, but the experience left me giddy.

My own verse continued to be conventional in form. I wrote a few sonnets and experimented with various kinds of stanzas. When I was sixteen, at the instigation of a woman visitor from the East, who praised my work highly, I submitted some of my poems to magazines for the first time. They were returned from *Poetry* (Chicago) with a penciled "promising" in the corner of the printed rejection slip, and from *Scribner's* with an actual note instead of a printed slip. I was sad, but at the same time I felt encouraged by the "promising" and the little note. It was my first editorial encouragement, and I felt hopeful. As it turned out, that was the last editorial encouragement I was to receive for a long time. This was in 1926. I continued to send poems out until, in 1935, I saw my first poem in *Poetry* after Marianne Moore had opened the door for me.

Although, as I have said, I enjoyed high school, by my senior year I was becoming restless. College was on my mind, not only the choice of a college, but the choice of a career. Of course I knew I wanted to be a writer, but I expected to earn money in some kind of salaried job before I could expect to earn my living by my writing. It seems to me fantastic that I ever, even then, supposed that I would eventually be able to earn my living by my writing, that is, by writing what I wanted to write.

I remember talking to Margaret Johnson one afternoon about the problem. She looked up at me where I stood before her desk, and said in an accent I have never forgotten, "Whatever you do, *don't teach!*" I was not seriously considering teaching, and her words confirmed me in my decision not to aim in that direction. (It was just as well, because, by the time I was out of college, there were no teaching jobs to be had unless the salaries were paid in un-cashable warrants. Only married women whose husbands could support them could afford that kind of job. They could gamble on being able to cash the warrants eventually.)

I considered majoring in journalism. The University of Washington was said to have a good school of journalism, and I thought I might go there. However, even on the playground at Arnada, I had been taunted with the cry of "Oh, *you'll* go to Reed!" It was probably my destiny, and in spite of a natural desire to prove the prophets wrong, I did go to Reed.

Although Reed College was only seventeen years old, it already had its detractors, especially in the Portland area. It was looked upon by the young as a school for dreary drudges because there were no Greek-letter fraternities and sororities and no intercollegiate sports. (This was the era of the raccoon coat and the hip flask—the F. Scott Fitzgerald period in American higher education.) Parents, on the other hand, viewed Reed as extremely dangerous. It condoned immorality, for one thing, because women students were allowed to smoke anywhere on campus (some sorority houses at this time had a "smoking room," but for the most part girls were expected to smoke on fire escapes). Also, the Reed dormitories were unsupervised by house mothers. And then of course the Reed faculty was considered dangerously radical. And to cap it all, the college was non-denominational. There was no compulsory chapel attendance, in fact, no religious services were held in the chapel, only concerts and lectures. Despite the staid gravity of President Coleman, a former clergyman, the rumor persisted that the principal subjects taught at Reed were "atheism, communism, and free love."

I was not frightened off by the reputation of Reed as a deadly place where no one had any fun, because two of my favorite teachers were lively, pretty, attractively dressed young women, full of fun, and right out of Reed. My parents were not frightened by rumors of Reed's radicalism and loose morals because they had common sense. But what really clinched the decision was a week-end spent as a visitor in a University of Washington sorority house. This was college? There was no privacy, no place to study. There seemed to be no books, no desks, nothing but a great flying about in dressing gowns, pealing telephones, and a general hurly-burly. By contrast, on a one-day visit to Reed I found dormitories with bedrooms *and* studies, the studies having proper desks, the desks loaded with books. I liked the small, quiet campus and the small student body, which was then about 450 (compared with 10,000 at the University of Washington). I attended one of Barry Cerf's Renaissance literature classes, and was in seventh heaven. There was no decision left to be made. I would go to Reed for two years at least if Reed would have me. My parents approved. They no doubt liked the idea of my being no more than fifteen miles away, though they put no pressure on me one way or the other. Reed, then as now, was expensive. Tuition was two hundred dollars a year compared with fifteen dollars a quarter at the state university. However, I had no qualms about that, and I doubt that my parents had any, though the lumber business in the fall of 1928 was already slipping off. Nobody, of course, had an inkling of the economic disaster waiting in the wings.

Chapter 2

I LOOKED forward to Reed with great anticipation, but a foreboding came over me when I entered the suite I was to share with a freshman roommate and saw on her desk just two books—the Bible and the poems of Edgar A. Guest. All my forebodings were fulfilled, and more. For four years I had been surrounded by good friends, but during that first year at Reed I made no friends at all. I had nothing in common with the other freshmen in the house, a sad lot, none of whom stayed the four years. The sophomores that year were all social butterflies, and I had nothing in common with them, either. The girls in the house who were later to become my friends (and are still friends after fifty years) were juniors and seniors. The gap was too wide for me to bridge. When I occasionally had dinner in the commons with them and their men friends, I was unable to join in the conversation because I had no idea what they were talking about. That situation fortunately lasted for only one year. By the second year I had found my feet, and my friends, and Reed College became for me the place I had imagined it might be.

The Reed curriculum was designed to give a good background in the humanities, not, at that time, through one integrated humanities course, but with parallel history and literature survey courses that were required of all freshman students. The courses began with the literature and history of Greece, continued with Rome and the Middle Ages, and wound up with the Renaissance in late spring. This would have been just my meat. As luck would have it, however, my freshman year was the year one of the social science professors persuaded the faculty to initiate a freshman course called Contemporary Society (Con Soc). We were not required to take it instead of history, but we were pushed. I pleaded to be allowed to take history instead, but to no avail. I was pushed into Con Soc, and as an entering freshman I did not know how to push back. By the next year, when I was being pushed into German instead of Greek, I was able to push back effectively.

As for the freshman literature course, which began with Homer, I was well-prepared by my high school Virgil course and got off to an excellent start. In a way, my proficiency in my first half year did me more harm than good, because it gave the literature department, in which I majored, an exaggerated idea of my ability. I am sure my professors never realized how much of the time in later years I was not waving but drowning.

Perhaps I should explain that Reed did not have English courses or English majors. In Modern Lit. we read Proust as well as Joyce. In Renaissance Lit. we read Montaigne as well as Marlowe. We were encouraged to read in the original language when it was one we were studying. The three men with whom I studied literature, Barry Cerf, Victor Chittick, and Lloyd Reynolds, were strikingly different. Looking back, I don't see how I could have done without any of them.

Barry Cerf was the classicist, a little man, very straight and perky, rather bird-like, with a bright blue eye and a resonant voice. I had had no idea of taking Greek until I heard the sound of it when he read one line of Homer in a freshman lit. lecture. It was a tiny seed that took root. Sometimes a small group of students would assemble in the evening to hear him read Homer aloud, in Greek. I was always present. He was an inspiring teacher when he was dealing with the classics, but no friend to modern poetry. I remember that he once lectured on "critical periods" and "creative periods" in literary history. Now, he said, we are in a critical period. It is impossible to write poetry today. This was in 1928–29 when Eliot, Frost, Jeffers, Pound, Cummings, Stevens, W. C. Williams and Marianne Moore were all in their prime, and Yeats was writing his late poems (*The Tower* was published in 1928). Critics today look back on those years as a Golden Age of poetry production. I needed the other two men to open a door on the modern world, but neither of them would ever have inspired me to study Greek.

Victor Chittick, a Nova Scotian with a doctorate from Columbia University, was as tall as Barry Cerf was short, and looked rather like a kindly eagle, very impressive in the evening dress he wore to symphony concerts. His speech was blunt and could be more brutal than he realized. He taught a second-year survey course dealing mainly with the Romantics. We began with Rousseau and continued with Wordsworth, Coleridge, Hazlitt, Keats, and so on. He also taught courses in modern literature and American literature. He was fiercely on the defensive against critics of the classical persuasion who disparaged romanticism, modernism, and American writing generally. He and Barry Cerf balanced each other nicely. Although I took all three of the courses I have mentioned from Victor Chittick, his greatest influence on my life at Reed was as sponsor, patron, or whatever, of a very informal organization known as the Gawd-Awful Society. It almost always met at his home, and whether it met there or elsewhere, he was always present.

This group was composed of would-be poets for the most part, and girls for the most part, though the membership fluctuated greatly from year to year, sometimes expanding, sometimes shrinking, sometimes with a number of males, and then again with few or none. In this group I encountered for the first time in my life other people who wrote poetry. We would meet on Saturday nights about once a month to read our Gawd-Awful poetry and our Gawd-Awful prose. Gawd-Awful was one of Victor Chittick's favorite adjectives, hence the name. I was invited to join almost immediately upon my arrival at Reed, a high compliment, I believe, because most members were juniors or seniors.

I remember the first meeting I attended, when everyone talked and talked about Huxley. Someone read a paper on a book by Huxley to start it all off, but I could not make out what was going on. The only Huxley I knew about was T. H., and I decided they could not possibly be talking about *him*. Eventually I learned that this Huxley's first name was Aldous. The book was *Point Counterpoint*. I had never heard of either the author or the book. If the Vancouver library had a copy, which I doubt, it was surely behind Mrs. Perky's desk.

Not at the first meeting, but soon after, I read a number of the poems I had written in high school. They were received with enthusiasm. It seemed that I was the only rhyming poet on campus. Everyone else wrote free verse. At that time the campus paper had an occasional literary issue, and my high school poems began to appear in its columns. I was much gratified.

Lloyd Reynolds, the third in the triumvirate that composed the literature department, was a young man who first appeared on the Reed campus at the beginning of my second year. He had only recently received his M. A. in English from the University of Oregon. In contrast to both Cerf and Chittick, he was in no way bird-like and only faintly academic, never even attempting (so far as I know) to get a Ph.D. Always a bit more of a guru than a professor, he stayed on at Reed, moving from literature into graphic arts and calligraphy, with excursions into other arts visual and theatrical, until his retirement.

I had no acquaintance with Lloyd until my third year, when I enrolled in his creative writing course. Under his influence my poetry changed dramatically, not so much in content as in style. I also wrote my first and last good critical papers for him. In his class, too, I first began to read the poets I think of as the real moderns: not Masters, Sandburg, the Benéts, but Eliot, Pound, H. D., Edith Sitwell, Hart Crane, and, I believe, Cummings. I am sure we did not get as far as W. C. Williams, who was still virtually unknown outside the range of the little mags. Marianne Moore, too, was hardly more than a name to me.

First, about the critical papers. My biggest difficulty in all my other lit. courses had been and continued to be my inability to turn in a really acceptable critical paper. I felt that I was expected to evaluate the work of the writer I was discussing, to make a judgment on it, and I never felt qualified to judge it. Anything that occurred to me seemed too obvious to set down, or, if I had some perception that seemed perhaps original enough to put on paper and submit on the appointed day, I was unable to spin it out to an acceptable length. I was reduced to handing in a paragraph when I should have handed in five pages. This inability to function as a critic caused both Victor Chittick and me much pain. Also, during my later college years the Depression was in full swing, the enrollment had dropped, and, besides, there was a flurry of enthusiasm for tutorial courses. Now the story about Mark Hopkins on one end of the log and the boy to be educated on the other is all very well, but as far as I was concerned, I needed the company of my peers. I was supposed to sit there and tell Victor Chittick about Keats? He knew a great deal more about Keats than I did. What was I supposed to tell him? What *could* I tell him? I was tongue-tied. It was only in Lloyd's creative writing class where discussion revealed what the other students were not perceiving that I discovered what I knew.

Furthermore, we were asked to write an entirely different kind of critical paper. We spent no time in class picking over each other's work. Instead, we read *Dubliners*, analyzing one story after another, paragraph by paragraph and phrase by phrase, to see how Joyce produced his effects. Then we were told to write out an analysis of one story, "A Painful Case," which we had not yet studied. I wrote a good paper. Before we read *Dubliners* in class, I had looked into the book and found it very dull. Now I realized that it was exciting. We were also assigned a paper on Joyce's poem, "I Hear an Army," and I wrote another good paper. I know that we also tackled a Hart Crane poem. I forget whether it was Victor Chittick or Lloyd Reynolds who set me to reading Edith Sitwell, but it was Lloyd who, when I was ready to give up in despair, sat with me in an empty classroom and showed me how to go about reading the poems. This was the tutorial system at its best. Once he said,

"Don't feel discouraged. Remember that when I was in college, Amy Lowell was considered difficult."

At that time T. S. Eliot was Lloyd's greatest enthusiasm. About 1930 Eliot must have been at the very peak of his fame. The early poems and *The Waste Land* had been so far assimilated that lines from them had become a part of speech wherever modern poetry was read and discussed. The Ariel poems were appearing one by one. As Eliot moved further into the shadow of the church, American literature, influenced by the concerns of the Depression, the Spanish Civil War, and the fear of rising militarism in Germany and Italy, moved further to the left. Auden's star rose, and Eliot's prestige waned. Between 1930 and 1932, however, it was Eliot, Eliot, Eliot all the way, until I was tired of the sound of his name.

This is not to say that I did not admire his work, but there was something in both the earlier work and the religious poetry that was foreign to me. Partly for this reason, partly in reaction to the adulation which seemed to me excessive, I veered away from Eliot and found myself drifting towards Pound.

The year before, my next door neighbor in the dorm had lent me her copy of *Personae* when I was doing some work on the troubadours. I had been interested, but not as interested as I should have been, perhaps because I was still using conventional meters and end-rhymes in my own poetry. At the beginning of my junior year when I enrolled in the creative writing course, I naturally showed Lloyd Reynolds a selection of my poems. Immediately he urged me to try loosening up, varying the line length, avoiding the sing-song rhythms, and dispensing with end-rhymes.

Here in my Brunnenburg apartment the other day I found a high school anthology called *The Pleasures of Poetry*. In the back of the book I was pleased to find a brief discussion of metric, with examples of iamb, dactyl, and so on. Good. Education, I thought, *is* improving. But then I turned a page and came to a section entitled "Write It Yourself" and here I found a recommendation to the student to select a paragraph of prose and chop it up into a free verse poem. This appalled me, and I was not reassured by the example given, or the further recommendation that it be prettied up with a few hyphenated adjectives ("grain-golden," "life-red") to make it more poetic. The poem obtained by chopping up the prose paragraph sounds exactly like the free verse that had always put me off free verse until Lloyd Reynolds took a hand. I no longer know which came first, the day I wrote a poem liberated, at least, from a whalebone corset, or the day when Lloyd wrote out several lines of Pound's poetry on the blackboard, waved his arms about, and proclaimed, "The man who could do that could do anything!"

Lloyd was given to making extravagant statements (enthusiasm, it seemed to me, was one of his greatest virtues), but still I was a bit startled, probably because he was not talking about Eliot, as I would have expected. I copied the lines in my notebook, feeling skeptical, yet intrigued. The lines were from the "Homage to Sextus Propertius":

> Since Adonis was gored in Idalia, and the Cytherean
> Ran crying with out-spread hair,
>   In vain, you call back the shade,
> In vain, Cynthia. Vain call to unanswering shadow,
>   Small talk comes from small bones.

They bit deep. I returned to Gill's bookstore the copy of the Harriet Monroe anthology that my mother gave me for my birthday, and brought home *Personae* instead. I was beginning to know at last the country I wanted to explore.

During my second year at Reed Rex Arragon entered my life to stay. He is still an important part of it. I should have taken his history survey course in my freshman year, but, as I said, I was shunted into Con Soc. The second year I did take it, and also I began to go to the Arragons' house for tea and scones on Friday afternoons. Rex was a Middle Westerner with a Ph.D. from Harvard; Gertrude was a New Englander with two Radcliffe degrees. Whether I went for the conversation or the muffins and marmalade I couldn't say now, but both were good. I always seemed to know more history majors than lit. majors; three of my best friends became assistants in the history department, one after the other; two friends lived with the Arragons, one one year, one the next, so that I was in and out of the house a great deal. By my senior year I was learning to change diapers on the new Arragon baby.

History had always been one of my favorite subjects, especially the kind of history we got at Reed, in which cultural history received equal time with political, military, social and economic history. It was for Rex Arragon that I had written the paper on the troubadours. We got on well together, but I never considered changing my major to history.

At least from the beginning of my second year I had had a subject for my senior thesis in mind: I would, I thought, write a thesis on Elinor Wylie, with Victor Chittick as my major professor. As my junior year drew to a close, I went to see Victor about it, to ask him if he would take me on, and what he thought of the subject. By this time there were other poets who interested me more, but Elinor Wylie had died rather suddenly in 1929 at age forty-three and she was at the moment being much talked of. Besides, I had had the idea for too long to want to give it up. I thought Victor would be pleased, but instead he eyed me grimly and said, "It's a job that certainly needs doing, but I doubt if you can do it." I was speechless with shock. I knew he thought I was deficient in critical ability, but I had not expected to be turned down. No more was said on the subject by either of us. I felt that I had been rebuffed, and ought to make other plans, which I did. The next fall I found out that during the summer he had been to see Carl Van Doren, who was a friend of his, to learn what he could tell or was willing to say about Elinor Wylie. He returned to Reed in the fall to find that I was proposing to do a creative thesis with Lloyd Reynolds. I think he was hurt, and I know that later on he upbraided me for having changed my mind without telling him. He denied that he had ever thought me incapable of doing the job, but I knew that I could not have imagined a blow to the solar plexus that temporarily demolished me. My mistake was in taking it as a rejection when it was apparently intended as a warning.

Although Lloyd agreed readily enough to the creative thesis, I ran into trouble when it was time for the Division of Literature and Languages to approve the project. It seemed that the very few creative theses in the past had been disappointing. Also, I was proposing to do a play. Barry Cerf was chilly to the idea. Victor was lukewarm—that is, he said that a creative thesis was likely to be a "flat-tire thesis," but that a critical thesis written by me would be even more likely to be a flat tire.

Lloyd managed to put my plan across, but had to agree to the stipulation that I should do it in verse ("We know that she can write poetry, but we don't know that she can write a play"). I have to admit that they were right about that, and that my first draft of a play was a failure. Lloyd told me so flatly. During a brief period of unhappy dithering about, Lloyd suggested that I change my major to history. Whereupon I wrote home that next I could expect Mr. Arragon to suggest that I major in physics. I did not consider a change to history seriously. It was too late for that kind of maneuver. Instead, I proposed that I make a collection of the verse I had written the year before and was continuing to write this year, salvage a couple of songs I had written for the play, and submit a volume of poetry for a senior thesis. Poor Lloyd had to take this idea back to the Division. After a certain amount of wrangling and a few "I told you so's," I was allowed to submit a collection of poems, mainly, I think, because it was too late to do anything else. This time the stipulation was that I should write a critical introduction stating my theories of poetry writing. Victor reported to me that he told them, "Well, she can do it, but it may be only ten lines." Barry Cerf shook his head over that, but Lloyd, bless his heart, muttered, "It may be only ten lines, but they will be ten perfect lines." Barry gave in.

The longer I live the more convinced I am that the art of taking a freshly written poem in hand and talking with the poet about it in terms that are actually helpful and illuminating to him is very difficult indeed. Lloyd seemed to be of the same opinion as William Carlos Williams when he wrote to me a few years later: "In general there are only two things to say about any poem. Yes and No." Lloyd sometimes said, "I think your poem is wonderful!" which made me feel good, especially as he bent a sparkling gaze upon me as he said it, but it told me nothing. Once he said of two poems I had put in his box, "It was a mistake to have written those two." When I handed in the final draft of the collection I had put together, he handed it back without comment, and said to type it for submission.

It was at this point that I first took my poems to Rex Arragon. I had never shown him any of my work, but the friends who lived with the Arragons had occasionally shown him a poem of mine and relayed his comments. I asked him to read the manuscript and help me to weed out the weakest poems. The conference I later had with him over this manuscript was the best I had ever had with anyone. He could say why one thing worked and another did not. He knew what I meant to say when I failed to say it, and could make me see at what point I went astray, though he never once suggested what I ought to do about it. Lloyd's "yes" or "no" was not enough. Victor, I always felt, had such reverence for the creative gift that he became clumsy in the presence of it. Also, he had a tendency to try to place me, to look for influences or to identify me with some school or other, a tendency common enough in English professors and critics generally, but unhelpful to the poet. At the same time, no one was ever more warmly appreciative of my poetry, from the first poems I read at the Gawd-Awful meetings to the Sappho translations. He was delighted with the thesis when it was at last in his hands, and summed up his satisfaction by saying: "A beautiful example of the pedagogic juggernaut being overturned by a butterfly."

To me, the most important part of the whole thesis-writing experience was that I had found myself a critic in Rex Arragon.

2

At the beginning of my second year at Reed another great change in my life began, although I was hardly aware of what was taking place until later. We saw the tall black newspaper headlines when the stock market crashed, but that meant nothing to me. I knew that my father had no money invested in the stock market, and, despite my course in Contemporary Society, which was supposed to prepare me to live in the modern world, I had no real notion of the association between the stock market and my bread and butter.

That, if I may digress for a moment, is what is wrong with most courses designed to prepare the young (sometimes even the very young) for life in the modern world. The course, in the first place, is likely to be more indoctrination than information; and, in the second, by the time the young are grown up enough to vote, the burning issues are entirely different from those included in the course. Thucydides might do them more good, yet history is gradually being eliminated as a course of study.

When, last year, we celebrated (if that is the word) the fiftieth anniversary of the stock market crash of '29, there was much discussion of economic factors, the evils of speculation, the length of the Depression, prospects of another such Depression, and so on. Now I admit that I have never understood economics, and after subject-indexing three volumes of Joe Dorfman's *The Economic Mind in American Civilization*, I knew I never would. I even wondered whether economists understand economics. But because I lived through it, I do know one thing about the Depression of the Thirties which none of the discussions I read or listened to last year even touched on.

The Middle West, from the Mexican border to the Canadian border, and almost from the Alleghenies to the Rockies, had seven years of drought. This does not mean that these states had less rain than usual, or insufficient rain, it means that many of them had no precipitation at all (rain or snow) for seven consecutive years. And this of course meant that farmers had no crops for seven years. And this in turn meant that the Midwest banks which regularly loaned money to farmers before they put in their crops, and were paid back when the crops were harvested, were unable to collect on any loans made. If they foreclosed on a mortgage, they were stuck with the farm. No one would buy it. Consequently, they failed. This seems elementary, yet in the recent discussion of the factors that brought on and prolonged the Depression, the reason given for bank failures was "unwise speculation." It may have been unwise to lend money to farmers, but that was what the banks were in business to do, and no one foresaw, or would have believed if they had been told, that a drought such as that one could last for seven years without a break.

I find that most of the younger people I talk with have heard vaguely of the Dust Bowl ("Was that in Kansas?"), and they recognize the term "Okies," which they associate with *The*

Grapes of Wrath. Steinbeck's book, and the movie made from it, seem to be the only things to keep the great drought of the Thirties alive in our collective memory. It is true that many poor southern sharecroppers, dislodged by drought, emigrated to California. Their plight was pitiful, and California tried to stem the tide by closing its borders to them. But Steinbeck seems to imply somehow that the heartless people speeding by in their Cadillacs were responsible for the Okies' plight and by extension for the drought. The Pulitzer Prize for 1934 was won by another novel (*Now In November* by Josephine W. Johnson) that graphically described the drought blighting the whole Midwest. This novel conveys the tension that built up in the farm families as they watched their crops wither first, then the trees, the drying up of creeks and ponds so that the scrawny cattle that could no longer be watered had to be sold for almost nothing while the sun blazed down month after month from a cloudless sky.

Of course we, west of the Cascade Mountains in Washington and Oregon, had rain. We also had our share of Dust Bowl immigrants, not so much the southern sharecroppers as the formerly prosperous farmers of German, Russian, and Scandinavian stock, who had been ruined by the drought in Montana and the Dakotas. In Portland we also had our dust storms, blown down the Columbia Gorge on an east wind. The first one struck on a fine spring afternoon in 1931 when I was studying at my desk in the dorm. There was suddenly a startling fusillade of casement windows slamming shut as a furious wind struck the campus. I sprang to fasten my windows and saw a yellow cloud extending half across the sky, approaching from the east. A few moments later the dust arrived, sifting through the windows, forming a thick layer on all the furniture, getting into one's teeth, eyes, hair. We had been hearing about the dust storms in the Midwest, but we now realized for the first time what less fortunate parts of the country had been enduring.

In 1936, at the very end of those dreadful years, I crossed the country from east to west, from Chicago to Portland on Great Northern's Empire Builder. Mile after dreary mile across North Dakota and Montana there was bare, brown, baked earth; there were unpainted and often abandoned farmhouses, windmills at rest and dilapidated, dusty stream beds, no cattle, no crops, no signs of life. I am not saying that the drought *caused* the collapse of the economy, but it was a major factor contributing to the misery of the nation during the early Thirties. And we were miserable.

If my parents ever had financial difficulties while I was growing up, I never knew it. My mother was brought up on frugal principles, not because the family was poor, but because waste was sinful. She carried on the tradition. What she bought was of good quality, but she never wasted anything. She turned and darned and made over as long as possible. She bought good cuts of meat, but never the most expensive, and she always found some way to use leftovers. She always saw to it that I had what I needed, but she never lavished gifts on me. In fact, I always had the impression, when I expressed the desire for something and did not get it, that somehow it wouldn't be good for me to have it. I don't think I ever attributed a denial to simple want of money. When the pinch came, it was hard for me to grasp the fact that we just did not have the money to spend even on some things I thought were essential.

The lumber market was slackening before the crash came, and by the spring of 1930, six months after the crash, we were beginning to be in trouble. That summer my mother had to have surgery, which lowered our reserves still more. By fall of that year I needed to start hashing in the commons, but I began as a substitute working only when the regulars wanted a day or a meal off. The campus was becoming depopulated. We were still going to symphony concerts, but single tickets for the cheapest seats were only fifty cents. Sometimes a faculty member gave us a ticket. My roommate and I usually rode downtown and back with the Arragons.

By my senior year, 1931–32, the campus was still more depopulated. One dorm was closed. Only one man in the previous graduating class had been able to find a job, and he had been taken on as an assistant at Reed for an annual salary of $500 (he was married). I was hashing three meals a day, five days a week, and substituting on week-ends when I didn't go home. I could not have finished that year if my mother had not used a nest egg she had put away for an emergency—a small bequest from that great-uncle who had gone to school with Riley. There was no thought in our minds of my applying for a scholarship or a loan. There were too many students who were worse off than I was.

Even that year we still occasionally went to concerts, most often entering the auditorium by a back door and sitting under the stage. The management must have known what was going on, but no one was ever thrown out. One fabulous evening when La Argentina was scheduled to dance in an almost empty auditorium, Mrs. Howard Barlow, whose husband was a Reed graduate, called the President's office and said to send Reed College down. That night we had orchestra seats, and we took taxis—by that time taxis were making a flat rate of fifty cents to take five of us downtown. (I believe there were only two student-owned cars on campus in 1931–32.)

There was more depressing news in the papers than the drought, the economy, and the Lindbergh kidnapping. Japan was moving into Manchuria. We had a talk in chapel by a Chinese gentleman who persuaded us that the Japanese were blackguards, and another by a Japanese gentleman who persuaded us they were nothing of the sort. Then we had a talk by a traveler returned from the Orient who told us that we need not worry about Japanese imperialism. There was no doubt that in taking Manchuria they had gobbled down more than they would be able to digest in the next twenty years—or was it one hundred? At any rate, there was no cause for worry. That, at least, was reassuring.

Mussolini was already in power, but I cannot remember that we were greatly disturbed about that. Then came the first newsreels of Hitler's goosestepping Nazis, and the old fear of Germany implanted in me by the World War I propaganda began to resurface. It should be noted, however, that we were all militantly pacifist, if that is not a contradiction in terms. The Vietnam generation, which thought it was introducing pacifism into the United States for the first time, did not realize how ardently pacifist most of the young were between the wars. We

Lyonesse sub mare/

my only queery is " poisonous " / what do you lose by omitting it.

possibly comma after light ,

and omit azure ?????

                    //

If you think well of any of these suggestions please
write direct to T/C/ Wilson and ask him to make 'em

on the mss/   2257   Bexley Pk. Rd
                                    Columbus
                                         Ohio

Am passing 16 poems for the anthol//   omitting

everything already used in College Vurrse.

(not sure , mebbe there are one or two more in mss/ Drummond

is Im looking over.

anyhow, you're bein' th starr border/ and I hope you wont **FLOP**

like H/Margaret   , and apparently the Bishop goil is a floppin '

already , unless Wilson has merely got a poor sample.

at any rate yr/ in the runnin fer the star lady purrformer

                    and the young lads need a stronger parental hand

than they   want.

You go on **CHAWIN** at them Sapphics/ with an Alcaic strophe on

sundays.   Remember the **SAWT** must strain against the

duration now and again , to maintain the tension. Cant

have rocking horse sapphics any more than tu **TUM,** iambs.

merry Xmas.   ciao   E . P .

They loathe me, because etc/ god damn 'em. But anyhow, any firm that has fallen for H. D. ought to repeat for M. B.

YOU mustn't get a swelled head and *say* that. Hilda hasn't answered my last. I don't think Bill has put her back up, perhaps he cd/ introduce you, the last address I had was

> Mrs. H. Aldington,
> case postale 72
> Latour, Vevey, Vaud, Switzerland

Either Bill or Marianne cd/ effect the introduction, or forward some of your poems to her, and ask her to recommend you to Houghton, without inserting my viperous name.
Bill prob/ better as he is by nature more enthusiastic. Tho' Marianne has expressed approval of both you and Wilson.

Send 'em (sen DUMB) the spare pages of the Westminster, so they won't see my connection with the affair.

> yrs
> EP

You'll be more comfort to Bill than to me 'cause he's got so much less to cheer him.

In May of 1935 he was still writing about sapphics, apparently in answer to further efforts of mine in that meter:

O/K/ keep at it till you get *your* basic, as distinct from Og's basic vocabulary so into yr/ head that you have no more difficulty about picking up quantitative dactyl, trochee or spondee, than J. S./B wd/ in knowing intervals of 3d, 4th and 5th and what they wd/ sound like before hand, not merely as intervals, but as intervals in transit.

Lavignac being any use?

· ·

Next step shd/ be to write sapphics without licherary words "clear as they are", is good to goodish, it contravenes strict greek or supposed idea of quantity, but it does throw the accent off the tumpty tum. *I* simply do not KNOW enough about question of quantity, I mean use IN english of greek supposed "rule". Keep on doing accented sapphics, if you like but also keep *trying* TOWARD the solution // can we in eng/ observe the measurements, short = short vowel and ONLY one consonant before the next vowel.

Can it be done without paralyzing the speech altogether. Sometimes I think my Arnaut Daniel is not so bad as I thought. It is emphatically NOT good enough.

flood of mail/ just in.

You might try to interest the great Marianna in the world about us. (nice job fer a young gal)

When Pound suggested that I write to W. H. D. Rouse about the possibility of writing quantitative verse in English, I did so. In reply I received an eight-page letter with a fascinating discussion of Greek scansion and an explanation of the way both accent and quantity were used in classical poetry. On the whole, however, the letter was decidedly discouraging. Rouse found some of my lines rather good, but seemed to feel that I was attempting the impossible. He feared that it was too late to Anglicize classical rhythms. "Chaucer might have done it, but hardly anyone since." *Evangeline*, he said, was "truly awful, not only the gabble, but the monotony."

In the fall of 1935 I was working in the relief office and feeling increasingly restive. With the publication of four poems in *Poetry* that year, I was cherishing a faint hope that when the magazine's annual awards were announced I might be the winner of the Young Poet's Prize, but I was delirious with joy when I received the Levinson Award instead. Of the four prizes given by *Poetry* at that time (the Levinson, the Guarantors', the Midland Authors and the Young Poet's Prizes), the Levinson was usually considered the most prestigious. The list of previous winners read like a Who's Who of modern American poets.

A little note saying that this year the awards were being given more for promise than performance did not diminish my pleasure in the least. By that time my father's business was improving; I had put some savings into a travel fund, and with this one hundred dollars of award money added, I felt that I could make plans at last for a trip to New York.

2

My first impressions of New York were so nearly those of every other young provincial with literary aspirations that there is no need to bore the reader with details. I took advantage of Southern Pacific's transportation bargain which included five days on its ship, the *Dixie*, sailing from New Orleans to New York; this meant that I entered New York in the most exciting way, moving through the harbor and up the Hudson one foggy morning in early April. A New Yorker who had been at my table on the ship stood at my shoulder identifying the towers as they emerged one by one from the fog. We docked at the foot of Bank Street.

In 1936 a number of my friends from Reed College were living in New York, and all of them, though living on a subsistence level, helped to make the visit memorable. The one who was my mainstay, however, was Charlotte Heaton. After her frigid winter at Cannon Beach, she had hitchhiked to New York with her former roommate, and after many adventures had finally gone into the window display business with Rex Sessions, whom she later married. Charlotte met me at the Southern Pacific dock and that same day took me out to find a furnished room not too far from her West Fourth Street apartment. We found one at 148 West Eleventh Street, across from St. Vincent's Hospital. Charlotte helped me to move in, then left me to my own devices. I had dinner at the diner on Sheridan Square and afterwards settled down in my new home with a map of the city, trying to locate myself and some of the addresses I had brought with me.

On my way to New Orleans, I had stopped off in California where I saw Xenia Kashavaroff, now Mrs. John Cage. John had given me the address of a woman poet, Clara Shanafelt, who was a friend of his, and I was pleased to find that she lived just down the street. I began to feel at home. But they had also given me Cummings' address in Patchin Place, and when I found that Patchin Place was in the same triangle I lived in, between 11th St., Greenwich Avenue and Sixth Avenue, my first-day revulsion from the noise, the soot, the wilderness of brick and stone and concrete, was all forgotten and I thought that this was not so much home as heaven.

There were some Reed couples in the Columbia University district ($8.00 per week for one room, the kitchen and bath being shared with a number of other people). Others, like

Charlotte, lived in the Village. I spent most of my first week with these friends: lunches, dinners, movies, plays, walking along the Hudson, riding the Staten Island Ferry, and just talking. I learned to ride the subway, and I wrote letters home. I also wrote to Dr. Williams.

I was feeling some diffidence about approaching in person the literary people who had corresponded with me. However, when I expressed this diffidence in a letter to Pound, he replied: "Ole Bill will be DEElighted to see you on his doorstep." With this reassurance, and the hope that Pound knew what he was talking about, I wrote to Williams first, and received in reply a note saying that he would be in the city on Friday, April 17th, and would call between five and five-thirty. A postscript suggested that I might have dinner with him. He was a little late, as he had said he might be, so that I had plenty of time to work myself up into a state of nervous anticipation that might have spoiled the evening. When he arrived, however, and throughout dinner, he put me at my ease (comparatively, at least) by doing all the talking himself. He regaled me with literary gossip to which I listened, completely fascinated, while making a mental note *never* to confide in Dr. Williams, if by any chance I ever had anything to confide.

If I remember correctly, I was startled and probably a little dismayed to find that he was so small and slight that I towered over him. At any rate I reported to my parents that he was

> not as good-looking as his picture (the only one I've ever seen) but he's every bit as enthusiastic as his letters, which makes up for it. He talks quite rapidly and nervously—reminds me a little bit of Dr. B—— as to his voice and manner of speaking. We went to an Italian restaurant [the Grand Ticino]. I believe he was in hopes of our seeing some celebrities, but we didn't. Nobody there but ourselves, as he expressed it.

I also reported that he was "rather bitter about his lack of success in publishing," and discouraging about my chances of publication in book form, a possibility that was already on my mind. He pleased me by saying I looked rather like Marianne Moore, until, a little later, he made a disparaging remark about her appearance and I realized that he had not intended the earlier

W. C. WILLIAMS, M. D.
9 RIDGE ROAD
RUTHERFORD, N J

April 14, 1936

Dear Miss Bernard:

Unless something
unforeseen prevents, I'll
be in New York this Friday
afternoon. I'll call sometime between five and
five thirty. If you are
not there I'll drop you
another line later.

Sincerely yours

W. C. Williams

Note from William Carlos Williams, April 14, 1936.

— or perhaps you'll
have supper with me
somewhere. I may be
a trifle late. But if
I am not there by 6:30
I will be because I am
stuck.

comparison as a compliment. He added that "I should see Miss Moore any place but at her home, because her mother is a dragon." As for the dinner itself, I said only that we had a lot to eat, and white wine to go with it, spumoni and demi-tasses of coffee for dessert. I don't remember what Williams had except for a huge slab of polenta, but the subsequent notes from him indicated that he had had a stomach upset afterwards, and I think he never quite believed that I wasn't just being nice when I said I had no ill effects.

After dinner we went back to my room where he looked at my manuscript and read four or five of my new poems. Suddenly he became enthusiastic and said "if nobody else would publish me, he would talk his friend Latimer into doing it—he would make me an exquisite little volume that would sell for $7.50 and be limited to 150 copies. That being what he did for Williams, and neither of us approving it in the least." He also decided at this point that I must meet more people.

> He suddenly said that he didn't want to bring down an avalanche on me, or anything like that, but would I mind if he wrote to some people and asked them to come to see me—Louis Zukofsky, the publisher Latimer, etc. Also he would write to Miss Moore and maybe she would drop around to see me. The only trouble was I wasn't staying long enough. And maybe I would like to come out to Rutherford sometime when the trees came out and the snow was off the roof. He knew a lot of other people but most of them were drunken bums—talented, but—. I should go to An American Place and see Alfred Stieglitz and he would talk an arm off me. I should go to see Miss Codman *at once*. James Laughlin IV broke his back while skiing and at the last word was off for Bermuda. He (W. C. W.) knew nothing of Wilson's whereabouts.

When he left, he took my manuscript and promised to send it back with his comments. It was nine o'clock. I sat down on the spot, and wrote the letter from which I have quoted.

One day during the following week I came home to my furnished room to find a note from R. L. Latimer of the Alcestis Press, who had called while I was out. The note was an invitation to a party at an apartment in Brooklyn. Williams was coming over to sign the colophon sheets of his new book, *Adam &*

Eve & the City; Miss Moore would also be there. Naturally, I went. Following Mr. Latimer's directions, I found my way over to Brooklyn Heights by subway. The party was in a penthouse apartment with a magnificent view of the Manhattan lights. I arrived early (a bad habit I have never been able to break). Dr. Williams and young Mr. Latimer, who had been having dinner together, arrived later, as did Miss Moore. Meanwhile I was in the awkward situation of having to introduce myself to people I had never heard of, who had never heard of me and could not quite imagine what I was doing there. Miss Moore arrived and was introduced, but failed to catch my name until Dr. Williams came in and greeted me. After that we tried to talk, but she was the center of attention, so that we had no private conversation though she promised to come to see me the following week. Only Williams, of the people at the party, had met her before, and he said that he hadn't seen her for years. I was delighted with her.

> She's a grand person. I'm very enthusiastic about her and not scared of her any more. [I had found her letters somewhat intimidating.] She talked a blue streak, and Williams said it was because she was frightened and was trying to build up a barrier of words to hide behind. I don't know about that, but she did get quite flushed, and she probably did realize that she was the center of the party. Anyway, she was most entertaining.

At this time Miss Moore was a straight and slender middle-aged woman who had not yet assumed her well-known trademark of the tricorne hat. She wore her once-red and still luxuriant hair braided in a coronet around her head, as she continued to do until the end of her life. At age forty-nine she dressed, not like my mother, but like my grandmother, in almost ankle-length skirts. In other words, she dressed like *her* mother. Her eyes were round and very alert, not sharp, but completely frank, open and observant—so observant that I tended to look instinctively for cover when they turned in my direction. Her voice, as is well-known from recorded readings of her poems, was nasal and unattractive, but listening to her talk I forgot the voice as I tried to keep up with her quick turns of thought. I felt as though I were one half of an unrehearsed flying-trapeze act. In a tête-à-tête conversation she would have been frightening except for her open, almost confiding manner.

When Miss Moore left, Latimer exclaimed that he had been trying to run that woman down for years. A young poet to whom I had already taken a dislike roused my ire by crying out that she was "just like Emily Dickinson!" Not to my mind. I could not imagine Emily Dickinson as editor of *The Dial*.

Sometime about midnight the party broke up. I rode back to Manhattan with Dr. Williams, across the already legendary Brooklyn Bridge, its towers disappearing into the night sky, Brooklyn Heights sparkling behind us and Manhattan glittering ahead. It is probably unnecessary to say that I felt the New York visit had got off to a flying start.

Miss Moore kept her word. On the 28th she came to see me and stayed two hours. My report to my family on that visit is unfortunately brief. "I couldn't begin to tell you what she said—" I told them, "she talked too fast." Apparently we talked about the manuscript I had brought with me, and which poems to include or exclude when I submitted it to a publisher. A letter had come that morning from Dr. Williams, who had made a list of poems I should leave out. It is not surprising that their opinions differed. We talked about his criticism, and "she said not to pay any attention to what Dr. Williams told me—as to content. As for technical advice, he might be very good. Then after some more, she said she was a menace, and I oughtn't to pay any attention to her either." I believe it was also at this meeting that she cautioned me against Dr. Williams and his friends: "It is NOT necessary to be Bohemian," she said firmly.

Finally: "She said she really knew very few people, but if she could help me at all she would be very glad to. She stopped on her way here to leave a note in T. C. Wilson's mailbox to tell him I was in town. She said he was dreadfully shy and maybe wouldn't look me up, at that. Also, he has had a very hard time. Sick, out of work, etc." She had surmised that I would be diffident about calling people to say, "Here I am!" because she found it almost impossible to do so herself. In London she had seen none of the literary people with whom she had corresponded, because she did not know how to go about letting them know that she was there.

260 Cumberland Street
Brooklyn, New York
April 26, 1936

Dear Miss Barnard,

If it would not interfere with something you had thought of doing, I could come to see you on Tuesday about two o'clock, for a little while. Do not be at the trouble to write if you would care to have me come, but please do tell me if you have plans for Tuesday that my coming would interfere with.

I hope you didn't take cold or find yourself too tired after the party Friday evening.

Sincerely yours

Marianne Moore

Note from Marianne Moore, April 26, 1936.

Almost immediately after Miss Moore left, Ted Wilson himself appeared and stayed about an hour and a half. Sometime after the *Westminster* debacle, I had had a letter from him saying that he was now poetry editor for a literary journal called *American Prefaces* published at the University of Iowa. He would like me to send him some poems. I did so, and he published two. By now, however, he was in New York, where he was doing a little reviewing, if I remember correctly, and reading manuscripts for Covici. He was a friend of Muriel Rukeyser and the Gregorys (Horace and Marya Zaturenska). Miss Moore seemed to know him rather well and to think highly of him. Poetically, he was associated with Pound, politically with the far left-wing. I never knew him well, and he always remained a bit of an enigma to me, but the meeting with him was to have important consequences. However, other developments came first.

The previous winter I had received a letter from Florence Codman of Arrow Editions, who said that she had been reading my poetry as it appeared in magazines "with increasing interest." She wondered if I had enough poems to make a book, and if so whether I would be kind enough to let her see the manuscript. Kindness wasn't in it. I was dying to let her see a manuscript. Arrow Editions had published *Tom* by E. E. Cummings, *Poems* by Robert Fitzgerald, and *Ten Introductions*, edited by Genevieve Taggard and Dudley Fitts, an anthology similar in intent to the Ann Winslow *Trial Balances*. R. P. Blackmur's *The Double Agent* also bore the Arrow Editions imprint.

Perhaps this letter first gave me the idea that I might be ready to have a book published. I did not send her anything that winter, but I brought the manuscript of a book to New York with me to show to Williams and Miss Moore. If they gave their blessing, I planned to show it to Miss Codman. I had also written to Pound about the possibility. His reply, written in February of 1936, was temperate. Without actually throwing cold water, he questioned whether I was ready.

> No, I don't see that I need issue VETO, and forbid you on pain (for whatever it wd. matter) of my displeasure to get a volume printed if you can manage it. BUT there are poets with

more to say than you have yet proved you have, who are still on
the waiting list. Not that proves anything save that they are
unacceptable to what the pubrs/ think is the public.

. . . .

Problem: whether you are content with remaining in the H. D.
// NOT as new in impact on the reader as she was.
          whether you wd/ go stale
if you dont have a book of yr/ own. . .
                     yr own
examination of conscience is all you can rely on.
           IS yr/ technical
achievement enough to warrant a repetition (pretty much)
of what H. D. had already said in 1913
                 ???
and wherefrom she advanceth not one inch.

. . . .

BUT I see nowt against your having a BRIEF book of yr/ own
if you can find a publisher. . . .

Williams, writing in April of 1936, also seemed to have
reservations:

> I've read your script through once and shall read it again in
> the next day or two and arrange it as I think it ought to be. I find
> the same charm—a bad word—that attracted me in the first
> place. Fine, clean writing.
>
> My chief comment so far would be that you are just begin-
> ning to do your best work. You are changing rapidly and get-
> ting better with each new piece. I mean, precisely, that the ear-
> lier pieces (or those which I take to be the earlier ones) are still
> somewhat conventionally restricted in their statement. But with
> more confidence you are allowing your personal reactions more
> leeway—you are feeling freer in the medium and will continue
> to develop with every contact you make with the world outside
> of Portland!

The last sentence especially interested me, coming from one
who had, as I thought, made a point of celebrating life in the
provinces and detachment from the New York scene. I was
equally interested when eventually I visited the Williams home
in Rutherford to discover that the Empire State building was
actually visible from the roof. At any rate, he concluded by

saying, "You ought to have a book now, but a small one," and that was what interested me most.

This note arrived between our tête-à-tête dinner and the evening in Brooklyn. After the party he returned the poems with another note. Asking how I enjoyed the evening, he said, "I hope your silence had no overwhelming significance. Marianne was in an extraordinary mood, through the curtain of words the frailty of her body made an affecting silhouette." My silence had signified only that I was scared, and too busy registering impressions to take part in the conversation myself—too much afraid of missing something, and also frequently at a loss to know what they were talking about.

Williams concluded this note, which contained a list of poems he would omit, by saying: "The poems improve on re-reading. To say that I have no way of foreseeing what is to become of you constitutes a true welcome into the small circle of those I admire." I quoted this in my letter home, and added, "I don't know what the last sentence means except that he said anything he liked (poetry, that is) seemed doomed to failure."

Miss Moore was in no way discouraging about the book—she only differed from Williams about which poems I should leave out. The very next day I called Miss Codman, who had an office at 444 Madison Avenue. This was the first skyscraper into which I had ascended, and I was mightily impressed. I found Miss Codman to be much younger than I expected, very smart in the conservative New York way, wearing one of the silly hats then in style—a perfectly flat, wide-brimmed black straw with a tricky little veil that she pulled down over her eyes while talking—I was entranced. She was a Wellesley graduate, but derided Wellesley as a "finishing school." Her accent, to my western ear, was posh East Coast, with a hint of British. Florence Codman also always remained a bit of an enigma to me. I never knew whether she was backing Arrow Editions with her own money, or acting for someone else. I may as well say now that she did not publish my poems, but she was extraordinarily kind to me, and did a great deal to make the New York visit even richer than it would have been without her interest.

She wanted to know where I had been, what I had seen, whom I had met. She took me out to lunch and to dinner with the Robert Fitzgeralds. We ate at the Brevoort, on the sidewalk behind the cedar hedge, surrounded by publishers and editors who were pointed out to me as they arrived. She took me to Harlem to see the John Houseman-Orson Welles production of *Macbeth* with an all-black cast (still the only production of *Macbeth* I have ever liked). At her apartment she showed me new books, avant-garde quarterlies, and played for me the recording of Joyce reading from *Anna Livia Plurabelle*—one of the most illuminating of my New York experiences.

One day when I met her for lunch I found her office full of people. I had no difficulty in recognizing one of them as he unfolded himself and stood up to meet me. I had already been told that Laughlin was six feet six inches tall, and knew it must be he. With him was his mother, a tall, handsome woman in the navy blue that all well-dressed New Yorkers wore in the summer. She said, "Oh, are you the girl who wrote *all those* poems?" Well, I did think he had published too many at once. I had sent them to him thinking he would make a selection, but he published them all. Besides the two Laughlins there was a middle-aged couple just returned from Paris. Robert Fitzgerald, who was working then for *Time* magazine, joined us. I had already written home when I first met Robert that he was "very young and sweet and serious—even younger and seriouser than Ted Wilson." Laughlin I found much less serious. In fact my first impression seems to have been that he didn't have very good sense. In 1936 he was twenty-two and dividing his time between Harvard and Europe when he was not recuperating from skiing accidents.

All of us had lunch at a large table in the Trianon Room of the Hotel Ambassador. I described it as having "fountains, soft music, much greenery, indirect lighting, etc." I had been budgeting one dollar a day for food, and the Trianon Room was not what I was used to. I sat next to Laughlin, but if we talked, I no longer know what we talked about except that he expressed surprise that I had been going to museums—the Metropolitan, the Museum of Modern Art (still in the old mansion that was its first home) and the Frick. He said that he loved painting, but *never* went to museums. The reason I remember the remark is that I was perplexed about where he could see paintings if he didn't go to museums. I finally realized that he no doubt saw Rembrandts and Picassos in the homes of his friends, if not in his own home. It boggled the imagination.

I don't want to overemphasize my own view of myself, in retrospect, as an awkward young woman with sawdust in her hair. How other people saw me, I don't know. It is possible that my naiveté may even have seemed refreshing. However that may be, I was thoroughly enjoying my adventures; but if I hadn't felt out of my depth now and then, I must have been obtuse; and if I hadn't been conscious of my home-made, too-colorful dresses, I would certainly not have been feminine. No one ever, at any time, by word or smile or raised eyebrow, did anything to increase my malaise. They were uniformly kind.

3

My original plan had been to spend three weeks in New York, go to Cambridge for a week to visit a friend at Radcliffe, and then, after another week in New York, to return home by way of Washington, D.C., Kentucky, and Indiana. I had not the remotest idea of staying on indefinitely, but I wished fervently that I had enough money to stay longer. My supervisor at the relief office had told me of a settlement house where I might get temporary work that would enable me to remain in New York for a month or two. I tried, but had no luck there.

Meanwhile I had been seeing Ted Wilson occasionally, sometimes alone and sometimes with a friend of his from Iowa. One night at dinner he suddenly said, "I know what you should do. You should go to Yaddo." I had never heard of Yaddo, and at first could not understand what he was talking about. I had heard of the MacDowell Colony at Peterborough, New Hampshire, where the widow of the composer Edward MacDowell provided sanctuary for writers, musicians, and artists to work during the summer months. It was much better known than Yaddo, in part because it was frequented by the establishment poets such as Edward Arlington Robinson, Elinor Wylie, William Rose Benét and the Untermeyers. Also, it is my impression that Mrs. MacDowell had to court publicity because she needed money, while at that time Yaddo was entirely funded by money from the Willard R. Spencer estate, and avoided publicity.

I learned from Ted that Yaddo was situated near Saratoga Springs. Like the MacDowell Colony, it offered hospitality to creative artists during the summer months. The will of the late Mrs. Trask so provided, in order that the hospitality she had extended to poets and artists in her own lifetime might continue indefinitely. Board and room were free. Applications were not accepted. One had to be recommended by a former guest. Ted explained that he would probably be going later that summer. Morton Zabel was on the Yaddo board of trustees and would almost certainly recommend me, but in addition I would have to be recommended by someone who had not only been a Yaddo guest, but had also met me face to face. This was Ted's first visit, therefore he was not qualified to pass on me, but he offered to introduce me to Muriel Rukeyser, who would also be there this coming summer and had been there before. She could certify that I was civilized. The only trouble was that the time was very short. It would be necessary to act with all speed. I was to write to Zabel, and Ted would set up a luncheon date with Muriel.

Writing home about this new development the day before I went to Cambridge, I said:

> I think it would be just the thing for me to do—because I'd see something of the East besides the metropolises, because I'd be available for further negotiations with publishers, if necessary, because of possible contacts 'outside of Portland', etc. But you can write your own reasons. I hope it isn't too late. Wilson . . . spoke to Mr. Covici about me, and Mr. Covici threw up his hands and said, 'Poetry! We don't want any more poetry! We're almost bankrupt now.'

My book manuscript was still with Miss Codman. She expected to have an answer ready for me when I returned from Cambridge. Like Williams, she felt strongly that I must remain in the East longer if possible, and she was encouraging me to try to place the poems with a commercial publisher whether or not she accepted the manuscript. I was to feel free to sign a contract with someone else until she actually announced publication *if* she accepted it.

We had had a miserable April in New York, but on May Day the sun came out. It glittered on the shining buttons of the mounted police as they paced slowly eight abreast down Seventh Avenue. Demonstrations were expected, but if they occurred I missed them; I was on my way to the subway and Grand Central Station. On the New York, New Haven and Hartford an elderly conductor unfolded my accordian-style ticket, which was still almost a yard long, and read it through from start to finish. "Well, young lady," he said, as he tore off the New York-to-Boston segment, "you're a long way from home. I hope you get back all right." I was delighted. New England, I felt, was going to live up to its reputation.

Spring came to Massachusetts, too, that week. We went to Concord, where the apple trees were in bloom, and to Salem and Marblehead. We went sight-seeing in Boston and viewed the treasures of the Boston Museum of Art and the Fogg Museum. I even had two interviews, one exploring the possibilities of a fellowship for creative work at Radcliffe, and the other an interview with a woman who was on the board of the MacDowell Colony. She was most discouraging, but the visit with her and the view of her apartment, the walls of which were covered with large, framed sepia photographs of Greek and Roman sculpture, provided another step in my education. The Cambridge spinster was not a legend; she was not even extinct. She lived and breathed and her every word was completely in character. It was like an encounter with the Phoenix.

Back in New York I took another room, this one on Washington Square South. I had moved in before I thought to ask about the telephone. When I did, I discovered to my dismay that there was none. This was not unusual in those days. Telephones were expensive. Mail was delivered four times a day, and a postcard mailed uptown in the morning was delivered downtown in the afternoon. Also, people used Western Union inside the city; if you were home, the hand-delivered message was put in your hand; if you were out, you found the message under your door when you returned. However, the lack of a telephone did complicate my campaign to get into Yaddo. My letters seem to be full of slip-ups that occurred when people had no way of reaching me.

All during the second half of May I was alternately down and up, leaving and not leaving, giving up hope and then hoping again. On May 13th I announced that I would leave New York a week from that day. I had had a friendly but not encouraging letter from Dr. Zabel. A luncheon date with Muriel Rukeyser had fallen through. I felt that it would be too expensive to stay on in New York with so little hope of getting the invitation.

The next day, however, I heard from Florence Codman. While she was not accepting the book because she felt I was not yet ready for one, she offered me $50.00 to live on while I continued the effort to get into Yaddo. It was not an advance, because she was not accepting the manuscript. However, she said, she would gamble that much on my coming through with a publishable manuscript later, and if I did, she would get her money back. This word sent me aloft again. I told her that if she felt it was that important for me to stay, I was sure my parents would back me for the extra week or so. "I feel like a race horse," I wrote them, "having somebody gambling good money on what a month in bluegrass would do for me. So I shall stay and make the attempt to get into Yaddo."

After this talk with Florence Codman I renewed my efforts to meet Muriel Rukeyser for lunch. One night when Ted Wilson was escorting me home after dinner, he had noticed her sitting in a car parked at the curb and had introduced us, but there was no chance to talk there. In fact, I had only a vague impression of her face in the half-light. After several abortive attempts the three of us finally had lunch together uptown. I saw her first far down the street, a large young woman in a striking lilac print dress and a large lilac hat. When she came up to us I saw her dark hair, large expressive dark eyes, and beaming smile. Her voice was soft, almost breathless, and she paused before she spoke. She was no chatterbox. By this time Muriel's plans for the summer had changed. She would not be going to Yaddo herself because the people she worked for had invited her to go to Spain with them. She promised to write that same evening declining the Yaddo invitation and recommending that I be asked in her place.

At lunch the conversation was of course about Yaddo.

When I asked whether it was a good place to make literary contacts, she answered that it was "the Magic Mountain with a vengeance." I learned about the mansion, with its fifty-five rooms, the studios in the woods, the lunch boxes set out on a marble bench beside an indoor fountain under a stained glass window. The bathtubs, she said, were six feet long, and her room had had seventeen windows. There were strict rules against interrupting anyone who was working. At this time Muriel must have been about twenty-two, or four years younger than I, but she seemed to have all the assurance I lacked. She had published *Theory of Flight* the year before, and was perhaps the best known of her contemporaries, although Elizabeth Bishop was also coming to the fore. It was the era of the Vassar girl: Rukeyser, Bishop, Eleanor Clark and Mary McCarthy.

So far so good, but when I wrote home on May 27th I was down again. I had had a note from Dr. Zabel "regretfully informing me that Mrs. Ames said previous invitations and acceptances would make it impossible to ask me during June." I would therefore leave for home on the following Wednesday. I continued:

> I'm to have lunch with Miss Codman tomorrow and I'll call Muriel to see what she thinks about whether they may have been counting her in on their guest-list. And if Miss C. doesn't have anything further to suggest, and I don't think she will, and if Muriel doesn't give me a lot more hope than I expect her to, I'll plan to come Wednesday.

When I called Muriel, she was more encouraging than I had dared hope she would be; she promised to write again that same day. Once more I postponed my departure for another week. However, by June 2, when five more days had passed with no word from Saratoga Springs, I was all set to leave on the homeward journey. Then the next day, June 3, I received a letter from Mrs. Ames inviting me to Yaddo for four weeks beginning June 12.

While these negotiations were going on, my social life and sight-seeing were continuing. There were few things I liked better than riding one of the open-topped Fifth Avenue buses downtown past those famous names (Brentano's, Scribners,

Macmillan) and under the arch into Washington Square. I liked the French tricolor flying at the Brevoort and the little Italian flag flying above the ice cream vendor's umbrella on the other side of the Square. I was pleased because I had been asked for directions five times, and had only had to ask twice. I was delighted because in this big city where one was supposed never to see a familiar face I kept encountering the people I knew. I no longer felt strange, even in the subways.

One evening Florence Codman and I were invited to the Fitzgeralds' apartment to dinner. The paragraph in my letter about this occasion contains the information that "I read some of the proof on a translation from Euripides that he [Robert] did with someone else. Harcourt Brace is bringing it out." The play was the *Alcestis*, perhaps the first truly modern verse translation of any Greek work. The "someone else" is, of course, Dudley Fitts, who was to write the Introduction for my Sappho translation more than twenty years later. I can hardly believe that I did not know, even then, who Dudley Fitts was; perhaps I omitted his name because I knew it would mean nothing to my parents. However that may be, coming events were casting shadows. Although we met only once in the interim, Robert Fitzgerald and I would both be at Brunnenburg in 1954 reading each other's manuscripts: his *Odyssey*, Book I, and my Sappho translation.

Soon after my return from Cambridge I invited Miss Moore to have lunch with me, but she countered with a suggestion that I meet her in her dentist's waiting room. I had told her about Miss Codman's rejection of the book manuscript, and she replied: "It is disappointing about the Arrow Editions, but a talent does not leave one and publication by degrees, in magazines, is in some ways I think even better than to begin at once with a book."

I met her as she suggested, and in a letter I wrote that evening, I said:

> I had quite a long and interesting conversation with Miss
> Moore—all about my poems and my future. I've hardly thought
> about anything else since. She gave me some advice I thought
> was very good and some I'm doubtful about. Also found out

that keeping up a correspondence with Ezra as long as I have without being insulted is a record. He even insults her. But maybe she would think she was insulted when I wouldn't. She was very pleased when I told her how nicely he always spoke of her in his letters.

Marianne Moore is the only person I have ever known who always said "Mr. Pound." She and "Mr. Pound" had not yet met, but had been corresponding for a long time, I gathered. She discounted the bluster, and emphasized his kindness. Once, she said, she wrote to him complaining that she was not getting anything published. Shortly thereafter she began to hear from editors not only in the United States and England, but from as far away as India and Australia. All the letters said the same thing: Ezra Pound had informed the writer that she might be willing to let him have some of her work for publication in his magazine.

She also chided me gently for not writing better prose. She had found my letters not very well written, and impressed upon me her view that a good prose style was very important to poets. I lamely explained that fright had probably helped to make my style a bit stilted; she nodded understandingly and said that she had thought that might be part of the trouble.

Sometimes Miss Moore seemed impossibly Victorian, as when she informed me that she never rode the subway alone at night, not because she was frightened (almost no one was, at that time), but because she did not consider it "suitable." She was also concerned about the kind of language Pound might be using in his letters to me. When I said, "Well, nothing worse than he publishes," she blenched and said, "I should hope not!" However, too much has sometimes been made of her primness. I was once told that when she was editor of *The Dial*, she refused to publish anything by E. E. Cummings, but that was not true. She published several of his poems, and she was the first person ever to tell me to read *The Enormous Room*.

During our conversation I told her about my visits to Concord, Salem and Marblehead, and especially about the cemetery at Marblehead. As I remember, it was on a small promontory overlooking the water. Among the graves there were a number of monuments inscribed with lists of names of men lost at sea, and just behind this green knoll we came upon a little pond where children were sailing toy boats with colored sails. There was the germ of a poem in it, but I never wrote the poem. Instead I told Miss Moore, who never forgot it. Several times in after years she mentioned the Marblehead cemetery, and once she told me that friends had taken her and her mother to Marblehead. She remembered about the cemetery, she said, and would have liked to have seen it, but unfortunately her mother was unable to leave the car, and of course she stayed with her mother. This kind of thing made me want to beat my head against the wall. And in this connection a letter she wrote me the next day after our talk is worth quoting almost in full:

> It strikes me in connection with the Concord group, what ascetics they were; how little they had materially, yet what great givers they were: their writings are lasting and we have to remember that they were the expression of what they—the writers—daily lived. I think young writers naturally feeling the weight of work coming can scarcely believe enough that often the foundation for it is in giving to others and taking care of their interests. Many things in life have been hard and I have often thought how much better it would be for me if circumstances were different; but a remark of Katharine Cornell—in a magazine—about her art stays in my mind since acting is the most obstructed form of expression perhaps that we have—: "Nothing is keeping me back but myself." But even the force in that idea does not enlarge one so much as the above idea, that in giving to others and taking care of their interests one has real self-expansion.
>
> I spoke of hoping that you will read the (Sheed and Ward) Henry W. Wells edition of Piers Ploughman; and perhaps you would care to read too when you can, Kagawa's novel, *A Grain of Wheat*.
>
> I hope you can feel too that opposition and advice are appreciation, not an illegitimate cutworm.
>
> Sincerely yours,
> Marianne Moore

I regretted that she herself found it necessary to give quite so much, but when, a few years later, I came upon her poem, "What Are Years," in the current issue of *Kenyon Review*, I had to ask myself whether the poem was not worth the price she had paid. It seems to me one of the great modern lyrics, and certainly one of the finest ever written by a woman.

4

The experience of living and working at Yaddo must of course be different for every individual. Marianne Moore quoted Morton Zabel as saying that it was "heaven on earth to be there." Others have arranged within days of their arrival to receive an urgent summons to return home. Still others have stayed, but only, I suspect, to collect notes for a satirical novel or short story. Perhaps others have stayed and suffered. In any case the Yaddo of forty-five years ago probably bears little resemblance to Yaddo today. I spent two summers there, 1936 and 1938, and even in two years there was a decided change: for instance, drinking was forbidden on the premises in 1936, which meant of course that it went on behind closed doors, but by 1938 that ban had been lifted. Also, the atmosphere necessarily changes with the changing guest-list as well as with changing times. I know very little about Yaddo today, but I assume that it is, as it was then, a good place for creative artists and writers who have so much work bottled up inside them that all they need is privacy and a desk to work on or a studio and an easel. They have an opportunity to work steadily, perhaps for the first time in their lives, and they produce an astonishing amount of work. If they can sublet their own living quarters while they are at Yaddo, they have not only free board and room, but a little nest-egg for the winter. It was a good place for me for other reasons. I had a chance to rub elbows with my peers and acquire some sense of the people behind the printed pages that had formed my only notion of the contemporary literary world.

An artist's wife once said to me that Yaddo was better or worse depending on the preponderance of artists or writers. "When the artists quit work," she said, "they *quit*. They are ready to relax and have a good time, but the writers are *always* working." I think she may have been right. Many of the writers, I felt, were constantly making mental notes, searching for the witty thing to say, jockeying for position. I was seldom really comfortable with them. With only two exceptions, the best friends I made during the two summers at Yaddo (that is, the people I spent the most time with while there, and continued to see later in New York) were not writers, but artists and musicians.

In the past, and I believe this is equally true today, the young or not yet established artists and writers were in the majority, with a sprinkling of editors as well as music, art or literary critics to give ballast and, I suppose, provide useful contacts for the young. There were no workshops or seminars. It was up to us to make our own opportunities for exchange of ideas or manuscripts.

Whatever the changing atmosphere from year to year, the mansion and the grounds provided the same sort of backdrop and contributed to an almost surrealist effect as the actors took their places or even as the working-men's black tin lunch boxes were set out on the marble bench beside the dribbling fountain. According to the terms of the Trask will, the furnishings of the mansion were to remain unchanged, and when I was there everything was still in place. Perhaps it still is. Acres of gold carpet seemed to extend into the distance as I entered the great hall. The larger-than-life portraits of the two dead children, clad in funereal black, dominated the music room, formerly a chapel. A canopied bishop's chair was attractive to the more daring guests; I don't remember that I ever mustered enough courage to sit in it. A bronze Mercury balanced on one foot on the newel post of the grand staircase. I believe he was holding a lamp aloft. The portraits of Mr. and Mrs. Trask, also life-size or near it, tried but failed to dominate the great hall. I have lingering memories of a rather buxom Mrs. Trask endeavoring to look ethereal in a diaphanous white gown with pink flowers in her hair, and her bearded husband in golf knickers and plaid socks. I always tried to sit with my eyes averted from them, and I may have misremembered the details.

The hall at the top of the staircase was a comfortable reading room on a more human scale. I was most impressed to see the periodicals that were laid out there, everything from *The Criterion* to *New Masses*. I found, too, that there was a fine record collection (fine by my lights, at least) in the music room. The freedom to browse among the magazines and listen to records whenever I wished seemed to me ample reward for the effort I had put into getting there.

Besides the current magazines in the reading room there were back files of literary quarterlies. In an old copy of *Hound & Horn* I found a description of the mansion: "The purest 1890 flowered into Yaddo, complete with Richardsonian granite, golden oak, pseudo-medieval stairways and diamond-paned casements." In this reproduction of Carmen Sylva's Romanian castle, Mrs. Trask had entertained Henry Van Dyke, and here she expected to entertain writers like him after her death. The coming-on writers of the Thirties, however, were cut from a different cloth. Hence the surrealist effect, which fascinated me.

However, if many of us were ill-at-ease in the mansion, we could relax in our studios. Mine was known as the Barn Studio. It was in a pine woods, and was furnished with a desk, wood-stove, cot, bookcase, and various chairs. This to me was home-like. There were also blotters, brooms, a fly swatter, a candle and a water jug. If it rained at noon, our lunchboxes were left on the doorstep. In sunny weather we picked up our lunch-boxes at the mansion and either returned to our studios or pic-nicked somewhere about the place, alone or in company, by appointment or by happenstance.

For me, walking was another pleasure. The grounds were extensive enough to provide a number of different rambling walks that I took alone or with someone else. After dinner, es-pecially the first year I was there, we sometimes walked to the race track tavern for beer. Or we might walk down to the race track before breakfast to watch the horses worked out. When Henry Roth was courting Muriel Parker, they walked every morning to the Spa, ostensibly to "drink the waters," but more probably to evade the observant eyes and attentive ears of their fellow guests.

Marianne Moore had also quoted Morton Zabel as saying the food was very good. This was an understatement. The cook was a Czech woman whose desserts I remember as the most delicious I have ever tasted anywhere, especially the perfect soufflés. Day after day she outdid herself, with few repetitions.

As I was still a beanpole, I was able to enjoy a blissful experience with no pangs of conscience. If tensions were building up around the table, I hardly noticed. I was concentrating, oblivious of my table-partners, on the lemon pie. So, at least, I have been told. My preoccupation with the food rather than the undercurrents of the dinner conversation seems to have been noticeable.

Of course there were tensions. If you gather together twenty or more artists, musicians, and writers (or anyone else for that matter) and isolate them on an estate, no matter how large, you can't hope to avoid tensions. One thing that contributed to tension was the personality of Mrs. Ames, the director. We never knew where we stood with her. We lived under a dictatorship, and there were times when a situation would develop that was almost Kafkaesque in its mysteriousness.

I had anticipated that cliques might form. I did not want to be part of one, or excluded from all of them, either. I wrote home that I was circulating "relentlessly" in order to do what I could against the cliquish tendency. As it turned out, that first year was open and easy. People arrived and departed and more people arrived, keeping the mix more or less fluid. It was a relatively small group and I think most of them were having a pretty good time, though some of the New Yorkers complained that there was nothing to do in the evening, and that birds woke them up in the morning.

It was at Yaddo that I first realized how little chance my poems had with born-and-bred New Yorkers who thought they heard hawks cawing in the woods, and supposed that all railroad trestles were of iron construction. I hadn't known of the existence of iron trestles until that summer. What I meant by a "mountain" was something quite different from what they meant by the same word. On the other hand, I wrote that I was now beginning to read the poems of my contemporaries with increased comprehension. The experience of those two months in the city had illuminated much in modern literature that had been obscure, but what experience was going to make my poems intelligible to city-bred readers? When they traveled they went to Paris.

Another difficulty was that all these writers were politically oriented, and I was not. It may seem odd that my social-work experience had not made a revolutionary of me, but actually, by giving me a first-hand acquaintance with one section of the proletariat, it had only convinced me that my clients and probably most members of the American proletariat were unrepentant capitalists. They only wanted more of the capital. The revolutionary aspirations of a Vassar beauty in pink linen culottes from Bonwit Teller seemed to me totally unreal and probably born of guilt combined with a desire to be in the swim. I could not take her seriously. The strong drift towards communism at that time was, in any case, inspired more by anti-fascist fervor than by revolutionary fervor. The Spanish Civil War broke out while I was at Yaddo; the shooting that we had all been dreading had started, but my pacifism had taken deep root and remained unshaken.

The social situation was made more difficult for me by the fact that when I arrived I was for the first time in my life surrounded by complete strangers, none of whom I had met before, most of whom I had never heard of before, and none of whom had ever heard of me. I had traveled alone all the way to New York, but that was different; conversations were casual and anonymous. At Yaddo I soon met two rather well-known left-wing playwrights, one of whom thought it was very funny when I asked him whether he was a writer. News of his successes naturally had not reached me in Vancouver. I had heard of Alfred Morang, who was a frequent contributor of short stories to avant-garde magazines. A little later Malcolm Cowley arrived. Of course I had heard of him. As literary editor of *The New Republic*, he was by way of being one of the best known literary men in the country, but I had not realized that he was a poet, and I put my foot in it again.

I was looking forward to Morton Zabel's arrival because, although I hadn't met him, we had corresponded and he at least knew who I was. When he did arrive, I was disappointed. I had been warned that I would find him stiff, but this was an understatement. In a letter home I said, "Mr. Zabel has arrived and I find him just as formal and precise as they said I would, but I fail to find him as charming as they said. Maybe I'll like him better when I get acquainted. He's very hard to get acquainted with." I also described him as the only man at Yaddo who always wore a hat. He was a great favorite with Mrs. Ames, who was delighted that her cocker spaniel Brownie was so attached to Morton. She alone seemed to be unaware that Morton regularly broke one of the strictest Yaddo house-rules and fed Brownie at the table.

For some reason Mrs. Ames seemed to take a fancy to me, too, perhaps because I was docile. My original invitation for four weeks was extended to July 27th. This was fortunate, because one of the friendships that was to mean most to me had its beginnings towards the end of my stay when Babette Deutsch arrived. I knew of her as a well-established poet, and also as the author of *This Modern Poetry*, which I thought the best book of the sort that I had come across. I guessed her age as about forty-five, but she was actually forty-one. I described her as soon as she arrived as "a small unprepossessing person with her hair in a short straight bob." Her name had suggested a chic little woman, but Babette's skirts were almost as long as Miss Moore's, and her shoes resembled what we used to call "Mary Janes." Her eyes were her most striking feature: dark eyes, clear and lively. I liked her immediately. We went for an evening walk together, and afterwards I gave her, at her suggestion, some of my poems to read.

I had been passing my poems about, and on the whole they were well received, but I was becoming increasingly confused by the different reactions to the same poems. The poems Miss Moore approved Dr. Williams thought I should exclude from a book when I had one. Dr. Williams thought I was just beginning to do my best work, and Florence Codman thought I was going downhill. Here at Yaddo the reactions of different readers were equally contradictory and confusing. Perhaps this was what Pound meant when he said that for the young too much criticism was often worse than none. I don't remember that Babette had specific comments, but she said in passing the next evening that "that was very exciting stuff" I had given her—the most heart-warming kind of compliment.

I no longer remember how much work I did that summer. I revised a few poems and wrote a few new ones. I wrote letters. I sat for my portrait to one of the painters, a provincial like myself from a small Pennsylvania town. A composer, Edwin Gerschefski, set one of my poems to music. I experienced my first East Coast summer with its hot nights and the violent thunderstorms that usually sent me scurrying from my studio back to the mansion in late afternoon. On the Fourth of July we had a clear balmy evening with a full moon. A group collected on the terrace. Someone provided sparklers. We ordered ice cream cones brought out by taxi from town. The moon shone brilliantly on the white petunias in their tubs around the edge of the terrace and shimmered on the vanilla ice cream cones. Malcolm Cowley mounted the balustrade and made a speech nominating Joe Gould for president. It was all very boring, or not, depending on how you looked at it. To me it was not.

5

In late July I left Yaddo and went back to New York for a brief visit, then on to Washington, D.C., for a day or two with Reed friends, and after that to Chicago with stopovers in Cincinnati and Indianapolis to see my cousins. The Empire Builder left the Chicago Union Station at midnight for Seattle and Portland, so that I had a free afternoon and evening in Chicago. I called the *Poetry* office and talked to Harriet Monroe, who immediately invited me to come out to 232 E. Erie. When I arrived, she explained that she was meeting her brother for dinner and afterwards they would be going over the manuscript of her autobiography, just completed. She invited me to come home with her for a glass of sherry when she left the office and also to have dinner with her and her brother. She was apologetic about having to turn me off after dinner. The conference over her manuscript could not be postponed because she was leaving for South America almost immediately. She was going (by sea, of course) to a P.E.N. conference in Buenos Aires and later would cross the Andes by rail to Chile. Harriet Monroe was then seventy-six, a tiny, dynamic, enthusiastic seventy-six.

When I was in her presence I realized for the first time how she had managed to do it—that is, induce one hundred wealthy Chicagoans to guarantee her the funding for a new magazine, and a poetry magazine at that, for five years. She had achieved that goal and put out the first issue of her magazine in 1912 when she was already fifty-two, and she had kept the magazine going for 24 years, through the first World War and the worst years of the Depression. She was at the same time engaging and indomitable.

It was always easy for the avant-garde to make fun of Harriet Monroe. She was an aging spinster, and they are fair game. Her judgment was sometimes faulty, like that of most editors and she must, sometimes, have had to think of the reactions of her guarantors. It was even easier for the literary conservatives, not to mention the Philistines who seldom read any poetry at all, to make fun of her and her magazine for the free verse she published, whether it was Carl Sandburg's "Hog-butcher for the world" or H. D.'s Imagism, Edgar Lee Master's *Spoon River* or T. S. Eliot's "Prufrock." Perhaps no modern literary figure has stood up to more artillery fire from both sides. Recently Daryl Hine, in his Introduction to *The POETRY Anthology*, has risen to her defense. I applaud the defense, though I think it might have been done without belittling what Pound did for the magazine in its early years. Perhaps Ezra Pound and Harriet Monroe did not need each other as much as I think they did, but surely American literature needed them both in the worst way. I can see no reason whatever to play down the achievement of one in order to exalt the achievement of the other.

Miss Monroe saw me looking at the photograph of Pound among the many portrait photographs on the office walls. It was one I had never seen before. "That is not a good likeness," she said. "Ezra Pound is a very handsome man!" She beamed. Then she settled me at Morton Zabel's desk where I wrote a few notes while she finished her work for the day. I have only a hazy memory of her apartment and no account of that visit in my letters because I was homeward bound. I know the rooms were pleasant, and I seem to remember that they contained mementoes of her recent trip to China; I believe the apartment was rather high, and looked towards Lake Michigan. I liked her brother, a substantial, professional type, amiable and courteous. We ate at a restaurant nearby. After dinner I took my leave and went off to the station. As I left, Miss Monroe said to me, "You

know, we expect great things of our Levinson Award winners."
It was an admonishment, but she seemed confident that I
wouldn't let her down. Of course I never saw her or heard from
her again. Our meeting was on August 5. On August 10th she
departed for South America and on September 26th she died of
a cerebral hemorrhage in Arequipa, Peru.

Boarding the Empire Builder was a homecoming in itself,
and by now I was excited about getting home. The Midwest
had been hot and parched by the drought, the trains dirty. My
first morning out from Chicago, I went into the diner and had a
huge bowl of fresh plump fragrant raspberries for my breakfast.
Ah-h-h-h. God's country again. The train crew, the porters, the
passengers, looked and spoke like my people. Next day we
would enter the Rockies, and the next morning when I woke up
we would be traveling along the Columbia as it flowed west to
the sea. I was looking forward to late summer trips into the
mountains and down to the coast. I boarded that train with
hardly a backward glance, and I was very happy.

I forget how long this euphoria lasted. A week? A month
perhaps? All I know now is that within a very short time I had
one immediate goal in mind, and that was to get back to New
York to stay. I had not liked coming home to live after college,
but now, after five months of travel and New York and Yaddo, I
found my situation intolerable. There is very little to say about
the two winters that followed. I did another stint at the relief
office and found it more depressing than ever. There was no
longer the hurly-burly of the early years, but with WPA in full
swing and more men working, we seemed to be handling only
the hopeless cases, and handling them in a predictable, cut-
and-dried fashion. The sense of crisis, of urgency was now
gone, but we had in its stead the dreariness of a long slow journey across a gray plain, a plain without landmarks and a journey
without a destination.

I remember only two flashes of light in those dreary winters: one, when James Laughlin skied down off a mountain and
took me to dinner at the old Portland Hotel, and afterwards to
see Greta Garbo in *Camille*; the other when John and Xenia
Cage just as unexpectedly turned up on their way from California to Seattle. If either Laughlin or the Cages had alighted from

another planet, their visits could hardly have seemed more miraculous.

The correspondence with Pound languished. After all, he had done what I wanted him to do; he had got me into print and introduced me to a few distinguished poets and some editors. Now it was up to me. I received one postcard from him, dated December 1, 1936:

> I have again a few moments leisure, if you care to report.
> NO royal road/
> in general read something MORE. read something DIF-
> FERENT, send me a few translations from greek IN orig/
> metres, picking what you feel.
>   also remind me what other languages you read/
>   and; on other hand/ what local energies can be released for
> textbook reform. and/or mobilizing linotypes under new deal.
>   y;v;t
>   E P

Energies: I was already sinking into a slough of despond, and to make matters worse, the Recession was about to begin, not so severe as the deep Depression of the early Thirties, but bad enough so that New York receded again into the impossible distance. I began to set myself a more practical goal. For all my familiarity with the back roads probing the Cascade Mountain fastnesses, and a considerable acquaintance with the Columbia Gorge trails, I had never done a real wilderness trip, a back-packing, camping-out trip, and I wanted to have that experience at least once. It became almost an obsession. When I had a chance to team up with two young women who were planning a hiking trip in British Columbia, I leapt at it. We went north in July, following the Frazer River to a hamlet called Lillooet, and hiked out from there into the steepest mountains I had ever seen: there was only enough slope on one side to allow an over-hang on the other. When we sat down on a trail to rest, we had to prop ourselves to keep from sliding to the bottom. We usu-ally camped in abandoned prospectors' camps beside rushing, foaming streams of cold green water. We encountered a few bears and had other adventures, all of them delightful. One night we slept on a narrow foot-bridge, head to toe, because the only other level ground had once served as a horse corral (fortunately no bears attempted to cross the bridge that night). Another night we slept on a lake beach within full sight of an Indian village. This was arid pine country; the nights were warm and there was no dew. I had not the stamina the other two girls had, but they were patient with me and cheerfully waited when I had to get my breath. It was an experience that produced a number of poems eventually, an experience I am thankful to have had, although I was never able to repeat it.

I read a great deal, among other things *The Enormous Room, Seven Pillars of Wisdom,* and *Ten Days that Shook the World.* Table-talk at Yaddo had made me feel how remiss I was not to have read the classic by Portland-born-and-bred John Reed. I had seen the Russian film (probably the first foreign film I ever saw) while I was at college, but I had never got around to the book itself. As it turned out, any impact John Reed's account might have had on my thinking was deflected every time I put the book down and picked up the evening paper. By some freak of timing, I found myself reading the book simultaneously with accounts of the Moscow Trials. The heroes of the book were appearing daily in the news dispatches from Russia as villains and traitors. They were standing in the dock actually beating their breasts and confessing their sins. Each account made the other seem unreal, perhaps even fictional. Of the three books I have mentioned, *The Enormous Room* made the deepest impression.

Meantime I was writing more poems and having a few things accepted and published. Morton Zabel, the new Editor of *Poetry,* took four, and Cowley took one for *The New Republic.* In the late summer of 1936 Laughlin had written asking me to select three of the poems he had published in *New Democracy* for republication in the first New Directions annual. He said there would be "no money in this venture, only glory, all kinds of large and small glory." When the volume arrived, the contribution that most impressed me was the Williams short story, "A Face of Stone." I was at an emotional low ebb in my social work experience, and Williams' little story in its spareness, simplicity (no modernist pyrotechnics), and raw truthfulness seemed to me the only satisfactory piece of *new* writing that I had encountered for some time. I wrote and told him so.

There followed, through the spring, summer and fall of 1937 an exchange of letters that did much to keep me alive—that is, alive as a poet. There was no question of my starving to death.

In reply to my comments on the short story, Williams wrote in a letter of March 4, 1937:

> It's much easier writing to a person I've seen and eaten Italian cooking with—not so hot that Italian cooking!
>
> Laughlin should receive fifty percent of the credit for that story of mine. You'd be surprised how many people looked askance at it before he printed it—and how many people have praised it since. The truth's a queer rabbit still in this world— and there's just enough of the sour truth in that story to frighten the life out of those who think they must be afraid to offend the Jews or this one or that one for fear lest someone should think this or that or the other. While they miss the whole point of the thing as being a story. Glad you enjoyed it.

He went on to describe the novel he had just finished (*White Mule*) and concluded:

> When you have your new collection of verse ready I'd like to see it. Send me the carbons if you care to. I'll promise to return everything in good order.
>
> Best wishes. I'm glad you saw Laughlin when he was out there. He came East again and promptly broke his arm. He's better now. Some day he'll break his neck skiing and it'll be too bad for poetry and prose.

I sent Williams a manuscript, a new collection, and the reply when it came provided enough nourishment for several weeks in barren country. On March 26, he wrote:

> I have taken great liberties. Forgive me. I have marked up your script as I pleased—but only because I enjoyed it. Pay no attention to what I have indicated unless you can do so impersonally. No one has a right to touch another's script—but if he does assume the right he should be completely ruthless and inconsiderate of all feelings.
>
> When your book is out send it to me. We'll trade. I enjoy your work very much. It is a sensual pleasure to read you. It is well worth doing over and over. There are places in your work that are unsurpassed in modern poetry. You have the summative

gift, the enclosing of deep feeling in the flash of an image which is the substance of the whole thing. That makes good reading. And, you don't overburden the attention with the fillgap too many others use—God knows why—perhaps in the illusion that they are writing a "story".

Hard to hold poetry to its natural bareness. We all want to make an impression on someone or something. Anyhow, you don't want to do that.

Best wishes. I enjoyed reading you. We'll meet again. You are a strange creature. Where in hell do you get your ruthlessness toward yourself combined with the will and courage to go—and face the modern without bitterness? Every once in a while I think of you as a romantic, then you stick something in my eye to wake me up. I wish you could circulate more in every way—I wish we all could. It isn't fear, it's lack of opportunity—and fastidiousness—

> Yours,
> Williams

Chapter 4

By January of 1938 my frustration with my life in Vancouver had redoubled, and the possibility of getting out seemed more remote than ever. The better times that we had experienced in 1936 had ebbed as the Recession set in; we were again decidedly short of money. The taste of New York had intensified my discontent, while the monotony of life in Vancouver actually increased. The friends who had come home from college when I did were now scattered, some of them teaching, some married. My contemporaries in Vancouver were completely occupied by domestic duties and child-bearing. The daily visit of the postman was the only thing I looked forward to. Finally all my waiting and watching was rewarded: I received a letter from Elizabeth Ames inviting me to Yaddo for two months beginning in July. We held a family conference and decided that we could scrape up enough money for the train fare. I would take only the clothes I already owned; I would need almost no spending money at Yaddo, and the free board would help to pay for the trip. From the moment we decided I would go, I had no intention of returning to Vancouver to live. I warned my parents that I intended to stay on in the East if I could find work. My father was surprised, but not opposed. My mother was not even surprised. She had seen my daily vigil at mail time, and she knew better than he did how lonely I was, or, as she said, "how deadly dull it is for you here."

The new development emboldened me to write to Pound again and send him the poems I had been writing. It has been said of Pound that during the late Thirties he lost interest in poetry and neither thought nor wrote of anything but economics. The letters to me written in 1938 show that he was still concerned about poetry and young poets at least occasionally. Now and then, in one letter or another, he recommended that I learn something about economics, but he did not insist when I simply ignored that part of the letter. He took the attitude, almost from the beginning, that the study of economics was not part of my job. In this I concurred.

In answer to my new offering of poems, he wrote, on February 18th:

Dear Mary,
    I thought there were a couple of good ones/ but the young must be judged by the young/ so I gave the best of 'em to R (not Raymond) Duncan, and he thought two fit for Townsman.

    and if they get by the pair of blue eyes which watch his activity I spose that will mean more than mere male susceptibility.

And it is now about time you *decided*
        whether you are going to be lorelai, or matriarch or blue stocking

        b/s to be made of good silk

        not that the latter need interfere with either of the other careers / or in fact that there is any objection to an A.I. standard female running the whole three lines/

At any rate I am past attending to the first two/ without undue inconvenience / but as to the third/ you better get a language and an author, greek, latin or chinese/ the latter being less occupied ground.
    .   .   .   .

There is Catullus' "Collis O Heliconii"
                still untranslated / well over a century since any female
tackled Homer/ and Rouse has made bread and butter of it/ At
any rate you shd/ take on a JOB something of interest in itself to
more than yourself

As to MEN / there was a likely lad passed through here six
weeks ago/ needs something above the average to look after
him.

No need of yr/ tying up and being sunk by the iceman.

As to the AUTHOR; you will want a SUBJECT by the time
you are 40/ may as well pick it NOW so that you will then
know something about it.

No real work been done on Chinese sound sequence/

If that is too difficult / there is always the Odyssey and the
Catullus longer impossibles.

yr venerable uncle

Ez P

I must have replied that I was going to be a bluestocking.
The retort came promptly:

WELL my dear M/B
        Every blue stocking has garters, AND we can't have you
relapsing into the cadence of Thanatopsis. EITHER you get a
FIELD, a job, or you have some EMOTIONS, something to
WORK on / / greek, if must, but *something*, and remember that
an "author" isn't registered at the police station, and you aren't
forced to monoandry of mind, even if it IS (I don't deny it) more
convenient for état civil (gamos, andros MONOS etc. . . . natural
in some cases; in others unnatural)

ANYhow you can't flirt with a frigidaire attachment, though
THAT and just that is what the U.S.A. tries (result uncle Bill
Wms/ "they are no use except six together on a bathing raft").

        There is quite a nice (minded) y/m doing a thesis of Dino
del Garbo, but I don't know what he LOOKS like/
· ·
I am not saying a mere cine star wd/ DO.

I forget what Yaddo is / can I be any use in landing you in a
teaching job?

Old Ford is trying to lure ME to a beanery in beyond mid
N.W. so there may be a vacancy. I don't say it is a nice way for a
young lady to spend her time/ correcting freshman themes
BUT . . .

if you won't grab a realtor / and if you want time to select
an accompanist . . .

at any rate . . . stave off the gradual and USUAL fade out of
the sweet girl graduate.
. . . .
and now mr cumming's COLLECTED have arrived and whatever else I may have had to say is lost /
le Whitman de nos jours?
the message of looseness?

AND turning back to yr/ letter/ I am not suggesting
HASTE/ bad girl but fast or etc/ with obviously monoandrous
inclination, error shd/ not be countenanced/

Also you needn't set out to translate the WHOLE of the Iliad/
but you CAN work on the juicier bits/ Iliad for exercise and the
Odyssey as an aim. no lady has since MMe Dacier and yrs/ wd.
be different.

OR Catullus . . . at any rate METRE

The poem in Cayoosh is mattressed and quilted down under the
verbiage.

and   EP

Ouch. In answer to the curious reader's inevitable question:
No, so far as I can remember, I did not revise; I pruned no
verbiage from "Fable from the Cayoosh Country," but I did not
forget the stricture, especially as Williams was writing in the
same vein. In a note appended to a letter of January 21, 1938,
he said:

You will see by what I have done to your poems what I am
after. By cutting out *all* explanation the poem gains in vividness
which *is* the only explanation that is sufferable in a poem. Maybe
I have obscured the precise sense of your intentions, if so, I shall
at least have reemphasized in yourself what you desire.

In this letter, written about the time I received the Yaddo
invitation, he also said:

It must be lonesome, in a sense, out there—when you feel, as I'm sure you must at times, that the corrupting heat of the metropolitan area might be turned to good literary uses in yourself and you not near enough to it to benefit. Fight it out somehow, I don't know how, but there's always a way for a person of imagination.

Then, either for my entertainment, or to indicate that I wasn't missing much, after all, he continued:

> The Poetry Society of America had Marianne Moore and me as their guests (among twenty others) at the annual banquet at the Hotel Biltmore last evening. I discovered while the speakers were at it that if you take a fern frond and lay it face down on an ironed table-cloth then hold the stem between your fingers and gently push the thing slowly forward tip end first that it appears to crawl like a turtle or a centipede or other entertaining creature. Try it. It's fun. Then if you take a fork in your right hand and toss the fern into the air you can make believe you are pitching hay in a field. You can even try to catch the thing on the fork if you feel real interested. I sat next to Margaret Widdemer who was really very nice. Neither Marianne nor I was asked to speak. What a break that was. Floss (Mrs. Williams) said she was itching to have me cut through that heavy atmosphere. No luck.

The autobiography that Harriet Monroe had finished just before her departure for South America was published under the title *A Poet's Life* in March of 1938, in time for me to read it before I left for Yaddo. In it I found more letters from Pound and Williams written to Miss Monroe in the early days of the magazine. They rounded out a picture for me—a picture of the two poets, as well as a picture of what the poet, any good modern poet, should demand of himself and expect of his editors.★ The poets' letters she included stayed in my mind as such an important part of her book, a part so well worth including, that they have influenced the form of my own book.

A few days ago, wanting to check on the exact circumstances of Harriet Monroe's death, I brought *A Poet's Life* home from the Vancouver library and found that it was the same copy I had read in the spring of 1938 before I went to Yaddo. Al-

---

★Read this as "himself or herself" and "his or her." I have to cope with the deficiencies of the English language as best I can, and I shall not mention the point again.

though it was accessioned April 2 of that year, it is still in very good condition, not even rebound. To be sure, except for the letters it is not very readable: however, its condition suggests, I think, something about Vancouver's lack of interest in poetry at the time I left, and something, too, about the lack of interest in Harriet Monroe's career once her activity as an editor had ceased. At least, the book has not yet been discarded.

2

My first arrival at Yaddo had gone smoothly. My second was anything but happy; I could only be thankful that I was at least on familiar ground. At almost the end of my long train journey (three days and three nights) from the West Coast, I arrived in Albany to find that the Saratoga train had changed schedule the day before. I had to send a telegram to Mrs. Ames, cross town to a bus station and take the next bus to Saratoga. Accordingly I arrived late, to be rebuked for not arriving when I said I would: it was most inconvenient for the staff. There was only time to wash my hands and arrive, late again, in a dining room where I found about twenty-five people assembled. This year, instead of being one of the earliest guests to arrive, I was one of the last. Muriel Rukeyser was there, but I only glimpsed her in the throng of strange faces. Aside from Muriel the one person I had met before was Mrs. Ames, who was displeased about my late arrival. To add to my misery, I happened to find myself seated next to a young man who was the most disagreeable, the most unpopular with everybody, of any Yaddo guest that summer or perhaps any summer. After one attempt at conversation with him I gave up and only longed for a bath and bed.

This time I had a large room that served as both bedroom and studio on the third floor above the reading room. It was called the "High Studio," and had a fine view of the grounds that sloped away in front of the mansion. On the whole I liked it very well. For the first few days I was chiefly conscious of the absence of the people who had been there two years before. I was glad to learn that one couple I had known then, Dan and

Susie Fuchs, were down at the North Farm. Wives were usually excluded from Yaddo invitations unless they, too, were artists, but some were allowed to live with their husbands in cottages on the fringes of the estate. In 1936 the husbands were expected to eat dinner at the mansion, but the wives dined alone in the cottages except when they received a special invitation to dinner. The arrangement was an unpopular one, and by 1938 the rules had changed to allow the husbands to dine with their wives except when both were invited to dinner. On my first night neither Dan nor Susie were there.

I also learned that the Hechenbleikners, an Austrian couple whose company I had enjoyed the year before, would be arriving in August. Morton Zabel, too, would be back. Although I had not been much taken with him in 1936, I looked forward to the arrival of any familiar face. This was the more true because I found that some of the 1938 guests already knew each other and had formed, with other New Yorkers, a circle that was not easy to penetrate. What I thought of as the New York crowd lunched together every day in the shade of a large tree that Kenneth Fearing called a "disillusioned elm," and others referred to as "the mulberry tree." They grouped themselves around Muriel Rukeyser and made it difficult for me to get to know her. They were not exclusive; the meeting place was near the mansion, and when I came outdoors with my lunchbox, I was often invited to join them. A time or two I did so, but the conversation was full of allusions to matters or people that I knew nothing about, and I gave up. At the cocktail hour the same people drank together. Evening walks were the one activity that broke up the group and formed new combinations, but Muriel Rukeyser seldom or never went on those evening rambles. Perhaps she worked in the evening.

Outside the "mulberry tree group" there were three men and one woman who rarely spoke to anyone. Fortunately, since we were so many that year there were still others who were sociable but unattached. During the early part of my stay, my most congenial lunching and walking companion was Muriel Parker, a musician who came to Yaddo from a midwestern college where she had been teaching, though she had traveled more than I and had even studied in Paris with Nadia Boulanger. She was a tall, rather athletic type with serious brown eyes and heavy eyebrows that gave her face extraordinary distinction. Dan Fuchs once said of her, "You know, that girl looks as though she had never told a lie in her whole life." Like Kenneth Fearing, she had grown up in Oak Park, Illinois.

Later, when the Hechenbleikners and Morton Zabel arrived, I lunched regularly with them. It was a very hot summer, but there was a spot under an elm at the top of a rather remote field where we could usually find a breath of air. The question was whether there was enough air to make up for the long walk to get there. I thought that Morton did a lot of complaining, but finally began to accept his ways as just part of Morton, who was rather nice, after all. He no longer wore a hat, and that seemed to make him more human. Gradually—very gradually—I began to get better acquainted with him.

Dan Fuchs and Louis Hechenbleikner had also come around to liking Morton very much. They told me that he was not a Jesuit, "not even a Catholic except that he was probably born one . . . Farrell started the rumor here, out of spite, because they differed in their views of Chicago, and it has persisted." Pound, I thought, probably used the term because Zabel was teaching at a Jesuit University. Wilson also spoke of him as a Jesuit "and I have gone on spreading the misinformation . . . It's also a myth about Muriel Rukeyser getting a pilot's license in order to write *Theory of Flight*, something that is repeated in print whenever her name is mentioned. She did attend aviation school, but never flew a plane, because she was a minor and her parents wouldn't give permission."

In a letter of August 16th, I wrote:

I don't know whether I told you that Muriel R. asked me if she could show me some of her poems. I was pleased, and said I'd love to see them. We hadn't got around to exchanging them, yet, but Sunday evening I went and got mine (I returned the compliment of course), and gave them to her while she was still talking to Morton. The result was that she handed some to him, and, though he had only glanced at them, and only at a few of them, he sounded quite enthusiastic, said he liked "Suggested Miracle" particularly, of those he had read, and asked about book publication. I told him how things stood, and he said he would think hard about it, and if he could think of any leads he could give me, he would let me know. As soon as Muriel gives the poems back to me, which should be today, I'll hand them over to him. If he can help me with a publisher, I won't hold it against him that he can't take a little exertion on a warm day, and a few scratches.

Another gratifying thing: a most unexpected letter arrived this morning from Joe Vogel, saying that he liked the poems in *Poetry*. [The poems Morton Zabel had accepted for the magazine in the fall of 1936 were published while I was at Yaddo in 1938.] About the *Partisan Review*: I had thought of sending them something, but could never see a copy of the magazine. There are four or five back numbers here, and I've looked them over carefully. They seem pretty good to me. According to what *Poetry* has printed about their policy, they claim to be left-wing but non-partisan. Apparently, however, they don't insist on their poetry having political implications. Anyway, since I've been here and heard more about who is who and what, it seems quite evident to me, as it does to the *New Masses*, that they are Trotskyite, though they still deny it. They record a brush with Williams, having written to him for poems, accepted a poem, and then sometime after, rejected it. After which, there was a brush with the *New Masses* à propos Williams and which organ he was writing for (it seemed he *couldn't* write for both, notwithstanding he is no communist of any hue), etc. That doesn't sound so good. But publication is publication, and I thought I might send them some of the things I'm pretty sure none but an experimental magazine would care to print. They've published Stevens, Cummings, Schwartz, Elizabeth Bishop, Edmund Wilson, Dos Passos, Blackmur, etc.

The above paragraphs move me to make two comments:

First, all my letters home were written in what could only be called a headlong style; I have refrained from tidying the original except for occasional correction of punctuation, capitalization or the like.

Second, the paragraph about *Partisan Review* brings out an important fact about the writing of the Thirties that has been almost as completely dropped from the record as the Midwest drought. Although so many of the important writers of that decade were politically oriented and avowedly of the Marxist faith, there was a division into Party members, who took Stalin as their hero and contributed to *New Masses,* and those whose hero was Trotsky. Recently I heard one of the most eminent men of letters of this century discussed in a radio broadcast, where it was emphasized that though he had "left-wing sympathies," he "never joined the Party." In the Thirties it was well known to anybody who knew anything at all (even in Portland) that he was a Trotskyite. The two factions hated each other perhaps even more than they hated the bourgeoisie. After the assassination of Trotsky, little more was heard from his disciples. Now the very existence of that faction seems to be almost forgotten.

I might add that although there were just as many left-wing writers at Yaddo in 1938 as in 1936, there seemed to be much less political discussion. I finally found out that in June all these writers had received a letter asking them to refrain from discussing politics at the table. Perhaps this was just as well. The war clouds were more and more threatening. Hitler had entered Austria in March; it appeared that Czechoslovakia would be next.

To return to the letter quoted above:

> Muriel gave me eight poems, all of which she had written since she had been here. One was two and a half pages. I was floored. She certainly is productive. Three of them I liked real well, some others I thought were good in spots, perhaps in all spots, but didn't hang together. They leave me with the feeling that she hasn't the ability to cut out good lines in order that the poems as a whole may be more perfect in form.

Apparently I was taking to heart the advice I had been receiving from Rutherford and Rapallo, at least where other people's poems were concerned. I still had some way to go when it came to trimming my own.

James Laughlin had published two more of my poems in the 1937 New Directions annual and had some in hand for 1938. While I was at Yaddo, he wrote asking if I would mind if he held them over until the next year; he found that he had too much material. Also, he wondered if I had ever thought of working for a publisher. I did mind about being left out of the annual, but of course I said it was all right and asked what he meant by "working for a publisher." He then explained that the young man who had the job of running the New Directions office at Norfolk might find the country solitude too much for him, and if so, would I be interested in taking over? Country solitude was not what I was looking for; on the other hand any job that kept me in the East, and within reach of New York, looked good to me. I said I would be interested.

One afternoon I found Muriel Rukeyser in the reading room with a strikingly handsome young man and a pretty dark-haired girl. I supposed the young man was Ralph Kirkpatrick, since Kirkpatrick was expected at any moment; but no, this turned out to be Delmore Schwartz and his wife. They had been there most of the day and were just leaving. According to my account, we did not have long to talk, and our conversation seems to have consisted wholly of "gossip about J. L. IV and N.D."

> It seems he has acquired a little hand printing press on which to turn out his advertising and acquire a little practical knowledge; and the first thing he turned out was a birthday card for his mother, in the form of a song printed on a handbill. The song being the one that goes "Don't kill your mother with a hammer just because she's old." Muriel said, "The Harvard humor—they never do grow out of it." Anyhow, Mr. Schwartz had also been invited to stay home from this year's N.D. party, but he stood up for his rights, which he could do easier than I since Jay is publishing his book this year, and it might supposedly sell some copies. Also, Jay, the hog, offered him a contract giving N.D. the right to publish his next *five*. Whereat Delmore said he thought that was a little excessive. Whereat Jay said all right, three then. Delmore agreed and then found out it was three after the present, when he thought it was three including the present volume. I decided that if a job were offered me, I should step carefully and show a stiff backbone to match the Scotch canni-ness and steel-bargaining instinct. . . . The Schwartzes said they hoped I would stay in the East and they would see me some-times, and Jay would know where they were, etc. . . . I almost forgot to tell you that D.S. said he wrote to Laughlin and told him he ought to get more people like me and fewer like Rex-roth. With which I could agree. I almost forgot to say, also, that Schwartz was supposed to come to Yaddo, but got married

instead, and, figuring that this would be a heck of a place to spend a honeymoon, as it would be, he is staying in Bennington.

Delmore was already, before the publication of his first book, being hailed as the white hope of our generation, not for what he had done, but for his potential.

I recently came across a statement by Gertrude Stein to the effect that there was no such thing as a one-book author. I suppose she meant that any author capable of producing one book was capable of producing several. However that may be, we had two one-book novelists at Yaddo that summer. Whether neither of them ever finished another book, or whether they were unable to get later work published, I do not know. I submit that it may be better in any case to write one good book and stop than to go on repeating oneself, as some authors do, through twenty volumes.

One of our one-book authors was Leonard Ehrlich, whose novel, *God's Angry Man*, had had a remarkable success for a first book. The other was Henry Roth, who was then about thirty-five. He had published *Call It Sleep* almost four years before to much critical acclaim, although it was now out of print. Henry arrived after I did, and so was not mentioned in my first impressions of people who were there when I arrived, but later I wrote: "Roth on first acquaintance seemed a kind of solid, blunt individual, but turns out to be extraordinarily sensitive—simply couldn't sit through the vampire play, is tortured by any kind of cattiness, and is said to be a beautiful writer." He deplored the heavy drinking and took no part in it. By this time he and Muriel Parker were going for their daily morning walks to the Spa. Most Yaddo romances are much like shipboard romances, and do not endure beyond a return to the normal routine of living. People who first encounter each other in the unreal Yaddo setting with its restricted activity can seem either more or less congenial, but in any case strangely changed, when they meet again in the real world. This can be true of friendships as well as love affairs on shipboard or at Yaddo, but the Roth-Parker romance was an exception. Henry's wooing continued through the following winter in New York and eventually they married.

There is almost nothing in my letters about Kenneth Fearing. He was, of course, one of the "mulberry tree crowd." I wrote at one point that I had come to like him for his dry humor (I came to like most of the people there, eventually). Once, when I had some conversation with him about poetry publishing, he told me that his practice was to keep on sending the same poem to the same editor, and, he said, "when it begins to sound familiar to them, they'll take it." I don't know whether he was serious or not. I also recall that one day when a young woman writer said that she simply had to have a drink before she could start writing, Kenneth snorted and said: "Whenever you have to do that, you might just as well crawl into bed with the bottle." This time I was sure he was serious and probably knew what he was talking about.

We had our ups and downs that summer: Kenneth sold a poem to *The New Yorker*, Dan sold two stories to *Colliers'*, which embarrassed him a little, and another to *The New Yorker*. On the other hand, Muriel Rukeyser received a letter from her publisher, Pat Covici, saying that he was going into bankruptcy. Several people won money at the race track. Several had cars, which meant that there were more excursions than before. We went to summer theater in Saratoga and Schenectady, to the Spa for swimming in the late afternoon, and occasionally we simply went driving into the countryside for fresh air on a hot evening. The excursion I enjoyed most culminated in a twilight visit to Gansevoort, where Herman Melville's Uncle Herman had lived —a delightful bucolic landscape, so much softer than Oregon, with "round-topped trees" instead of the spiky Douglas firs I was used to, rolling hills, and large old houses set in wide lawns.

Compared with Yaddo in 1936 this year the atmosphere was less cozy but more lively. As for the food, I thought the meals were better than ever, especially the desserts. There were no starving artists at Yaddo. The lunch-box lunches were not elegant, but they were ample.

At that time Yaddo was completely supported by the Trask Foundation. It did not need assistance from outside; it accepted no applications, only recommendations from previous guests; therefore it was the policy of the board to avoid publicity of any kind. One of the first things Muriel Rukeyser told me before I went to Yaddo for the first time was that guests were expected *not* to write about it. In early 1938, however, Louis Adamic, who was a former guest and formerly on the board of directors, published an article on Yaddo in *Esquire*. He deplored not only the management but the whole concept. I believe the article led some people who had expected to go to cancel, and others almost canceled, but were happy that they had not done so. Perhaps it was the *Esquire* article that alerted other magazines to the proximity of good copy up there at Saratoga Springs. Mrs. Ames was busy fending them off that summer. Among others, *Life* proposed to do a picture story. She told them that the artists would have to make the decision. When the question was put to us, we voted against it unanimously. The following September there was a personal attack on Mrs. Ames in *Time*, and the next year a picture story on Yaddo appeared in *Life*. I have no idea whether there was a cause-and-effect relationship in this sequence of events. I shall never know, either, what benefit the public was supposed to receive from photographs that showed Morton Zabel making his bed and Marguerite Young sitting crosslegged in the bishop's chair.

Memories are tricky things to live with. For twenty or thirty years, at least, I have believed that Morton Zabel accepted my poem "Shoreline" after Pound suggested that I send something to *Poetry* and mention his name. When I was writing Chapter II, I discovered by a comparison of dates that the poem was accepted after Marianne Moore suggested I send poems to *Poetry* and mention *her* name. The poem was accepted before Pound wrote to the same effect. Similarly, I have believed for years that I enjoyed Yaddo more the first time I was there; but I have discovered a letter written at the end of my second Yaddo summer in which I say that I enjoyed 1938 more. However, in matters of this sort one's letters home are not entirely reliable, either. I might have been fudging a bit. Fortunately it is of no consequence to anyone now, least of all to me. I mention my doubt only as an illustration of the difficulties facing a conscientious autobiographer.

3

When I arrived in New York on August 24th, everything began to go wrong. In the first place, the Hechenbleikners had offered me their apartment while they were at Lake George, but in the end they did not go to the lake; they returned to New York when I did. Muriel Parker then invited me to stay with her in her sister's apartment, which she was to occupy while the sister and her husband were on vacation, but when she arrived in the city, she found painters in full possession. She fled to Connecticut. I had to go to a hotel. To be sure, the room cost only a dollar and a half a night, but that was a big bite out of my budget. I urgently needed a job and a roof over my head. After that the next project was to be the preparation and circulation of a poetry manuscript.

All my New York friends rallied round to help, and this time they included not only the Reed graduates (Marian and Bryce Wood at Columbia, Claudia Lewis in the Village, and, above all, Charlotte and Rex Heaton-Sessions on West 23rd Street) but the Yaddo friends (Muriel Parker, the Hechenbleikners, the Greenhoods, the Gerschefskis, and Babette Deutsch). They had me to lunch and dinner repeatedly, some of them gave me shelter when I needed it, and most of them knew somebody who knew somebody who might be able to speak to somebody who might be able to give me a job.

My first move was to find housing. I was delighted when I found a little furnished room for five dollars a week on East 75th Street near the Hechenbleikners. It was very neat, had a nice outlook, and the Swiss landlady was most friendly and accomodating. I wrote home giving my new address and asking for a check to tide me over until I found work. The answer came by return mail. My father sent two ten dollar checks, but wrote that I would have to come home because things were bad and getting worse. He promised that I would be able to return later, as soon as the situation improved, but that right now he could not afford to subsidize a stay in New York. What he did not tell me was that he was facing a law suit. He felt sure of winning it, but in the meantime he needed every cent he could scrape together in order to fight it. Not knowing that fact, I felt that he was being unreasonable, and that neither of my parents understood how very cheaply one could live in New York. Also, of course, I was perfectly confident that I would find work soon. I was resolved to stay, but it was obvious that I would have to give up the furnished room.

At this point Claudia Lewis, who had an apartment on Greenwich Avenue, offered me shelter until the end of September when she would be leaving for a job in Tennessee. She was as broke as I was, but at least she had a roof and an extra bed. Just as I was about to move, she called to say she had had a chance to sell the extra bed, and had done so. Charlotte and Rex then produced a folding bed belonging to a friend of theirs, and the Greenhoods moved me and the bed in their car to Claudia's apartment. After two weeks, when I still had not found work, I had to get out of Claudia's way so that she could pack. I was in despair again until Charlotte and Rex offered to let me set up the folding bed in the little room they called their office. They were in a loft, most of which was their display studio, with their (illegal) living quarters at one end and the office, containing a desk, filing cabinets, and a telephone, at the other. They also offered me board for forty cents a day; all three of us took turns cooking dinner. I moved in with them September 27th.

For a month I had been going to employment agencies and following every lead offered to me, but with no results anywhere and very little encouragement. In the first place, I had experience in only one field, social work, but no school-of-social-work training, and by now there were enough trained social workers to fill all the jobs. In the second place, the time was unpropitious; there was not only a Recession, but we were going through the Munich crisis that month, and even I had come to feel that war was probably inevitable. The commercial world, including every form of publishing, was marking time. I was still sure that I would find work eventually, but I obviously could not go on living in the window-display office:

> I couldn't possibly be living in a more upset condition than I am here, but I've got quite used to it and hardly mind at all. I've left practically everything in my suitcases. My dresser is a cleared

space on a shelf full of art supplies. My closet is a cupboard full of the same supplies. My hat is parked in a bag on the filing cases. The floor is so littered and grimy I can't put my feet down. We have no bathtub. Etc. But I'm having a good time. Not but what I want to get a permanent place as soon as possible, for their sakes as well as mine.

This time I was not fudging. I *was* happy. I was hopeful and excited, but I now began to answer classified ads offering a room in exchange for services. Doctors, especially psychiatrists, wanted someone to answer the telephone, but most of the ads offered a room in exchange for baby-sitting. I had several interviews, but someone else always got the job. Finally I realized, or perhaps Charlotte did, that my problem might be the fact that I still had no daytime employment. People might well wonder: would I stay on once I had daytime work? Would I starve on their hands? Would I be underfoot too much? We therefore concocted a "job" for me. I was doing office work at the display studio. For a start, I could overhaul their picture files. I have never been a good liar, but in my next interview I posed as a young woman employed at a low salary, who would be willing to baby-sit in return for a room. I was hired on the spot and moved immediately to the apartment on West 70th Street not far from Central Park. I had the maid's room off the little back hall leading from the kitchen to the back door. There was a big bed taking up most of the room, and a tiny bath all my own. The children were aged two, four, six, and eight, and a fifth was on the way. I was to have Friday night off, and any other evening that Mrs. M. decided to spend at home. I began my life here on October 18th. This was my first real break in almost two months of hectic hunting. I found the place, not through an ad, but through the Columbia University student employment service, where Marian Wood had taken me to register.

My arrangement with Charlotte and Rex continued. I would come to the studio every morning unless I was making the rounds of the agencies or had some other appointment. I could continue to board with them for forty cents a day for lunch and dinner. Breakfast (cooked cereal or toasted muffin, fruit juice and coffee) was fifteen cents at the 72nd Street Automat. Beginning on the first night and continuing throughout the winter, Mrs. M. insisted that I have a glass of milk before I went to bed. She may have thought I was starving because I was so thin. Although I was not starving, the glass of milk was welcome.

One of the reasons I had been so determined to stay on in New York when I came down from Yaddo was the possibility of work at Norfolk for New Directions. By August 30th, however, Laughlin had dashed that hope with a letter saying that the present incumbent would remain through the winter. He softened the blow somewhat with a kind remark about the poems in *Poetry*, but I was much disappointed. At the same time, however, I received an invitation from Williams to come over to Rutherford with Fred Miller. As it turned out, the Williamses had just returned from two weeks as Laughlin's guests at Norfolk. They were able to shed much light on what had been obscure before, and they raised my hopes again.

Fred Miller had been the most silent of our three silent men at Yaddo that summer. I knew he was a writer who published occasionally in the little magazines, and I somehow associated him with Williams, who published in the same magazines. When I let him know that I knew Williams, he finally thawed a little; we had some conversation, and he offered to take me out to Rutherford when we both returned to New York. The Millers lived in Brooklyn. I wrote of this invitation: "I hope it will be nice. Knowing Fred only as the Silent Man, and Mrs. W. not at all, I dunno. Anyway, Dr. W. himself is talkative."

The evening proved to be a memorable one. We rode the Paterson bus through the Lincoln Tunnel and across the Jersey marshes to Rutherford. Fred brought his daughter Diane, aged eight, who was a lively little piece and prevented any prolonged and awkward silences. The Millers, I found, were on intimate terms with the Williamses. As soon as we arrived Diane ran off to find a little iron cat that was her plaything when she visited there. Mrs. Williams had had carpenters in the kitchen that day, and had given the maid the day off, but we had a delicious dinner served without any fuss or flutter. We were seven at the table, the four Williamses and the three of us, with Diane racing round and round the table, chattering and teasing the boys.

I like the boys, each very different from the other, and both different from their father. The older one [Bill] is in med. school in New York. The other [Paul] at the University of Pennsylvania. Older one quite silent, younger very talkative. Both are taller than either of their parents. W. C. W.'s mother, who is eighty-four, and quite deaf, and nearly blind, and has broken her hip twice, but is still keen of mind, was away.

I remember that one of the boys, probably Paul, asked me to explain modern poetry to him. I could not believe my ears. "Dad's, for instance," he went on. I looked at the doctor, who laughed a little ruefully, I thought. I begged off. Not long after that I met a girl who had known young Bill in college. She said that he spoke of his father as "interested in poetry." Even when she was invited to their home, it had not occurred to her that her host was anyone she had ever heard of until halfway through dinner when she suddenly realized that she was having dinner with William Carlos Williams.

After dinner we were taken on a tour of the house. I described it as "quite an old one, nicely furnished, of course, with very modern pictures. There are two entrances, one being the doctor's office, and a big upstairs, the attic being on the third floor. The house is right in town, only about a couple of blocks from the station. The lights of Manhattan, as well as the moon, were visible from the little roof-porch we went out on."

One of my memories of this visit concerns an upstairs hallway, a roomy space at the top of the stairs with numerous bookshelves in one corner. I was taking particular note of the books, all modern, all in dustjackets, most of them by well-known poets and novelists. Dr. Williams explained that they were all presentation copies sent by the authors. I looked at them in awe, but then he spoiled everything by saying with a grin, "Some day I'm going to read them." On those few occasions when I have had a book published, and feel the impulse to send out presentation copies to other authors whose work I admire, those words come back to me, and I hesitate. Once in a while I send one, anyway, but not often.

My mother's comment on this tour of the house must have been to the effect that she would hate to have dinner guests visiting *our* attic, because I replied, "The Williams attic has been, if it is not now, the poet's study (not the doctor's office), and by that you will know it bears little resemblance to ours." It was full of little magazines and much other literary debris, including unsold copies of Williams' books, and a trunkful of letters. Before we left, he gave each of us several of the unsold pamphlets and paperbacks, all of them now collector's items. My letter continued:

> We . . . came away about eleven o'clock loaded down with booty in the form of paper-bound books, pamphlet poems, and I loaded down besides with invitations from Mrs. Williams to come back any time, and to come over to stay all night as soon as the boys were off to school. She seemed to take to me, for which I was very glad. All in all, I had such a good time, I didn't sleep for thinking about it. And about all the things I learned about this and that—much too much to repeat, but especially about the Norfolk job, and I'll try to put down some of that for your benefit.
>
> The present incumbent is just out of Harvard, name Jimmy Higgins. There are three reasons why he may not stay very long. But first—Robin Hill is apparently something like Yaddo in layout. Big house, inhabited by Jay's aunt and uncle, Mr. and Mrs. Carlisle, known as the "manse." Lots of other houses spotted around—a mile this way, half-mile that way. Higgins lives in one of these. Every luxury. All you have to do is push buttons. Cleaning woman comes over from the manse. He doesn't cook but I could. Electric stove. Everything. But, Jimmy is WILD to go to Paris. Can't talk about anything else. Jimmy is being chased by a girl. W. C. W. seems to think one of two things is bound to happen. Either the girl will carry Jimmy off by main force, or Jimmy will have to flee to Paris to avoid being carried off . . . in either case the place will be open. Also, Jimmy is not the type to get along with the Carlisles, which has to be done. All four Williamses agreed that I would fit in much better. Went so far as to say "perfectly," I believe. Spoke of interceding for me. I wouldn't be alone, exactly, since I would be often at the manse, and "many interesting people come there." Also, I would have all the room in the world to have company. I *don't* know whether I could get a salary in addition to all this luxury, or not. Important item. Also, I don't know about visiting New York. . . .
>
> We talked about publishing, and *not* publishing, and I heard

some harrowing tales. Editors requesting articles, certain number of words, much research to be done, time limit, and *then* rejecting them. And much more along the same line. *White Mule* just paid for itself. *Passaic River* did not. Macy's refused to stock a single copy of *White Mule*.

In the next letter I reverted to this subject, saying, "They say the bookstores simply wouldn't stock it because Laughlin spent only four hundred dollars advertising it. 'Spend three thousand', they said, 'and we'll stock as many copies as you can give us.' And it got good reviews everywhere."

About three weeks later I saw the Williamses again, not in Rutherford but in New York, where I had dinner and went to a play with Dr. and Mrs. Williams and Paul. This was a much less satisfactory evening. We paid a quick visit to the Museum of Modern Art, which was housed temporarily in Rockefeller Center while the present MOMA was being built. Then we went to dinner at a Japanese restaurant, and afterwards to see *You Can't Take It with You*, the Pulitzer drama award winner of that season. Judging by my account of the evening written the next day, I seem to have enjoyed the food more than the play or the company. Paul could talk only about the opening of the football season; Mrs. Williams seemed much less cordial than before, and said nothing further about a week-end in Rutherford. As for the doctor, "all our conversation was so spasmodic that it served only to tantalize me, and at the same time I'm a little dubious that there will ever be another one. I'd rather have had more talk and less expensive entertainment—what with the museum on a pay day, and an expensive dinner and orchestra seats at *You Can't Take It With You*, I feel they've done everything they could possibly be expected to do for one visiting poet—and more too, and done it all at once."

Our brief talk left me with the feeling that I was not measuring up to expectations, a feeling that was confirmed by a long letter he wrote to me a week later. I had sent him the poem that I considered the major production of the Yaddo summer, "The Rapids." It contained five four-line stanzas. I was shocked to see when he returned it that he had struck out the first and third stanzas. My first reaction was, "Oh, NO!" After much pondering, however, I realized that I was being guilty of exactly the same sin I had pointed to in Muriel Rukeyser's work. I was unwilling to cut out eight good lines in order to sharpen the impression made by the remaining twelve. I capitulated, took out the two stanzas, and forgot them. The rest of the letter was harder to forget. I give it in full, although I still wince when I read it. He now made it plain that I never had measured up, despite the praise he had earlier given my work, and the defect was perhaps not so much in my craftsmanship as it was in *me*. Or was it a matter of craftsmanship after all? I give this entire letter of October 6, 1938, because of what it says about his attitude to his own work.

> You won't do what I'd ask you to and I wouldn't ask you—
> but your poem needs to be shortened for the sake of intensity.
> I'd cut out the first and third stanzas. Maybe you want to say too
> much. Why bother? There is usually one intense note in a short
> poem, the objective of the writer can't be much else than to
> make that as penetrating as possible.
>
> That can't possibly help you. Nor can I, especially in my
> present state of indifference. I look at some of the continuing
> writers in the various magazines, not to mention *Poetry*, and I'm
> glad I'm not among them. Why continue that way. If there's
> nothing to add to what has been done then why for the love of
> God do anything?
>
> Maybe you're right, you've been too closely surrounded by
> a small adulatory group. That's why you're in New York and
> living not too easily here. But I don't see that in the form of
> your poems. I don't see any flaws in the masonry as if something
> had hit you. I believe you don't want to write just to be writing.
> Then what are you writing for? Nobody can teach you anything
> much.
>
> Your objects don't seem to me to be or to have been looked
> at in moments of sufficient emotional stress. You see them and
> you put them down clearly but you don't seem much hurt or
> elated. The reason I wanted you to go see Cummings was to
> have you sneeze unwanted in his face and do it anyhow. It isn't
> fatal.
>
> As to form: all I can say is that, to me, the form is in the fit
> of the words to the sense intended and nothing else. Opposed to
> that is traditional form. One or the other. I remember you used
> to do some fine work after the Greek models. Pound wanted
> you to go on with that.

I'm a poor one to say anything when I haven't much to say to myself. I want to write more colloquially, more after the pattern of speech, maybe I want to discover singable patterns. I don't want to write pictures. I don't want to do what I've done before. I don't want dilutions, there won't be any. I especially don't want to say anything that I don't very particularly mean and mean as I'd mean it if they asked me if I wanted to have my hand cut off and I'd say, No—or Yes.

Don't pay any attention to me. Go on writing.

Yours,

W. C. Williams

In the meantime, one of the poems from the group published in the August issue of *Poetry* had been picked up by the *Herald Tribune* and published in its Sunday poetry column. Williams had found it "while waiting between twins" (it was a home delivery). He said it "looked good," but that was small comfort. What ought to have been a comfort, if I had thought of it, was the fact that he had taken the time out of a very busy life to write a letter that he hoped might do me some good.

4

All during September and October, while I was moving about with my folding bed and searching for a permanent shelter at least for one winter, I was not only continuing the search for daytime work, but also preparing and circulating my poetry manuscript. There is no need to go into detail concerning all the leads I followed and all the rebuffs I encountered as I scoured Manhattan for the kind of work *I* could do. It seemed to me there must be something. There is no need, either, to recount my interviews with publishers, or the form their rejections took.

A day or so before I left Yaddo, I had had a conference with Morton Zabel over the manuscript. He advised me to arrange it like a book, with title page and table of contents, group the poems under Roman numerals, and write a letter explaining the grouping. All these things, he said, affect a publisher and a publisher's reader. He was encouraging about the poems, and insisted that I should make all the rounds.

I had no typewriter with me (I had rented one in Saratoga), but Christl Hechenbleikner offered to let me use hers. Accordingly, I bought some Supre-Macy Bond and went to work at once, typing in spurts between the moves and the job interviews whenever the typewriter was available. By September 16th the manuscript was ready. In my covering letters I always mentioned that I was looking for work, but I did not find anyone who was willing either to hire me or to publish my poems.

Strangely enough, my spirits remained high. We were enjoying the beautiful, crisp fall weather, brisk and sunny, that is the best part of any year in the Northeast. Every day I expected rain, but except for a few hard showers, the sky remained clear. I found the job-hunting itself actually exhilarating. I was almost lyrical over my first view of a morning rush hour in the financial district:

> It was just nine a.m., and a cold bright brisk morning with blocks of light and sea air at the ends of the street, but the streets all in shadow of the skyscrapers that looked cold and empty, and the sidewalks all massed with the quickest-stepping quiet crowd, not a saunterer, nobody loitering and wondering where to go next, nobody coming *out* of a building, no evidence of life that had lasted overnight, but *everybody* coming out from underground and pouring down the streets and into the buildings.

Fortunately, the rebuffs came one by one, when I was already feeling hopeful about two or three other prospects that seemed to me much better. By the time those had come to nothing, I was hopeful about still others. In any case, every attempt was a new experience that I welcomed.

When I had been about ten days in my new home, which I found very satisfactory—the children being no trouble to speak of and Mrs. M. most considerate of my comfort—I was startled and thrown into a quandary by the arrival of a telegram: WOULD YOU LIKE WEEKS WORK ADDRESSING CATALOGS HERE BEGINNING MONDAY WE PAY THIRTY CENTS AN HOUR AND BOARD IN VILLAGE AND TRAIN FARE HERE AND BACK IF ACCEPTABLE PLEASE ADVISE JAMES HIGGINS MY OFFICE HERE WHAT TIME TO MEET TRAIN AT CANAAN CONN

MONDAY TRAIN LEAVES FROM GRAND CENTRAL

LAUGHLIN. At first I thought that I could not possibly go, now that I had my baby-sitting job; but after more thought, I decided that I wanted very much to go in order to look over the situation there, and I felt that Mrs. M. would probably not object to my being absent for a week, especially if I offered to get one of my friends to substitute for me in an emergency. She lived up to my expectations, was perfectly agreeable to my going, and said that I need not provide a substitute. Accordingly I went off to Connecticut, and, as it turned out, stayed ten days.

My letters are full of detail about this interlude at Norfolk because I was still thinking in terms of going up there to live and work, if not that winter, then the next summer or fall. Because the history of New Directions is by now a part of the history of American letters, or ought to be, it seems to me that an intimate glimpse of its beginnings may not be out of place. I shall therefore quote freely from my letters. Perhaps I should say at the outset that forty cents an hour, with no room or board included, was standard student pay in the Thirties, and fifty cents as much as I could hope to get on a typing job. Thirty cents *with* room and board was munificent.

I left early Monday morning:

> The train trip was lovely, and I got more and more excited as we nosed into the reddish brown hills, following a rocky river that was probably the Hackensack [actually the Housatonic]. The day was clear and crisp, with a few white puffs of cloud and white puffs from the engine, and white bare birch trunks, a few pines, stone walls, square white New England houses set on the hill slopes. . . . Jimmy bounced into the Canaan Station five minutes late. He's snub-nosed, very young, very industrious—works like a trooper twelve or fourteen hours a day. . . . My landlady-to-be being gone, we came on out to the office, which is spacious and just pleasantly barny. I got in four and a half hours work yesterday—mostly running the hand printing press, which was a lot more fun than typing. I also addressed envelopes and stuck on stamps. We ran out of stamps, and the catalogues to stick into the envelopes didn't come, so I didn't have much variety today.
>
> The Carlisles are gone, apparently, but Mrs. Carlisle had

"arranged everything." Best arranger he ever knew, says Jimmy, I think a bit ruefully. My room and board is provided at a very pleasant place. The room is as New Englandish as can be—rag rug, patchwork quilts, white painted furniture, white dotted swiss frilled, tied back, at the windows—two sets of bay windows. . . . Jimmy eats in town and we ride back and forth in the Robin Hill car. It's a nice little drive—about a mile and a half. It's very cold and clear tonight. The stars fairly snap, and there's a half moon. Norfolk is a beautiful little village of big white houses, pines, a stony brook with a waterfall, a beautiful church with a tall white spire. By contrast the New Directions office might be a Paris attic except for its cleanness. Abounds in books, photographs (including Cummings and Williams) magazines. . . .

Gradually I began to fill in the picture for myself and pass on the bits and pieces in my letters like random pieces of a jigsaw puzzle. I had learned from the Williamses that Laughlin's mother, who did not live at Norfolk, was "unsympathetic to J.'s endeavours," or so they believed. They had never met her. His aunt, Mrs. Carlisle, was the one who encouraged him and offered him the building on the Robin Hill estate for an office. He was further encouraged by a woman named Miss Demarest, a former history professor who was tired of teaching, was interested in modern literature, and was willing to take over the office. She had lived on the estate and done the office work until her death the previous year. Jim Higgins was her successor.

I sent some snapshots, with the following description:

The building which houses New Directions was built as a caretaker's house. It is of big bricks or stones painted white. The doors are blue, darker than turquoise. It's a three-way affair, including cottage, what was originally intended for a stable, and a four-car garage. The Carlisles lived in it while they were building their house. They liked it so much that they used it for guests instead of servants, and in that use, they decided a stable was inappropriate so they made the stable into a big living room for the cottage, built a big stone fireplace in one end, and where there was an open shed-roof to drive a wagon under—I don't know what you call it—there is now a sloping-roofed alcove with windows which were bought for the big house and not used in it—quaint octagonal-paned affairs. In the alcove is a big table, a soft gray rug, the printing press, and a long wicker settee. The sun comes through the low windows that look out into the birch woods, and it's the pleasantest place imaginable. That's where I usually worked. Jim's desk was on the other side of the room, and all about are bookshelves, charts, book-jackets, pictures, etc. There is a little bare room just off the office, up a couple of steps, towards the passage way to the cottage, which is used as a packing room. The scales, paper, cardboard, etc., are out there. The parts of the building are connected by a passage way which is a kind of open arcade in summer, but has battens put up this time of year. Even in the summer the deer come right into the yard, and in the winter they scare them away with slingshot—or try to.

The cottage has a big kitchen with electric and wood ranges, a lavatory off the kitchen, which was for my use, two bed rooms and a sitting room, a nice bathroom, and an upstairs which I didn't see. Half the garage space is closed off from the other half, and is now a storeroom for New Directions books, etc. . . .

One of the things I especially liked about the drive out from Norfolk was a snake-rail fence along a level field surrounded by steep little hills, elms on either side of the road. Something that looked like our red-berry shrub, the prickly stuff, was growing in the angles of the fence. The weeping willows were still yellow, and so was the little apple orchard divided from the cottage by a low stone wall. . . .

About the deer, most of the countryside around there is wooded. . . . There are some pretty steep hills, and the ground is so rocky that it's no good for cultivation. I couldn't get over the feeling of strangeness at seeing such a prosperous village, small, but with big, well-kept houses, and big churches, and a fine-looking library, surrounded by wooded hills, cut off from the railroad, and without an apparent excuse for being. That's New England.

There is a great deal of wealth, of course. The two sons of the Carlisles' caretaker have jobs as butlers close by. Live at home.

Laughlin was there very briefly, to meet and be interviewed by a *Time* reporter, Robert Cantwell. An announcement that New Directions would publish Henry Miller in the United States had made the press sit up and take notice. Laughlin and I had no conversation so far as I remember, but while I was at

Norfolk my view of him was radically changed. I suppose, because Laughlin was a perennial Harvard student and a wealthy young man who went jauntering about Europe calling on the likes of Ezra Pound and Gertrude Stein between visits to Alpine ski resorts, that I thought he was necessarily a dilettante. While I was at Norfolk I realized that he was very much in earnest about what he was doing, and trying his best to demonstrate to his family and other publishers that it was worth doing. Jim was bombarded by dozens of instructions that arrived daily from Harvard, and when Jay was on the spot, he threw himself into the office work. I said in one letter, "I think Jim is a prodigy of industry, but he sighs and shakes his head over the way the boss works, so Jay must be a marvel. He's certainly putting a lot of energy into this thing."

Also, I was excited about the books appearing under the New Directions imprint. The catalogue I was sending out announced the publication of *The Complete Collected Poems* of William Carlos Williams, *Culture* by Ezra Pound, *Maule's Curse* by Yvor Winters, *In Dreams Begin Responsibilities* by Delmore Schwartz, *One Hundred Poems from the Palatine Anthology* translated by Dudley Fitts, *An Exagmination of James Joyce*, and the 1938 New Directions annual in which I was not represented. Even the mailing list for the catalogue was exciting. I was never bored. Sometimes I came to with a start and wondered how I happened to be where I was, and then I remembered that it was the Pound Connection that had worked the miracle. "Jim says that Jay wrote Ezra once when he was in Europe, and said he had much admired his writings and would like to see him, might he come to visit. And Ezra . . . wired back and said, 'visibility high.' Which is how it started on that end."

I also liked Jim Higgins. I wrote that his passions were "swing music, football, Paris, prose and poetry. We get along fine. He thinks Ezra must be a swell guy, and he's sure W. C. W. is."

The Carlisles were away when I arrived, but returned a day or so later.

> I met them about Wednesday, saw no more of them until Saturday, when Mrs. C. asked me up to the house for lunch. One of

her cousins, young woman from N.Y.C., was to be there. We had a very light meal served in elegance by a black butler. I behaved as well as I knew how and didn't upset my soup plate. They mostly talked New York politics, which I didn't enter into. When I left Mrs. C. said she would show me the way to a path through the woods back to the office. She did, but she also walked all the way back to the office with me and in talking with me, said, well, I knew more about the work now, and I would know her nephew better, etc., indicating that I was on the inside track for the job when Jimmy left. I certainly felt I had passed an acid test. After twenty-four hours of thinking about our conversation and all the considerations, and Jim talking again about going to Paris in the spring, I couldn't hold in any longer, and told him about what Mrs. Carlisle said. I said, "I don't know how much say she has about who's to have the job," and he said, "She has *all* the say!" Then we consoled each other on our feelings during the luncheon-looking-over which he had also gone through. Consoled is not the proper word, but I'm writing too fast to be accurate. Of course she might change her mind or Jay might change it for her, but it looks as though I could come up here in May or June if I liked.

It seemed clear that the Carlisles had not taken to Jim Higgins, and I didn't know why not.

I think he's a very circumspect young man. True, he did turn himself and Jay over in the car one time,★ but that sometimes happens in the best of families. . . . Jim says Mr. Carlisle is always grumbling about 'these long-haired poets,' so one day somebody mentioned Williams at that juncture, and oh, says Mr. C., such a perfect gentleman! such vitality! such this and such that! But apparently he never made the connection.

I summed up the pros and cons, putting into the negative column first, the isolation, the lack of transportation between Norfolk and Canaan, then the fact that I was physically incapable of handling the heavy work of packaging and sending out books in the rush season, and finally my misgivings about living in such close proximity to people who had more money

★JL believes that I was misinformed about this. Perhaps, but it is also possible that he has forgotten.

than I would ever conceivably have. I quoted Louis Hechen-bleikner, who had said of a similar situation, "You are neither fish nor fowl," neither a servant, nor one of the family, and yet a part of the ménage. It is not a comfortable role to play.

5

By Thanksgiving Eve of 1938 my earlier elation had disappeared. Almost every lead had given out, and I had had a letter from my parents pressing me to return home. I was, as I told them, no longer able to write that I would surely get work soon; I had been saying that for almost three months. My round trip ticket, good for six months, was soon to expire, and I had to make up my mind whether I was going to use it or turn it in. Of course it seemed to me that the longer I stayed the more severe my defeat would be if I gave up and returned to Vancouver. By now I felt that I could never face myself again.

Thanksgiving Day, however, was satisfactory in every way, and when, a day or so later, I received a letter from Laughlin proposing that I do a little work in New York, copying mailing lists and the like, I took heart again. Also Florence Codman, who had been away earlier in the fall, reentered my life with encouraging if vague ideas of temporary work sometime in the near future. I had lunch with Florence and Robert Fitzgerald one day. Robert reported that three or four girls had recently left the staff of *Time*, where he worked, and suggested that I might apply there. At that time no women were employed as writers for the magazine; they were hired only as researchers. I thought I should prefer research, and I did apply, but nothing came of it.

Florence and Robert also encouraged me strongly to write to Laughlin and ask him to make up his mind whether he was going to want me to come to Norfolk in the spring, or no. The answer came in early December, and it was no. Jim Higgins wanted to stay until August. Thereafter, Laughlin expected to have the books shipped from New York and do the office work himself. This was a blow, but I promptly decided to stay on in New York no matter what happened. I braced myself for a difficult letter from home; I knew it would not be emotional, or wounding, but I did not expect the cheerful letter I received. My parents took the decision gracefully, and even—almost— approvingly. It may have been at this time that the threatened law suit was finally dropped. For the next two months the financial situation was easier at home, and I had work coming in little dribbles, all of it temporary, all of it paid by the hour, from the day after Christmas until late spring.

The first job was the one Laughlin had proposed (and forgotten about) in late November. The next was a little typing job that Florence Codman gave me, I think perhaps to try me out. When I returned the work to her, the job she had mentioned vaguely at an earlier interview took definite shape. My letter of January 19th explains:

> She [Florence] had me come out to her Park Avenue bookstore Tuesday to bring something. I just poked my head in, shoved the papers at her, and was so overcome by the general ritzy atmosphere and her hat, that I scooted out without looking around. There were some other people there that she was talking with as I went in, and I thought they stopped and stared at me a little more than was seemly. Anyhow, she called yesterday and said the young man at the bookstore (there are four people involved in this store, it seems, including herself) was working on a bibliography of Aldous Huxley's work. The cards were all made, ready to be typed for the printer. It would be a job requiring great care, but not speed necessarily. He had found someone who would do it for $15.00 (a week's work, probably), but she wanted me to have a chance at it if I was interested. I said I was. She had told him that I would have an advantage over the other person in that I would have an understanding of the material, and also that I had a head to use. Apparently she doubted that the other person did. . . . When I took the typed letters out to her—26 of them, a page single-spaced, she thought they looked movvelous. She couldn't see the wastebasket, though.

The above paragraph was written in the morning; I had an interview with the gentleman at his apartment at two that afternoon, and finished the letter when I returned from the interview.

I found . . . when I got out there, that I already had the job. I was very pleased, needless to say. Mr. Duval is a young man with red hair and specs. . . . I arrived on the dot and had time to look the place over before he arrived. It looked like Yaddo with a Chinese flavor. The five portraits ornamenting the walls were much better, but date from earlier periods, and are quite likely not portraits of the Duvals. It's a pleasant big room, if you don't think about dusting it. A corner, third floor, over-looking Park Avenue and 60th. There is a maid named Flora and a Siamese kitty.

Well, Mr. D. came in, and brought out the card files and the book on which his is to be modelled (the other done by his aunt, published by Arrow Editions). He explained various points, and decided, after some discussion, that I might as well start work Monday. I work from ten to five, with time off for lunch. I'll copy the whole business, then he'll proofread it—for his errors as well as mine, and I'll do it again. After that, he said he might like me to do a little research for him at the library, if I would like to. It's beginning to look more like three than one week's work to me. I hope so.

As it turned out, I worked on the Huxley bibliography off and on, typing, researching, with a week or two off now and then, and only an hour or so a day, some days, until summer. I worked alone at the Duval apartment, and went to the display studio only on week-ends.

By Christmas my need for more and warmer clothing had become critical. I had been wearing a borrowed tweed coat without an interlining; worn over a wool suit, it was barely adequate, but no matter how much its owner insisted that she didn't *need* it, I wanted to return it at the first opportunity. As soon as the bibliography job was definite, my first act was to buy a warm winter coat for ten dollars at Constable's. Gradually I acquired a few replacements for garments that were disintegrating, and even a custom-made hat through Charlotte's good offices (she did the window decorations for a Madison Avenue milliner). In reading over my letters I am constantly struck by the importance of *hats*. One could not go hatless to apply for a job. In fact, it was only in the Village that young women could appear hatless on the street (and even in the Village no woman could appear on the street in slacks unless she was prepared to brave the jeers and catcalls of passing males). These were years when a despondent woman could, if she had enough money, give herself the equivalent of a "fix" with a new hat. If she had to go about in an out-of-date or out-of-season or shabby hat, that in itself was enough to lower her into a chronic depression. My custom-made hat from the Madison Avenue shop did me a world of good.

All of my job hunting had been done more or less in concert with Christl Hechenbleikner, who had made the rounds before and could give me much good advice on agencies to go to, what to say, what to expect, and so on. If either of us heard of work that we ourselves couldn't do, but the other might be interested in, we exchanged the information. As it turned out, I was instrumental in finding steady work for Christl, and later she brought me in to assist her temporarily.

In January of 1938 I had received a letter from Williams in which he mentioned a projected new magazine: "There's to be a new twice a year magazine out soon. It's to be called Twice a Year. It sounds as if it might turn out to be good. Plenty of money back of it."

Sometime after that I must have received a circular from *Twice-a-Year* asking me to send some poems, which were rejected. In January of 1939 I talked on the telephone with the editor, Dorothy Norman, who said that Florence Codman had spoken of me. She asked me to send more poems, and she took my telephone number in case she had some typing for me to do. She was looking for a part-time stenographer, but wanted someone who could take shorthand. I recommended Christl, who went for an interview and was put to work on the spot.

By the end of January I was working for Duval in the daytime, and assembling another mailing list for New Directions on the week-end at the display studio. If I was not on duty at the M.'s apartment, I worked on it in the evening. The New Directions job was soon finished, but then at the end of February Christl called me to help her address envelopes for Mrs. Norman. The work on the bibliography was now intermittent; Hanson Duval even left town for a month during March, and I managed to juggle my time so as to keep both jobs going temporarily.

Twice-a-Year was a book-sized, soft-cover periodical, strongly political in tone, but also featuring avant-garde writers and artists. The artists tended to be those who showed work at the Stieglitz gallery. The magazine's official address was that of An American Place, but we were working at first in Mrs. Norman's Park Avenue apartment:

> The Norman apartment makes the Duval one look like about thirty cents. And the M.'s like a tenement. It's modern, in contrast to the Duval period and Chinese interior. It's large and luxurious. There are a couple of maids, a butler, a cook, and a governess besides the editorial staff (us). Christl told me Dorothy Norman was young and good looking, but she was even more of both than I expected. I've only said "good morning" to her. She does all her dictating in her bedroom, after breakfast in bed, and emerges at noon in hat and coat (squirrel, I think . . .) and off she goes. We're getting out circulars. . . . We work in a lovely big room, very quiet, lots of light, and one wall all bookshelves clear to the ceiling. And all over the room are literally dozens of Stieglitz photographs and Marin and O'Keefe paintings. . . . The only drawback is that there's no good cheap place to eat in the vicinity. Even the drugstore is high. Fifteen cents for a bowl of soup, and Campbell's at that.
>
> Mrs. Norman has two children, girl eleven or twelve, and a boy about nine or ten, I should judge. She was having a dinner party tonight for twenty-four or -six, from the looks of things.

Of all my odd jobs, especially the odd literary jobs, this was one of the most irritating, because I felt that I was wasting so much of my time in inefficient activity. Of course I was being unreasonable; I was paid by the hour, and when the work was done, I would be laid off. Nevertheless, it annoyed me that we had to waste half an hour every morning laying newspapers down on the lovely rugs, setting up card tables, bringing out our card files and envelopes and getting set up for work. At the end of the day we wasted another half hour putting everything away again. We had several card files of names and addresses, many of them duplicated. I wanted to make a master file immediately, but Christl explained that Mrs. Norman was not sure that she would bring out any more numbers of the magazine; therefore we were to check each name as we came to it against the files that were already done. This was maddening, and took several times as long as making a master file. For the same reason, Mrs. Norman was unwilling to rent a proper office. Later I worked a day or two with Christl at An American Place where we were stuffing envelopes. Here, although we were doing work that we could more comfortably have done sitting down, we had to stand because there was no place to sit, even to rest for a moment. Ansel Adams, telling on a recent television program of his first interview with Stieglitz, said that he had to perch on a cold steam radiator, because there was nowhere else to sit. At the time of his second interview, there was steam in the radiator, and he stood, perforce. We also stood. By the time the issue was on its way to the post office, my work there was at an end, and I was thankful for it.

The people at the Park Avenue book store permitted me free run of their rental library and also provided a point of contact with other potential employers. Through them I met a young man who needed a master's thesis copied. He also lived on Park Avenue, this time in a duplex apartment, but I did the work at the display studio. I was surprised when he called, because it seemed to me that there must be many copyists available at Columbia University, where he was a graduate student; but after I talked with him I decided that he was shopping around for someone who would do the work for a few cents less. I did the work for less, but I disliked him (I think he disliked me, too), and the copying was distasteful because the thesis was an editing of a bad restoration tragedy. I could not get the sound of the lines out of my head, even when I slept. Dreaming in blank verse is bad enough, but dreaming in bad blank verse upset me.

One more, very brief bit of work turned up. Brief as it was, I think my account of it deserves to be quoted. My employer was a young woman who lived in the East Fifties and did a bit of writing. I copied an article for her one Sunday afternoon and earned two dollars, but I reported that she could neither spell nor punctuate, and I thought the article (about Fifth Avenue shops) was stupid. Later she called on me again:

> Yesterday I masqueraded as Miss X's secretary from the *Times*, and addressed envelopes for a charity doings with some of the

young society women of New York. Ex-debs. They had called wanting her to help address invitations, and she didn't want to and said she had to do some work for the *Times*, which was "perfectly true"—she was working on a thing for the *Times*, and she had to get it finished. But Mrs. Y. understood she was on the *Times* staff, so she sort of let that go, but she said there was a girl she could send, and Mrs. Y. understood she meant her secretary, and she sort of let that go, too. If I wanted to go out and address envelopes for her, and not let on I was hired for the purpose, and then surreptitiously let her know how many hours I put in, she'd be happy to pay me. I deduced that she would be in the doghouse if she hired someone to do the work she was supposed to contribute, but that if she sent out someone who was in her employ anyway, or in the *Times* employ—though Mrs. Y. must have a fantastic idea of what that would mean, if she thought a staff member could send a stenographer out to do private work for a charity—that would be all right and perfectly decent.

So here's the picture which looked excruciatingly funny to me, the longer I looked at it: I sat and addressed envelopes by the dozens to Tuxedo Park and Long Island and Greenwich, Connecticut, and the Ritz Tower, so Miss X, who can't write for applesauce . . . can have time to write for the *Times*, and . . . addressing with me are young society matrons who dashed into town from Long Island or Connecticut just for the afternoon, and who are, at great sacrifice, taking an hour or two between luncheon and cocktails to address envelopes for invitations to a ball or banquet given by a charity, not for benefit of the charity but in honor of somebody who has been decorated by the D.A.R. . . . when I would be only too happy to address the whole smear at fifty cents an hour. But that's outlawed. I couldn't even suggest it, or let on that I was at that moment doing it for pay. Miss X was actually doing more in the way of charity by letting me have the job, than she would have been doing if she had done it herself, but had to cover up to do it. Can you make any sense of it? I can't, but there it is, and since you can't do anything about it, it's nice it's funny.

6

What with juggling two or three daytime jobs, intermittent as they might be, and looking after the four little M.'s, there was not a great deal of opportunity for social life. I was in touch with Marianne Moore from time to time, but did not see her. At Yaddo the summer before, I had asked Morton Zabel whether he thought Miss Moore was annoyed by one's importunities if one tried to see her, or did she feel neglected if one didn't try? He burst into laughter and said, "Probably both!" With only this judgment to guide me, I tried, but did not press her. In a telephone conversation she indicated misgivings about my decision to stay on in New York. Perhaps that was one reason I did not pursue her after being put off at least twice.

In January I was invited to dinner with the Delmore Schwartzes. It is deplorable how often, on occasions such as this, I described the menu instead of the things I should like, now, to remember; but I have always enjoyed good food and never more than when I was eating regularly in cafeterias and Automats. A young poet named Finnegan came in after dinner. As I had guessed after only a brief meeting with Schwartz at Yaddo, he was an indefatigable talker. There were no embarrassing silences. In my first letter after the event, I said:

> Wish I could tell you more about last night, but I can't think of anything unless I started recounting anecdotes and I don't believe any of them are interesting enough. Wallace Stevens wrote Jay (Jay having written and asked him for some publishable statement on Schwartz for advertising purposes) that in publishing Delmore Schwartz New Directions was for the first time doing what it set out to do—and suggested he "might print that bright remark." He also said that Schwartz was too good to need any help—which is nonsense. All young writers need it. Jay sent Delmore the Wallace Stevens letter and his own lengthy and heated reply. Delmore said sadly that Jay was going to have everybody down on him—which is quite likely true.

Other bits and pieces of that evening's conversation came out in later letters. For instance, we talked about *White Mule*, and Delmore said that Williams had shown the book to his mother-in-law (who figures as Gurlie in the novel) and that she said anyone who wanted to know the true facts should come to *her*. I remarked that the doctor had "a lot of nerve for a man of his size." Also: "Delmore said the *Partisan Review* people really were genuinely interested in my work and they do pay three dollars a page, which isn't much, but is something, and I should surely send them some poems." He also encouraged me to think that Laughlin might publish a volume of my poems, but he added, "I imagine he would want to get you mentioned around a bit, first." I suddenly realized that those names of poets continually cropping up in reviews of other poets' books might be *planted*. I did send a few poems to *Partisan Review*, and Delmore, who by that time was poetry editor, took two.

A week or so later, I went to dinner at the Hechenbleikner's and found another friend of theirs whom I had heard about and never met. This was John Cheever, who had been a great favorite at Yaddo in previous years. "I fully expected to like him, and did—he's a very straightforward, unassuming sort. I wouldn't say Delmore Schwartz was unassuming, but I would say it would be a wonder if he hadn't had his head turned recently—if not before. I think John is to have a book published soon by Harcourt."

About this time I received one of the two letters from Pound to arrive that winter:

Dear Mary
      continuin'
Ole fatty Ford (M. Ford) is at Ten, Fifth Ave / encourager of young talents. . . . I don't know whether he has a phone/ but you don't need a letter of introd/ if you say I sent you. GOD knows what sort of people he now plays about with/ probably the best (mentally) he can find
      I forget whom I have told you to meet/

Yr/ choice EF you are going to look after other people's kids instead of yr/ own /// is between bein an old maid and bein a fussy old maid.
. . . .

I forget yr/ exact age but it is too young to relapse into Thoreau and solitude/
. . . .

if you WONT work on verse technique/ the next best career for
the amenities is licherchoor in general/ Plenty of small mags
NEED thoughtful criticism / do you get Townsman?
. . . .

You might try civilizing one or two of Jas's friends if he has any
left. preferably males of yr/ own generation.

Thos Hardy lost nowt by practical writing. dont be too sniffy
about trying to break into current PUBlications (I mean the
LOW-got-damnit-brow pubctns or dyly nooz wypers.

You might even tell me about new American publications or
persuade Jas to turn N.D.'s annual into a serious or meritorious
publication.

I did write to Ford and immediately received a reply saying
that certainly any friend of Ezra's was welcome in his house,
and that Mrs. Ford was at home on Thursdays from five to
seven. They would be glad to have me come. Mrs. M. was
usually very agreeable about changing my night off if I had a
special reason, and this time there was a "Living Poetry" program I wanted to attend later the same evening. Accordingly, I
asked for Thursday off and went to the Ford's at five-thirty. It
was, I said,

a very strange experience. Nothing like what I expected. When I
left I still didn't have any idea whether they knew how I happened to be there. Most of the time there was just one other
guest, a young woman, friend of Mrs. Ford's, non-literary to say
the least. She seemed to be doing most of the conversing. Mr.
Ford appeared even older than I expected him to—a big man
with a wheezy speech plus an English accent that is always difficult for me to understand. He seemed to speak with a certain
difficulty, and said very little. Mrs. Ford is much younger, was
friendly in a very casual way, served tea, attempted a sketch of
her husband (she's an artist) because they had just got a wire
wanting a photograph for publicity purposes and they couldn't
find one that would do. The tea cakes were lovely, and we talked
about the big bund meeting—suppose it got in the Portland
papers—relief, etc. My watch stopped and I stayed longer than I
intended. I was glad I went—at this stage of my career—but I'm
glad Dr. Williams was the first literary light I met. My present
opinion is that I could never have found anyone who was easier

to get acquainted with. Maybe it's because Ford is English that he seemed so remote.

The apartment was rather gloomy and bare, and looked as though they were only camping in it, which was probably the case. Ford's expression hardly changed except that two or three times his eyes suddenly came alive with a brilliant, curious, penetrating look that gave me a glimpse of the Ford I had read and heard about. Later, Florence Codman told me that Ford Madox Ford was not at all well, and probably had not been feeling well the day I was there. She had been there twice, and said that he was *very* entertaining both times. He had monologued all evening on different topics, including, for instance, the French theater. This might have encouraged me to try again, but I never had another opportunity. The Fords spent part of the spring in the South with the Tates, and in May sailed for France, where he died on June 26.

At least twice I had dinner with Babette Deutsch and her family. I found her husband Avrahm Yarmolinsky a quiet, scholarly gentleman whom I liked, though he had no sympathy whatever with my enthusiasm for the wilderness. Babette herself regarded Cape Cod as the farthest conceivable remove from civilization. One of the things I enjoyed about dining with them, besides the food and the conversation, was the feeling that I was in a home, a house, even, rather than an apartment, though it actually was an apartment in a large building. I remember that she was much pleased when I told her so. My younger friends were most of them in make-shift quarters or studios, and the apartments of my Park Avenue employers might have been show windows or stage settings, but Babette's apartment was a family home.

I saw the Williamses just once that spring. One day in late March, I did some errands for Duval, and when I reported back to the bookstore I found him mourning because he was unable to find a certain copy of *The Little Review*. When I said I would bet it was in the Williams attic, he said, "How much is the fare?" I went over after lunch next day, a beautiful spring day, and found both the Williamses at home. I also found the magazine, as I had thought I would, and had a visit besides. They were both still smarting because, when they were invited to New York especially to meet Muriel Rukeyser (she having set the date) they drove through rain and snow and slush to get there, and, they said, Muriel neither showed up nor sent regrets nor did they hear from her afterwards. They were disgusted. Williams had spoken to Cummings about me and I was to go see him—perhaps. The only thing I remember now about that afternoon is that I bought some Wenatchee Winesaps at a fruit-stand in Rutherford while I waited for the bus. According to my letter, the doctor was in a facetious mood. He said I was looking "sick," but my comment on that was that I thought he was trying to drum up trade. Charlotte thought I was looking unusually healthy.

Although time and money were both in scant supply, New York, New York, was a wonderful town, and one way or an-other I managed to take in a surprising number of events, the-atrical, musical, and so on. Babette, for instance, gave me a pair of student tickets for a matinée concert that two of her friends were giving in Town Hall. Because I had to sign the tickets when I used them, I found myself on the Town Hall mailing list for student tickets, always matinées, which were more conven-ient for me, anyway. One presented a ticket, paid fifteen cents, and walked in to hear the Pasquier Trio, for instance. Because the tickets came in pairs, I was even able to repay a little of the hospitality I owed my friends.

Hanson Duval gave me a ticket for a New York Philhar-monic concert, my first symphony concert outside Portland, and very exciting. The mother of one of my friends sent me a dollar for Christmas, and with that I bought a seat for my first Metropolitan Opera performance. I chose *Don Giovanni*. I also managed to see *Henry IV*, Saroyan's *My Heart's in the Highlands*, (which I loved), Humphrey and Weidman, besides an occa-sional movie (*Pygmalion* and *The Lady Vanishes*, for two).

Poetry readings were almost unknown in those days, but I did attend one group reading called "Living Poetry." I went from tea with the Fords to the reading later the same evening. Muriel Parker went with me. The affair was sponsored by the *New Masses*, and all the participating poets were far to the left of center, including Muriel Rukeyser and Kenneth Fearing. Maxwell Bodenheim had not been invited to participate, but was on the platform, obviously drunk. They put up with him, and even allowed him to read a long poem, as long as most of the other poems put together. The young poet I had taken a dislike to at the Latimer party back in 1936 was also on the program. I still did not like him, but I wrote that the others were all "pretty good, very serious, and quite intelligent. . . . Afterward there was a dramatization of one of Kenneth's poems, and a couple of other skits." I regret to say that Bodenheim's behavior is all I can remember now about that evening. We talked to our Yaddo friends afterward, and I went home feeling that I had had a very literary day indeed.

In late spring of 1939 another crisis was building up, not only in Europe, but in my life. The M. family would be moving out of town permanently in June; I would be homeless. There was no prospect of further work from any of the people I had already worked for, once I finished the bibliography. The possibility that I might find a permanent job at the beginning of the summer was almost non-existent, though I did attempt to get something at the World's Fair. To make matters worse, the lumber business was on the skids again. I was as loathe to return home as I had ever been. In this dilemma, I thought of trying to get another invitation to Yaddo. While I was dithering over this and other possibilities, Muriel Parker, whom I had been seeing frequently during the winter, asked me to come to dinner with Edna Guck.

Edna had been one of the most conspicuous members of the "mulberry tree crowd" at Yaddo, a born and bred New Yorker, who had lived in Paris and the south of France, a painter and sculptor (and an extraordinarily good one). On first acquaintance I found her a little bizarre because her style was rather dramatic: it would, in other words, have turned heads in Vancouver, and sometimes turned them in Saratoga Springs. She always wore slacks in the daytime, when slacks were still considered suitable only on the beach. She almost always dressed for dinner in one of the new long, summery evening dresses and wore a white flower (from one of the petunia pots) in her hair. I gradually got acquainted with her because she liked evening walks as much as I did, even scrambling over fences in her billowing flounces "without showing her ankles." She had been at Yaddo before, and was already acquainted with the Hechenbleikners, among others. The more I walked with her, the better I liked her, and when I went to her studio one evening and saw her work, I was delighted. However, she still seemed someone who was and always would be out of my orbit. I had seen her not at all during the winter, because she had been in Tennessee on a WPA art project. Now she was going to a country schoolhouse she leased for a summer studio, and she asked Muriel to go with her. When Muriel decided against going, Edna invited me to go with her to stay until July 1st. This was on May 15th, and she was eager to get away as soon as possible. I am sure she did not especially want my company, but she did not want to go alone. I had misgivings about how it would work out, but accepted the invitation on the spot with a feeling of immense relief. What would happen after July 1st, I did not know, but there was a chance I might be able to visit Jane Ruby in Cambridge for a month. I knew that Edna and I could live together in the country for almost nothing, as we did. Also, I had still a little work on the bibliography to do, and this I could take with me. On my last visit to the Park Avenue Bookstore, I admired the window display of Arrow Editions and New Directions books accompanied by handsome photographs of the two publishers. Duval said that the display was attracting much attention; many people were dropping into the shop, not to buy books, but to inquire for the addresses of the publishers. They wanted to send in their manuscripts. And Laughlin was writing me that he was losing so much money that he might publish only the annual in the fall of 1939.

Chapter 5

A REVIEW in a recent issue of the *Times Literary Supplement* begins with the statement: "Ezra Pound embarrasses his admirers." Not invariably, chum; not invariably; but his arrival in New York in April of 1939, which was splashed all over the front pages of the newspapers, took a deal of living-down. Psychologically we were already at war with the Axis, and Pound was extolling Mussolini in his interview with the New York reporters. The Pound case has been tried so often, in publication after publication, that I can add little or nothing to the evidence. I intend only to give a glimpse of him as *I* saw him that first time in New York, shortly before war broke out in Europe. I did not understand his admiration of Mussolini, especially not after Ethiopia, but I have never excluded from my friendship people with whom I disagreed about something, or even most things. It would have been a lonely life.

I agreed with Pound about certain things that were of great importance to me, and he had, besides, been extremely helpful. Of course I wanted to meet him. I would no more have refused to meet him because of his politics than I would have refused to meet the communist poets because of theirs. I thought they were both mistaken, but politics was not what I wanted to talk with him or them about. I wrote a note to him, care of Cummings, saying I would like to pay my respects. After a week or so I received a postcard from Washington, D.C., saying simply: "Thanks E P". While I was getting ready to go to the country with Edna, I heard rumors that he had returned to New York. Then one afternoon only a few days before I left the city, he called to ask if I would be free to meet him immediately at the Restaurant Robert. I was, and I did.

Not long ago Mary de Rachewiltz asked me how I would describe her father's manner when I met him in New York that May. She said she had heard such fantastic stories of his behavior during his visit to the United States, stories that sounded completely unlike him as she knew him, that she would like to know how he seemed to me. How did he behave? After some thought I said that I could best describe his manner as punctilious. Mary was startled; she doubted that the word "punctilious" had ever before been used to describe Pound, and she hoped I would use it. Very well, I have used it, and I still have not thought of a better one. I was with him only for a couple of hours, and we discussed nothing of much importance, but the meeting had large consequences for me, and I remember it vividly. My account of it in my letters, though brief, helps to fix some of the facts.

In the first place, I need hardly say that I was on edge. This thing of being confronted and looked over for the first time is not easy. He, too, seemed somewhat constrained, and said at one point that these first meetings have to be got over. I arrived at the restaurant about three o'clock, and found it deserted except for the waiters and Pound, who had been having lunch there with Mencken—another first meeting. The newspapers had emphasized that Pound was traveling first class, and when interviewed was wearing expensive tweeds. I don't know what had become of the tweeds, but that day he was wearing a dark blue pin-stripe that can never have been expensive, and now needed the attention of a valet. The only eccentricities of dress were the wide collar and large, broad-brimmed black hat. The beard was neatly trimmed, but of course any beard was conspicuous in the Thirties. The waiters may have looked askance at the brown paper parcel he was carrying, though it was not large—in fact I thought it hardly large enough, when he explained that it was his overnight bag. He was on his way to Patchin Place to stay with the Cummingses. We settled down at one of the numerous empty tables, and he offered me a drink, or tea. Since I had been invited to tea, I took tea, which was probably a mistake. A drink might have helped, but as he was apparently not drinking, I chose tea. I did not yet know that he almost never touched alcohol.

We had tea and talked about his travels and my plans, or lack of them: still no job, and no place to live when I came back from the country; no prospects for next year. We talked about Marianne Moore, whom he had also met for the first time during this New York visit. I was amazed to learn that they had never met before; from my surprise he inferred (mistakenly) that I had been misled by a woman, a Ph.D. candidate, I believe, who had surmised in print that Mary Moore of Trenton and Marianne Moore were the same person. He smiled, and said that Mary Moore of Trenton was in another department of life altogether. When I asked about Marianne, he said that he thought she was "having a thin time of it with that old mother of hers." He talked of introducing me to an old friend from his Hamilton College days, a woman who lived in New Jersey. He thought I might find her interesting, but seemed a little doubtful (this woman turned out to be Viola Baxter Jordan, who lived in Tenafly). He suggested that I might possibly be able to stay with her when I came back from the country, while I looked for work.

I also asked about *Furioso*. Vol. I. No. 1 had not yet appeared, but I had received a prospectus and sent some poems which were rejected, though the editors wanted to see more. Pound said he thought I should contribute, though he really didn't know a lot about the taste of the young men doing the job; at any rate, they had a lot of energy. The young men were then, judging by the return address, students at Yale. Pound also said that one of the editors, James Angleton, had turned up in Rapallo and taken the best picture anyone had ever taken of him.

Presently Pound proposed that we go down to the Museum of Modern Art, now in its new building. I assumed that he wanted to see the exhibit there, but when I found that he was going, instead, to see Iris Barry, the Curator of the Film Library, I quickly offered to take my leave. He reassured me: No, no! I was to come along. We were going there with a purpose; now that the museum was in its big new building, surely people were being hired to staff it, and there might possibly be a job for me there. He then told me more about Iris, whom he had known in London when she was a very young poet, and to whom, as I later discovered, he wrote letters much like those he had been writing to me. He told me that she had, herself, been very hard up, and would understand my problems. As the letters reveal, when she first came to London from the provinces, she was counting her pence as carefully as I had been counting my pennies.

Accordingly, we left the waiters, who had been lined up along the opposite wall carefully not watching us, to their own devices, and stepped out down Fifth Avenue to the MOMA. I was inclined to dart through traffic New York style, while he protested, "Don't take grandpa along so fast!" We ascended to the museum offices, and I was introduced to Iris, who was very handsome and looked twenty years younger than she must have been, judging by what Pound had told me. At this time, all women executives, curators, editors, and the like, wore hats when in their offices, and what hats! At first I assumed that these ladies were on the point of going out, and had paused a moment to see me, but finally I realized that they always had the hats on, perhaps in the hope of giving exactly that impression, or perhaps in order to distinguish themselves from secretaries and file clerks, who could be summoned by a buzzer. Iris's hat was wide-brimmed and absolutely stunning.

She handed Pound some mail that had come for him, care of the Museum. As he took it, he said casually, "Now, while I look over my mail, give Mary a job."

Iris gave me a quick, inquiring look, and I said, yes, I was job-hunting. Pound said that I wrote very decent poetry. "but we'll skip that," meaning, I suppose, that a prospective employer would not consider proficiency in poetry-writing a recommendation. I found it difficult to explain myself to Iris while he sat beside me interjecting comments, and no doubt sensing this she said, "Why don't you write me a letter and tell me all about it? If I were you, I would rather do it that way. Wouldn't you?" I most thankfully would.

After that, Alfred Barr came in, and I was able to relax while Pound and Barr discussed Gaudier-Brzeska and Wyndham Lewis. Iris put in a word for a young man who was most anxious to meet Pound, but he shook his head. "I can't see *everybody*," he said. That was comforting. Then we went into another office where I met Iris's husband, John Abbott, who was Director of the Film Library. The conversation that ensued meant nothing much to me because most of it related to John Abbott's brother, who seemed to be collecting poetry manuscripts, perhaps for a university. It seemed that Pound was not cooperating. About five o'clock he and I left. We found a taxi, and I rode with him as far as 23rd Street. During the ride, he said that he did not know whether he could offer any stimulation in an interview that he couldn't give by letter, and he added, "My medium is the typewriter." He also amazed me by saying that he would very soon be going back to "the peace and quiet of Rapallo." My first thought was: But doesn't he know what is coming? Peace and quiet for how long? I realized that apparently he did *not* know, though the invasion of Poland and England's declaration of war against Germany were only three months away. Of course we did not know the date, but to us a European war seemed, by May of 1939, imminent and unavoidable. Pound's remark lodged in my memory beside another statement published in *Partisan Review* a month or two later (Summer, 1939). The editors had sent out a questionnaire to a number of authors asking (among other things) their opinions on the role of the writer (that is, writers generally) in the event of war. Gertrude Stein replied: "It does not seem possible for any of you to realize that most probably there will not be another general European war, the more America thinks there is going to be one the more suspicious the continent gets and the less likely they are to fight." I am tempted to say that both Pound and Stein were out of touch with reality, or at least with the reality of current events, and for the same reason. But then I am suddenly reminded of all the experts on world problems whose crystal balls have proved to be equally clouded, perhaps for other reasons.

The meeting with Ezra took place on Monday, May 22nd, and I left for the schoolhouse with Edna on the following Friday, but during the three intervening days I wrote the letter to Iris, had a reply from her, and went to the museum for an interview. After I had a little talk with her, I was interviewed by a member of her office staff, who gave me the biggest lift I had had in months. I reported that "they treated me like the Queen of Sheba instead of an applicant for a job." I received some pointers on how to look for summer substitute work, and encouragement about the possibility of clerical or even, possibly, research work at the museum in the fall. Iris Barry said the first money she ever made was from *Poetry*, a payment for some poems Ezra had sent in. She offered to put me up for a few days when I came back from the country, if I should be up against it. She also said she would let me know if she heard of anything interesting while I was there.

I went off to the country full of hope and excitement, though still wondering about how Edna and I would get along for a month of almost total isolation in a one-room schoolhouse. I thought that I could get along with almost anyone for a month if I put my mind to it, and I intended to try. As it turned out, that summer was an idyllic one for both of us, and when another of Edna's friends who was to come in July had to change her plans, I stayed on.

We had one big room with curtains to pull for privacy; blackboards for doodling; an entryway where we had an oil stove and an ice box; a Girls and a Boys; an old upright piano, two beds, two or three school desks, a couple of tables and assorted chairs. There was a huge oak tree beside the school house to give us shade; under it a few rocks and a grate made a fireplace where we did most of our cooking. The landscape was wholly bucolic: no houses near us, a meadow behind us, and a brook at the bottom of the meadow. A few wooded hills broke

Neither Mrs. A, Mrs. B nor Mrs. P. having
celebrated the 4th as I expected them to I have
to report that I am tied here until further
notice. I can't be counted on when these
situations occur, all these ladies being now
past due they may very well select Friday for
their childrens' birthday. I just have to sit and
wait. By the way, I wonder if you got my last
communication, I thought I might have a reply by
this morning's mail. I'll still come next
Friday afternoon (unless you tell me not to)
~~if~~ if I can get away but the nearer the time
approaches the more the difficulties mount. I
seldom get a clean break.

Mary Barnard
Lake Schoolhouse
Warwick, N.Y.

R.D. 1

Postcard from William Carlos Williams, July 5, 1939.

the skyline. We were only forty-five miles from New York City, but when we took the train to Chester, on our way to the city, we had to flag it down with a large white handkerchief Edna kept on hand especially for that purpose. The train was a freight with two box cars and one coach, half baggage-car and half passenger-coach. The interior looked as though it had not been dusted since Lee's surrender, but at that the coach was in better condition than the New York, New Haven and Hartford coaches that I rode on a few years ago. At least the windows were not broken. Unfortunately passenger service was suspended during the summer of 1939, and Edna's schoolhouse became inaccessible except by car.

Edna usually worked outside. I had Hanson Duval's typewriter, which I used for my own work as well as his. For our marketing we sometimes hitched rides with a neighbor who trucked milk into Warwick at seven o'clock every morning. We were on delivery routes for ice, meat, and mail. Vegetables, eggs, and milk were available at neighboring farms. We carried water from a spring, and bought honey from a nearby bee-keeper.

The summer was uneventfully happy. War still held off. A mourning dove in the elms at the bottom of the meadow moaned gently through the hot summer days. I wrote and revised some poems, sent poems out and had some accepted, tried my hand at a play. Simply getting into slacks and going hatless day in and day out was blissful. I thoroughly enjoyed the New York countryside: fields full of daisies, mint and violas by the brook, wild iris, wild roses, new mown hay, fireflies hovering over the meadow at night and dragonflies over the brook in the daytime. The only difficulty was that as August approached I began to be more and more worried about my next move. I could not stay on at the schoolhouse after August first. New York was hot and dirty and more or less depopulated. I was brooding over a number of possibilities, most of them rather impractical, unattractive and unpromising, when all my problems were solved at one blow by the arrival of a letter from the University of Buffalo offering me a job. It arrived on July 22nd, and the writer of the letter, Mr. C. D. Abbott, Director of Libraries, who introduced himself as Iris Barry's brother-in-law, would like me to begin work on August 1st or 15th, that is, if I were interested in the position. He was sure I could do "more than competently" what he wanted done. I wondered how he knew. He also felt pretty certain I would find the work interesting and stimulating. Just what my duties would be I could not make out, and I had never at any time thought of Buffalo as a desirable place to live, but I was in no position to think twice about the matter. I replied immediately that I *was* interested, and thereupon was appointed Curator of the Poetry Collection at the Lockwood Memorial Library of the University of Buffalo. The title was loftier than the salary, which was meager, but I was promised short hours and plenty of time for my own work. Later, when I saw Iris Barry again in New York, she filled in the story behind that first letter, which seemed to have come straight from heaven.

Earlier in the month the John Abbotts had paid a summer visit to the Charles Abbotts, where they heard more about the poetry collection. The books, letters, and manuscripts were accumulating satisfactorily, but an assistant was needed to help carry on necessary correspondence and catalogue manuscripts. There was a grant from the Carnegie Foundation which would provide a salary for an assistant for two years, but where was a suitable person to be found? One woman had been approached, but was not interested. Charles Abbott was not looking for a trained librarian (he was not one himself). He wanted someone passably intelligent, someone who was knowledgeable about modern poetry and could write a good letter. "Well," said Iris, "how about this girl Ezra brought in? She seemed bright." He thought not. I was too far away. He preferred not to hire an assistant without a personal interview. When Iris returned to New York, however, she sent him the letter I had written to her. That was enough; he wrote immediately offering me the job. For this position, the fact that I wrote "very decent poetry" was not, for once, a liability, but an asset. The fact that I had been working on a bibliography may have been a factor, also. Some familiarity with collation proved to be very helpful. The letter itself, however, told him what he needed to know about my letter-writing ability; I had put all the skill I possessed into that epistle.

I went immediately to New York, even before I received the second letter appointing me curator. I had to retrieve my scattered possessions, copy the manuscripts I had been working on, and say goodbye to my friends. As a base for operations I took a furnished room on West 22nd Street, not far from Edna's apartment. As soon as possible I went to see Iris Barry at the Museum. Ezra had warned me that some people could not stand her, but so far as I was concerned, she was perfect. I believe he said that because she was English, she was more outspoken than most Americans, and that put some people off. To me she was kindness itself. She said my job was to be mostly writing letters and "being nice to poets," with some research. She told me more about the Buffalo Abbotts and the collection of working manuscripts. The interview was brief, but a few days later I received a note from her with a check for twenty-five dollars enclosed. She thought I might "like to have a new dress or something." I was dumbfounded. I had not had twenty-five dollars at one swoop since I could remember. I confess I had no impulse to return the money, but the note that accompanied it was phrased with such delicacy and understanding that the impulse, if I had had it, would have been curbed at once. Obviously, she *had* been very hard up herself one time, though she did not say so.

As I called people to tell them about the new job in Buffalo, and to say goodbye, I was surprised to discover that several of my friends knew both Iris Barry and Charles Abbott, but no one had ever mentioned either of them to me, or me to them. With one or two sentences casually spoken, Pound had made the connection between me and the one job in the country that I was best fitted to do. Chance played a part, but for some reason, whenever Ezra made one of those moves that changed my life, something more like fate than chance seemed to be operating.

With the twenty-five dollar check from Iris I bought the new dress she suggested, a pair of sandals, and went to see the exhibit of Italian art at the World's Fair. On August 7th I got away at last. I hated to leave New York; I still knew almost nothing about Buffalo or the work I was to do, but two years would not be long. Then, I thought, I could return to New York and try again to storm the ramparts, this time with two years' worth of respectable employment on my record. On the whole, I was satisfied and excited about the future.

2

I arrived in Buffalo's palatial new Union Station hot, tired and dirty after a long day-coach trip from New York. I was looking for one of Charles Abbott's two secretaries, who was to meet me in black and white checks. I expected to see someone middle-aged and academic-looking, but the crisp black and white checked suit was on a very young woman with big brown eyes, clusters of brown curls and a most unacademic air from her high heeled pumps to the hat with a little veil. We identified each other; she took me to a hotel where a reservation had been made for me, and afterwards treated me to dinner. Her name was Anne McCarthy; we still exchange letters on the anniversary of that meeting.

Next morning I went out to the library, met the Director and his other secretary, Mrs. Sweeney, and was introduced to the Poetry Collection. The University library was a new building, built with money given by Thomas Lockwood, Mrs. Abbott's Uncle Tom, as a memorial to his parents. Since he also gave his collection of rare books, the library was provided with a large "Librarian's Study" lined on one side and one end with glass-fronted bookcases to house the books. Off the study at one end was a strong room containing steel files for manuscripts and letters, as well as two safes for the most precious volumes: the Shakespeare First Folio, the first edition of *Lyrical Ballads* and the like. At the other end of the long study, which was carpeted with a purple carpet and furnished with the Librarian's desk and a long refectory table, was a square corner room containing card files and two desks, one for Mrs. Sweeney and one for me. Anne's office was on the other side of the building on the same floor; a balcony above the main reading room led from her office to mine. There was also on that floor a large room filled with exhibition cases and another room that would eventually house the Poetry Collection. Outside, the four-storey library reminded me of Grant's Tomb; inside it was pleasant and well-equipped.

After a look around, I took a list Anne gave me and went in search of a furnished room. The University at that time had about three thousand students, but many of them were in either the law school or the medical school, which were in other parts of the city. Most U.B. students lived at home. The campus had no dormitories, but some families living near the campus rented rooms to students. I found a room, but was determined to find an apartment, a task much more difficult than I had anticipated. After a week or so I found a tiny apartment built into the back of a house on Winspear Avenue, just off Main Street and very near the campus. It was probably made from a boarded-up back porch—a dump, really—but all my own. The fact that only a curtain separated the kitchen from the bath bothered me not at all. It was not a maid's room in someone else's apartment; it was not a window–display office; neither was it a folding cot in a friend's apartment. Tiny as it was, it had everything: a complete bathroom, a sink, a little gas stove with an oven, and it was all mine. I even had a private entrance. It was completely furnished, and the rent was six dollars a week.

Meantime, I had made inroads on the work that was waiting for me. The Abbotts had recently returned from a collecting tour in England. There were masses of manuscripts and letters to be sorted, catalogued, and filed away in manila envelopes as well as unanswered letters to be taken care of. Also, another collecting tour was in prospect, this time across the Midwest to California. I had the job of making out a list of poets to be visited; I believe I also wrote to them. Besides all the un-catalogued materials, there were overlapping lists of poets and no clear record of who had contributed what. I have always enjoyed bringing order out of chaos (one of the most satisfying forms of creation), and this was a golden opportunity. I started out immediately with a master card file of poets, English and American.

I found as I got into the work that while Charles Abbott, who as a Rhodes Scholar had frequented those famous houses that were open to young Oxonians of literary bent, naturally knew much more about modern English poets than I did, I knew more about the Americans than he did. This was promising; and what was still more promising was that we usually saw eye-to-eye on the merits of the poets we both knew. Unfortunately, according to the terms of the Carnegie grant we had to collect *everybody* whose poems were published by the leading publishers (Carnegie did not trust our taste). On our own account we added books published not by vanity publishers but by reputable small presses.

For the remainder of the month of August I was busy and happy at the library but lonely when I was not at work. Anne and Mrs. Sweeney were native Buffalonians with families and a large circle of friends. Classes would not begin until September, and the campus was empty. However, on the last week-end of August I was invited to visit the Abbotts for the first time. They lived on an estate called Gratwick Highlands about sixty miles out of town in the direction of Rochester and the Genessee Valley. This was another of those big estates with several houses inhabited by different members of the family (Mrs. Abbott's family), but in this case the money was gone.

Wyndham Lewis's description of the estate and its gardens (in *America, I Presume*) is overdrawn like his characterizations of the Buffalonians he met. After all, the book is a satirical novel, not reportage. However, he does evoke the atmosphere of neglect and decay where "nothing had been touched since the Depression hit these gardens like a typhoon." The high-walled kitchen garden with its espaliered fruit trees and mingled weeds and vegetables gone to seed of course reminded me of *The Secret Garden*, but this and the flagged pavements where grass sprouted, the "stone seats decorated with bird droppings," the clogged fountains, were "purest Chekov" to Lewis. "A Slavic melancholy pervaded them, and their desolation was like a political tract." The rather melancholy beauty appealed to me, at least when the sun was shining, and I seldom saw them in rain. On one visit (at Easter) they were buried under four feet of snow, but usually I saw them (and contributed to the weeding) in bright summer weather.

The following week-end was our Labor Day week-end, when Hitler invaded Poland, and England delivered its ultimatum. All over Europe and America the radios blared; there was no music; the voices went on and on and on. I had not yet bought a radio, but from all the open windows in the neighborhood I could hear those voices, strident, urgent, without being able to distinguish their words. The tension was almost unbearable. Christopher Milne, in his autobiographical volume, *The Path Through the Trees*, describes that week-end in England. He and his father were huddled over the radio, waiting with everyone else to hear what England would do:

> Four years earlier my father had published a book called *Peace with Honor*. In it he had written: "I think that war is the ultimate expression of man's wickedness and man's silliness."
>
> He had now just finished his autobiography. In it he had written ". . . it makes me almost physically sick to think of that nightmare of mental and moral degradation, war." He had been a pacifist before 1914; he was a pacifist again from 1919 until 1939. And he was now, it might seem, about to betray the cause of which he was one of the more eloquent champions. He who had written "A nation has no honour" was now about to thrill with pride that Britain was doing the honourable thing.

This seemed to me one of the bitterest pills my generation had to swallow. At the time when the young men were taking the Oxford Oath, my father had said: "It will all depend on what the next war is *about*. Then we shall see." This made me very angry, because we young people thought then that we knew what every war was about. All wars were stirred up by propagandists in order to make money for munitions manufacturers and the like. Atrocities were fiction invented by warmongers, who repented and confessed when the war was over. But the leading propagandists for peace were now, in 1939, in favor of war, except for those Communist Party members who, less than a month ago, had been thrown into reverse by the Stalin–Hitler pact. Others left the Party at that point, never to return.

Finally the unthinkable thing that I had been dreading for almost a decade happened. England, followed by France, declared war on Germany. After those first three weeks of August, all the events, all the developments of my life in Buffalo took place against a background of war. There was the war, and there was the weather. If the weather predominates over the war in my letters, that is because my parents were reading the same news dispatches I was reading. There was nothing I could tell them about the war, but I had plenty to say about the weather.

On a radio news broadcast recently the announcer remarked: "Well, now it's official. The weather bureau has announced that Buffalo is the snow capital of the nation." A study of snowfall in the major cities of the United States during the last decade had revealed that Buffalo outstripped all contenders by I forget how many inches. This was no surprise to me. Coming as I did from a part of the country where three inches of snow is enough to close the schools, I was totally unprepared for Buffalo weather, even after a winter in New York City.

The snow, however, was only one aspect of Buffalo's bad winters. On April 15, 1942, I wrote that we had had five inches of snow on the previous Friday, and more on Saturday. I continued:

> The other night the paper had an article on the weather in fifteen of the large cities of the nation, and the statistics are as sad as my wholly emotional view of the subject. Buffalo has the lowest average temperature—47 degrees, I believe it was. Ties with New York for the highest wind velocity—Chicago coming fifth. Has the highest humidity of any. And only Seattle ranks lower on amount of sunshine. We get 50% and Seattle something like 47%.

Besides the snow, the wind, and the cold, there was ice underfoot all winter long. Sidewalks were cleared of snow, which was piled on either side of the walk, but a slight warming in the daytime would cause some of the snow to melt and form a puddle of water on the sidewalk; at sundown the puddle invariably became a treacherous sheet of ice. Crutches, slings and plaster casts abounded on campus. During the frequent blizzards, pedestrians clung to ropes stretched on downtown streets. The combination of ice and wind made it almost impossible to stand up, let alone proceed, without the assistance of the ropes. Doors on the windward side of public buildings were kept locked when the wind rose, because once opened they could not be closed again. Weather reports invariably referred to a wind clocked at sixty miles an hour (a "gale" on the Pacific Coast) as a "fresh wind."

One of the things that struck me as especially odd about Buffalo was the fact that the Buffalonians were actually proud of having the worst weather in the United States. In fact, I finally came to the conclusion that it was the only thing they were proud of except the fact that McKinley was shot there.

To add to the discomfort, the transit system was also ranked, according to the local papers, as the worst in any major American city. Instead of being able to dive into a subway as I had done in New York, or wait a very few minutes for one of the frequent New York buses, we had to wait sometimes twenty minutes or half an hour for an ancient, virtually unheated street car. People who owned their own cars always carried a shovel as well as chains, because a car once parked usually had to be dug out of a drift when it was time to go home. Taxis, so far as I was concerned, were out of the question because of the expense. Under these conditions very few things really seemed worth going out for. Fortunately there was a good neighborhood movie house within about two blocks of my apartment. I probably saw more movies in Buffalo than I have ever seen before or since.

When people ask me, "But Buffalo does have nice summers, doesn't it?" I like to quote the man who said that the nicest winter he ever spent was one summer in Buffalo. The warm weather was humid, often rainy, and the sunny weather was definitely cool. Also, summer was short. The icebreakers operated on Lake Erie in *May*.

Before I went to Buffalo, I had thought that even my small salary, since it was regular, would relieve me of constant worry about money, but I found otherwise. For one thing, I was run down. My blood pressure was low, my blood count was low, my nose was causing trouble, my teeth and my eyes needed attention. The internist was a long-time friend of Anne's; his charges were minimal and he gave me medication instead of writing prescriptions; nevertheless, all the repair work cost money.

Besides the doctor and dentist bills, a considerable outlay was necessary to re-stock my wardrobe. I was a little dismayed to find that the library gave teas, had exhibition openings, and other social functions at which I would be assisting, passing cakes, filling teapots, or even pouring. To make matters worse, the part of Buffalo that came to these affairs belonged to what I thought of as the white-kid-glove segment of society. Even Anne and Mrs. Sweeney considered white kid gloves an indispensable part of one's wardrobe. I had never had a pair in my life, never wanted them, and have managed to outlive any need for them without once owning a pair, but I absolutely had to have decent dresses and shoes to wear on social occasions such as these. Not only that, I had to outfit myself with snow-boots, mittens, hoods, sweaters and a much warmer coat than my ten-dollar one from Constable's. I was able to get by until the first of the year, when I used a fifty-dollar Christmas check from home for a warmer coat.

One time when Diarmuid Russell and I were comparing our odd-job experiences, he said that his oddest odd job was selling children's underwear in Marshall Field's basement. Of all my odd jobs, the one I have been most embarrassed about was a little moonlighting that I did when I first went to Buffalo. A Miss Anita Browne wrote to Mr. Abbott on stationery bearing an address in Radio City, though her return address was one that Mrs. Sweeney recognized as a Buffalo nursing home, she believed for mental cases, or nervous breakdowns. Miss Browne identified herself as the Founder of National Poetry Week, and asked whether Mr. Abbott would like to undertake some poetry criticism in his spare time, or if not, whether he knew of someone who would. He would not, but turned the letter over to me in case I was interested. I was of course willing to look into almost anything that might bring me a little extra money. Accordingly, I went to see Miss Browne and carried home several book-length poetry manuscripts that she wanted criticized or corrected. They varied, but most of them were unbelievably bad. The would-be poets were illiterate. Miss Browne had told me that when I found fault with the rhyme or the syntax or the metric (there was no free verse), I was to suggest a substitute line or construction. At first I tried to get away with indicating dissatisfaction and, sometimes, suggesting several possibilities. However, when I returned the manuscripts, Miss Browne was very unhappy. She insisted that I must emend as well as criticize. I finally realized that what I was supposed to do was make these verses fit for publication—by her, I assumed. She was apparently a vanity publisher, but the manuscripts she received were too bad even for vanity press publication without being re-written. I have tried to forget that I connived in the prettying up and publication of these impossible manuscripts. However, I could make five dollars in an evening, correcting two manuscripts, and I needed the five dollars. This desultory labor on the shady side of Mt. Helicon continued for perhaps a year or even longer, though gradually Miss Browne asked me to do less "criticizing" and more "judging." I preferred judging. I am glad to report that she recovered from her collapse and was able to leave the nursing home. I hope the people she published were happy about their books.

In mid-October of 1939 the Abbotts departed on their cross-country trip. When they returned in early December, my boss informed me that I looked "one thousand per cent better" than when I first arrived. He surmised that Buffalo agreed with me, but Buffalo never agreed with me in summer or winter. The improvement simply showed what a difference even four regular monthly paychecks could make.

3

The Poetry Collection at the Lockwood Memorial Library was the first of its kind, so far as I know; that is, it was the first archive set up for books, manuscripts and letters of modern and in most cases still living poets. (Chronologically the Collection began with Yeats's first volume, and Yeats was still living when the Collection began to take shape.) It was also the first to solicit working manuscripts that showed the process of composition. It would be difficult to say which of these two aspects of the Collection excited the most ridicule. The English were the first to double up with laughter; there was even a cartoon in *Punch*. To the English the joke was all the better because the manuscripts were to be collected in a city with the barbarous name of Buffalo. They found the whole idea simply hilarious and have not yet stopped poking fun at the quaint American notion of what constitutes a scholarly archive. While attempting to put myself to sleep last night with an English detective story, I came upon this: "American universities have fallen on hard times. Most of them have stopped buying second-rate authors' cast-off underwear." Honor Tracy has written a whole novel about an impecunious writer who was busy manufacturing a "working manuscript" of his last book. Ah well, yes. We were asking for papers that would otherwise have gone into the trash basket.

The idea that it was part of a university's business to collect materials for research into the work of modern poets was as strange (not to say scandalous) to most American professors, including those on the U.B. campus, as it was to the British. No self-respecting scholar would think of wasting his time on living writers. Charles Abbott himself believed that the Collection would come into its own "perhaps in a hundred years." The scholars would begin to come when we were long gone, he said, but the time to collect materials was the present. He was collecting for posterity. Living poets would one day be dead, the present would have become the past, the scholars would eventually become interested, and by that time the materials they needed would be much more difficult and expensive to obtain. This was surely true. The fifty dollars we paid for Williams' little pamphlet called simply *Poems* (Rutherford, 1909) seemed fantastic even to me, but thirty-five years later, the same book sold at auction for sixteen thousand. Undoubtedly we were collecting a lot of junk, too. The terms of the Carnegie grant would have made that inevitable, even if we ourselves had been sure that we knew what the scholars of the twenty-first century would consider junk.

Besides the books and magazines we were buying, we were asking for donations of manuscripts or other papers, and this involved a great deal of correspondence, most of it my job. While I was in Buffalo nearly all my letters from poets were part of my business correspondence and went into the library files. I retained only a few personal letters that came in response to letters of mine that had included a request for manuscripts.

I wrote immediately to Pound to tell him the result of that visit we paid to Iris Barry, but I did not request manuscripts because I knew it was useless. I seem to have had no answer to my letter, and did not write again until the war was over and he was in custody in Washington, D.C. I also wrote to Williams and Marianne Moore, explaining about my new job and soliciting manuscripts. Marianne replied on October 14, 1939:

Dear Miss Barnard,

No amount of preoccupation or even distress prevents one from wishing the situation for others were better, and it indeed does me good to know of your having this work, and of your liking it. I shall remember about the manuscripts. It is not probable that I have saved what might have value for students, but if I come on such work I shall offer it to you.

Your word of greeting at Christmas reached me, and this summer when my mother and I were in Gloucester for a little while I thought of what you had told me of Salem and Concord and Marblehead. I hope that sometime it may be possible to see something of those places, but we were unable for sight-seeing this year. Last winter was, for my mother, illness upon illness till June; and the aftermath has lasted till now. But our doctor has heard of a remedy, in use now at the Mayo Centre (for the kind of neuralgia my mother has) and we are hopeful of it. That she has not been able to use her eyes nor wear glasses since her illness, has been a handicap for us both, the use of another person's eyes never being a real substitute. Perhaps we shall find this present aid our deliverance. And even hardships have their good side. One is ashamed to elaborate personal difficulty when the world is in anguish.

It was a pleasure to see Ezra Pound, even briefly, and as I said to him, I think we in America need him and have a right to him, and that he should live over here. That he is not easily dissuaded from his decisions, however, is perhaps part of his value.

My own library work was of a very routine sort compared with your present work, but I liked it and am encouraged to hope that what you have begun will give you more and more satisfaction.

Sincerely yours,
Marianne Moore

I enclosed a new poem or two in my letter to Williams, and had in reply another of those disconcerting letters in which he deplored my shortcomings. It is dated January 8, 1940:

Dear Mary:

The world's in a parlous state. I don't know what we as poets can do about it either. Perhaps we should have gone to bed together or something, at least we might have bettered the general state of poetry a little by it and so in sum have benefitted the world also minimally.

Meanwhile thank you for a friendly letter and I wish you might be filing away scripts of mine as you should be if I had any to send you. I have a lot of junk lying around which I can bale up and dump on your lap if you want it but I can't imagine that it will be of use to anybody. Anything you want, ask for it. It's yours—with one or two exceptions, such as the script of the second volume of White Mule, now in the writing. I've promised that.

The poems, Mary, have you in them, your excellence which is great and your—reluctance, too concerned to explain. To hell with it. You want to explain too much. Let them go to hell. Make designs and dedicate them to yourself. They will be more transparent than you imagine. You cut your verses down but you cut them too much, too much of the details of you while leaving in too much of consideration for the others. Write you, write it intricately, as intricately and as finely, to the last detail of a thin line. I won't say make them, the poems, deliberately incomprehensible but I mean something like that while, at the same time, you labor to make them lucid within themselves, as poems. Spend every possible effort to make them explicitly lucid as designs of what you intend—but don't, oh don't ever explain. Take FOREST FIRE. I don't know how you are going to do it but you've got to leave out the line beginning "Aged five . " and the one that follows. Tell *me* to go to hell.

You are so damned good, that . I don't know why I say anything at all. Anyhow, I'm the masculine element that's no use to you. You're a woman and write like one . I ought to shut up. But I would at the same time like to see you sharpened to your essence, a passionate femininity without which you would not be writing at all. Somehow or other you've got to let it go— retaining the keeness.

Happy New Year.

Bill

The complaint that my poems lacked emotional intensity was a familiar one to me. I had been hearing it ever since my college days. Marianne Moore, on the other hand, felt that I expressed perhaps too much emotion. A young poet could easily become confused by criticism coming from contrary directions; but, in the end, I could only be myself, too emotional for one critic, and not emotional enough for the other. As for "Forest Fire," I later turned it into a prose fable.

With the new books coming in regularly and with all the current little mags and literary quarterlies crossing my desk on their way into the archive, I was keeping in close touch with everything that happened in the world of poetry publishing. Besides the news I learned from the printed word, rumor and gossip traveled to Buffalo with the visiting poets. I was naturally interested in developments at New Directions. Rumor had it that Laughlin was having difficulties. I heard first that the office had been removed to Cambridge after Higgins and Laughlin had each turned the car over again. Later I wrote to Kenneth Patchen and received a big pack of manuscripts mailed from Norfolk. (Interesting. But perhaps he was merely domiciled there?) In the 1939 issue of the New Directions annual, Laughlin announced that he would in the fall of 1940 publish a volume of poems by five or six poets in their twenties who had not yet had a volume of verse published. It would be, in effect, five or six first volumes of about thirty poems each between two covers.

I pondered that bit of information for some time, but decided to wait and see. My last offerings to N.D. had been rejected with the explanation that my writing was "not wild and woolsy enough." I might be rejected this time for the additional reason that I was celebrating my thirtieth birthday in December of 1939, although all the poems I would be submitting were written in my twenties. Besides, I still hoped for a book of my own, and I still hoped it would be published by a commercial publisher. I decided that I would wait for Laughlin to approach me if he felt so inclined. He knew my work; he knew my address; and if he wanted my poems he could ask for them. In February I had a letter asking whether I would like to submit a manuscript. I got it off promptly, and then I waited. After two months I inquired what was happening; in reply a card from Sun Valley advised patience.

In the meantime I had had a conversation with my boss

about commercial poetry publishing. It was most illuminating, and I gave a full account of it in my next letter:

> I still haven't heard a word from Jay, needless to say, but Mr. Abbott brought up the question the other day and we discussed it at some length. He said that if Jay didn't take it, he would be glad to mention it to Mr. Morley of Harcourt Brace, and following that, I got a lot of information. Charles Pearce, the man I talked to at H. B., has left and started a company of his own with two other people, something Sloan and Pearce I believe. We've had several of their books already. Morley is Christopher's brother, used to be with Faber . . . in England, and has now come over to take Pearce's place with H. B. Louis Untermeyer is *the* financial power behind H. B.—put up most of the money for it, and his word goes. If he's interested in a young poet, and . . . thinks he or she will sell, he says so to H. B., and H. B. publishes the book. If he's interested in the young poet, but thinks him or her too grave a financial risk, he mentions the poet to another company with which he has influence, but in which his money is not sunk, and persuades them to publish the book. As for instance a young man named John Ciardi who has just had a book published by Holt—the young head of that office having told me that they didn't publish any poetry. Well, it seems that Holt does publish Robert Frost, and Untermeyer is a man who can and does sell poetry. "Sell" it you know. Not over the counter, but by advertising it in lectures, critical writing, and so forth. Not, as Mr. Abbott remarked, that Frost isn't a good poet, that Untermeyer doesn't think he is a good poet, or that he doesn't deserve his popularity, but there is no particular reason why Frost should have been popular if Untermeyer hadn't "sold" him to the American public by singing his praises continually and without stint. Therefore, if you follow me, Holt is exceedingly in debt to Untermeyer, and dutifully publishes Ciardi, though if he'd had good salable qualities, they'd never have had the chance. At this point Mr. Abbott aptly remarked that it was "all a racket, all a racket."
>
> . . . I've known all the time that there were things like this behind the scenes, but could never get anyone to open up and tell me what was what.

More weeks passed, and more New Directions gossip came to Buffalo with the visits of John Wheelwright and Wyndham Lewis. Patchen had left Norfolk, and Delmore Schwartz was now in charge of the N. D. office, but in Cambridge. Finally on August 10th a letter signed "Jack Rip" informed me I was "raised to glory." I objected to the inclusion of holograph copies of poems, photographs of the poets, and critical notes, in that order, but of course in the end I complied with all of it. I did, however, reject a plea to expand my critical note. The book was published in November of 1940 as *Five Young American Poets, 1940*, and included collections by John Berryman, Randall Jarrell, George William O'Donnell, and W. R. Moses, besides my own "Cool Country." I had finally found the title, after much groping, while I was preparing the manuscript in New York the winter before.

Iris Barry had said that part of my job would consist in "being nice to poets." When poets visited, I was usually very much in the background, but I learned at second hand what being nice to poets can entail in the way of nervous strain and household crises. We had a number of visiting firemen who lectured or read their poems or simply dropped in for a tour of the Poetry Collection. Usually they were entertained at Gratwick Highlands, hence the household crises.

Wyndham Lewis was the first, completely unexpected arrival after I joined the staff. He appeared immediately after the outbreak of war in Europe and shortly before the Abbotts left for the West Coast. He and his wife were rescued from the Buffalo Statler where they had been nonplussed to find that the dining room always closed at eight o'clock, just when they were ready for dinner. He was taken to the country for a visit, introduced to Buffalo society, and negotiations were undertaken to secure a portrait commission for him. He was, it seemed, very hard up. Of course I was interested in Lewis because of his long association with Pound. My report on *l'Affaire Lewis* includes the following paragraph from a letter of September 19, 1939:

> Mr. Abbott has taken Mr. Lewis out to lunch with the Lockwoods, trying to get him a commission for a portrait—which is what Mr. Lewis is hanging around Buffalo for. Mr. Abbott said that he did one of Ezra, which was bought by the Tate Gallery in London and hung beside Whistler's portrait of Carlyle, and that Ezra was as pleased as punch. He has also done one of Eliot which caused a great stir because the British Academy rejected

it and three famous British painters, including Augustus John, left the Academy as a result. Augustus John has done a portrait of Mr. Lockwood, which hangs in Mr. Abbott's office, so he thought maybe Mr. L. would be a good bet for one by Lewis. He said Mrs. L. would fall for him, but she would fall much harder if Mrs. Lewis didn't go along. When he called Mr. Lewis, it turned out that that was already arranged—Mrs. Lewis was *not* going. Mr. A. said, "They *are* so funny about their wives!" Mrs. S. thought he meant Englishmen, and I thought he meant geniuses. Maybe both.

A postscript written the following afternoon continues with the information that Mr. Lewis was coming next day to sketch Mr. Abbott:

> Mr. A. brought in a colored reproduction of the Pound portrait. For my special edification. Very nice. The green sketch on I think it's my third letter from Pound is also by Lewis, and is one of the best likenesses of him as he looks now, I think. That and the colored portrait. Lewis said he told Pound he thought it was a better portrait than the Eliot one and of course Pound exploded and said why wouldn't it be, since he had so much better subject matter! . . . In the article that accompanies the portrait and other reproductions [of Lewis's work] Eliot is quoted as saying Lewis is the most fascinating personality of our time. Of course I was introduced as a protegé of Pound, and he asked if I had ever been to Rapallo, but that was about all the conversation.

The negotiations were successful. Mr. Lockwood put up half the money, another wealthy gentleman more or less related to everybody (I never managed to straighten out the relationships between Buffalo's Old Families) put up the other half, and a portrait of Chancellor Capen was commissioned. Lewis stayed on and painted it while the Abbotts were away, then left and returned in the spring for a lengthy stay at Gratwick Highlands where he worked on a book he referred to as a "pot-boiler"; his publisher wanted him to do something embodying his impressions of America and Americans. This book, *America, I Presume*, turned out to be a very block-buster of a pot-boiler when it dropped on Buffalo later that year. Compared to some of Lewis's satire it is mild indeed; but Buffalo was unable to understand how he could be so *ungrateful*. The trouble is, of course, that most people resent having to feel grateful, especially in matters of money; there is always, smouldering under the surface, a lingering resentment that may burst into flame, and in the case of a writer, the flame unleashed can be devastating. No doubt it is true that Lewis was an especially hard case, hypersensitive and likely to imagine that he was looked upon as an object of charity whether or not he had grounds for it, but his demonstration of ingratitude should not really have surprised anyone. One is kind to geniuses at one's own risk.

That same spring Dr. Williams was engaged to come for a lecture and reading. The Lewises were still with the Abbotts, and for a time we thought the Williamses and Lewises would be there together:

> One new complication is that the Lewises are going to stay until next Tuesday or Wednesday, which means the Abbotts will be entertaining them and the Williamses at the same time. I should think the Williamses would be very easy to entertain, but how Wyndham and William will hit it off at the same dinner table is another question. They're both friends of Ezra's, but that would give me qualms as quick as anything. I'm pretty sure Williams wouldn't take offense—or at least would have too much respect for his host to take offense—at anything Lewis would say, but Lewis is awfully touchy and likely to fly off the handle at something Williams is most likely to say—because he's impetuous and certainly doesn't weigh well his words before he speaks, though he's willing to laugh almost anything off, himself.

As it turned out, the Lewises left before or immediately after the Williamses arrived.

> Mrs. Abbott reported yesterday that she was finding the Williamses "very restful." . . . The doctor was autographing books in the study, and he autographed my copy of the collected poems. . . . We had a little chat, during which I learned that James Fourth is still at Sun Valley! Williams was pretty cross about it himself. Laughlin is bringing out the second volume of *White Mule* next fall. Also he has put his advertising and distribution in the hands of Duell Sloan and Pearce—the Pearce who was so nasty about my manuscript at Harcourt Brace.

Perhaps I should explain that this was the first time I had heard Williams perform in public. His coming had been partly my doing, and I was on edge about how the evening would turn out. He had read a few poems one evening when I was at Rutherford, probably when I was there with Fred Miller, and I had not thought he did them justice by any means. Mrs. Williams apparently felt that he did not read well, because she said, "Oh, no!" when he offered to read to us. I knew that he had done very few public lectures or readings up to that time, although on this trip he was appearing at Penn State, Dartmouth and Middlebury. My chief concern, however, was whether anyone would show up. At this time the Buffalo Public Library contained not a single volume of his work, poetry or prose, and interest in modern poetry (by anybody) was almost non-existent on the U.B. campus outside the second floor of the library. All in all, I was afraid the audience would be limited to a handful of people who would wonder why he was there. I need not have worried. My letter continued:

> The lecture was good. I was afraid he'd be nervous, which he was, and that that would make him stiff, as it does some people, instead of natural, but he very successfully got rid of his own nervousness and the audience's stiffness by being very natural indeed and he had everybody laughing at least half the time, I should think. The crowd was respectable, and certainly seemed to like him. When he mentioned quitting—drawing to a close, some girl behind me whom I didn't know, said "Oh, no, no!" very fervently. Most of the time he read from his poems. At the end, instead of asking whether there were any questions, as they usually do, Mr. Abbott said anyone with questions should come up and ask them personally. He won't do it again. A group of students, a large group, and I'm sure not from U.B. (never saw any of them before and I can't imagine where on earth they came from) literally mobbed him and wouldn't leave. Mr. Abbott told me enthusiastically that he thought the lecture was "swell" and Dr. Williams inquired whether he had disgraced me and Mrs. Williams invited me to be sure and come to see them next time I came to N.Y. Which I would like to do, but I wonder when I'd squeeze it in.

One poet who came that winter was well-known even in Buffalo. We had no worries about filling seats in the Fenton Auditorium when Alfred Noyes gave a lecture and reading. He was then about sixty-seven, and surely one of the most popular living English poets. If I had had a chance to meet him when I was thirteen or fourteen, I should have been thrilled to the tips of my toes. At that age I read Alfred Noyes avidly. I even read *Drake* and *A Forest of Wild Thyme*, but by the time our paths crossed in Buffalo, I had only a mild curiosity about the man. He struck me as altogether unremarkable. I barely mentioned the visit in my letters, and I retain only one memory of it.

The Collection contained prose by poets as well as their poetry. In the case of novelists like Hemingway, Faulkner, or Graham Greene, each of whom published a single slight volume of verse before settling down to novel-writing, we acquired the one volume of verse and let it go at that. In the case of writers like D. H. Lawrence and W. C. Williams whose poetry and prose fiction went hand in hand, we collected both. We had the fiction as well as the poetry of both Alfred Noyes and John Masefield, who was then Poet Laureate of England. While the visitors were being shown through the book collection, I heard Mrs. Noyes exclaim: "Alfred! John has more shelves than you have!" This remark struck me as bitterly funny. I believe there were about four shelves of Noyes and five shelves of Masefield at that time, but, as everybody knows, the Muse has scales that do not weigh by the pound of paper printed and sold. Quality is not necessarily in inverse proportion to quantity, but there is, as Pound was pointing out in early letters to Harriet Monroe, a danger in over-production. At least the Noyes and Masefield shelves were not filled with poetry alone. That would not bear thinking of.

I was more interested in the invitation extended to Robinson Jeffers. He was much in vogue when I was at Reed, and I had read several volumes of his poetry. I preferred the shorter poems, especially those descriptive of the headlands and surf on the California coast. I knew the one picture of him that everyone knew, a rugged profile silhouetted against a stone wall. When Una Jeffers answered the letter of invitation, saying: "I should be very glad to have Robin speak at the University of Buffalo," I was stunned. Later, when I told Bill Williams about it, a shocked expression crossed his face, he paused in the act of carving a roast, and exclaimed: "Good God! No wonder he writes about ROAN STALLIONS!" I found Jeffers a gentle, unobtrusive man who spoke to me kindly about my poetry. I thought I might have liked to know him, but I wondered whether anyone ever did, Una so dominated the stage. I no longer remember anything about his lecture and have no account of it in my letters.

Among the women who came, I especially liked May Sarton, a very attractive young woman with a fine profile, an apple-blossom complexion, and prematurely gray hair worn Alice-in-Wonderland fashion. She talked to a group of students about America, which she had been discovering in her travels. She was charming, but my feeling was that the students were merely politely puzzled. Genevieve Taggard stopped in to see the Collection, but did not lecture. Leonora Speyer, however, gave a full-scale performance:

> I think I wrote you that Leonora was coming. She came. Did I write you she was bringing a trunk? She called it "small" in her letters, and later said it contained her "little all." We had an idea her all was not little, and it wasn't, and it did come with her. A full-size wardrobe trunk. Eleven pairs of shoes she brought for the week-end.

Leonora Speyer was a tall, imposing woman in her late sixties. She had the bearing and style that went with her title of Baroness (which she did not use) and the stage presence of a concert violinist, a career she forsook for poetry. She had won the Pulitzer Prize for poetry in 1927 with *Fiddler's Farewell*. At the lecture she wore a most impressive formal gown, satin as I remember it, with an amply flowing floor-length skirt. As she was being introduced she forestalled any incipient tedium by lifting the hem of her skirt and giving her glasses a good polish.

> I was a little irritated by the lecture, and more so (in a way) because everybody else seemed to like it so well, and she's the least good poet we've had, in my opinion. Of course that's why they liked her, and it was nice to have somebody people liked. I softened, however, when Mr. Abbott told me she was disappointed not to meet me because she had read some of my poems, and liked them, and she said she had already ordered "my"

book. She has written poems that were better, I think, than the program she gave that night. . . . Mr. Abbott had said quite positively that he was bringing her in Saturday morning to look at the manuscript collection. I thought I would have time to visit with her then, and all you can say after a lecture is that you enjoyed it—which I hadn't, particularly. Mr. Abbott also felt that she would have done better to leave out the preliminary remarks (poking fun not very cleverly at the experimental poets) and have confined herself to reading the poems.

As it turned out, Mrs. Speyer spent all Saturday morning re-packing her trunk and did not reach the library until three o'clock. By that time I had gone home.

Another visitor, the Bostonian John Wheelwright, was al-most unknown to the poetry-reading public. I had seen his work in the *Westminster* anthology and *New Directions*, but found it too strident, or too obscure, or both. However, when he sent us a batch of manuscripts, I found as I worked on them that they had a certain fascination. He was a tall, thin, middle-aged man, very intense and difficult. Ignoring the ash tray placed for his convenience, he deliberately tossed a burning cig-arette end on the highly polished refectory table. In one respect at least, he left his mark. He had a way of charging headlong into traffic with no regard for traffic lights or crosswalks, and in that manner he met his death not long after his Buffalo visit. He talked informally with a small group at the library one after-noon. The question-and-answer period proceeded at a good pace. Someone asked him what he thought about Pound's *Can-tos*, and he dismissed them in a few well-chosen words while heads nodded vigorously. Then someone asked him that inev-itable question: "How do you go about writing a poem? Where do you get your ideas? How does inspiration come?" Wheel-wright replied that he opened a book—any book—and without looking, put his finger on a word (as in the *sortes virgilianae*), then put his finger on another word, and then put the two words together to see what the combination of words sug-gested. Suddenly no one seemed disposed to ask any more questions. The session ended flatly. I have never been able to decide whether he disliked the question and therefore gave an answer intended to be insulting, or whether he was telling them the simple truth. I think his audience was also in doubt, but found both interpretations equally disconcerting. It seems to me most probable that he was telling the truth. I have always meant to try the method one day to see whether it worked. The inception of a poem is something difficult to watch: if one watches, nothing happens; but my impression is that the inception most often takes place when two heretofore unrelated images or concepts come together in my mind to form a new combination. Perhaps Wheelwright's *sortes* would induce this kind of generation.

4

While my work at the library was as interesting and stimulating as I had been assured that it would be, life outside working hours continued to offer no stimulus at all. I met a number of people, and I find, looking through my letters, that I had more social life during my first winter there than I have any memory of, but none of it was an improvement on Vancouver. In April, however, there was a turn for the better. We arranged an exhibit drawn from our manuscript collection, and one of the people who turned up at the opening was a young poet, Reuel Denney, whom I had met at Yaddo in 1936. His arrival in Saratoga had almost coincided with my departure, and our acquaintance was so slight that when I came to Buffalo, I was not willing to try to track him down. In the meantime, a volume of his poems, with an introduction by Stephen Vincent Benét, had been published in the Yale Younger Poets Series. He had also married, and when he came to the opening I met his wife, Ruth, for the first time. From then on for about a year, I had more congenial company outside working hours. The Denneys entertained me, and through them I met Mark Howe, then head of the U.B. Law School, and his wife, the Irish novelist Mary Manning. The Howes and the Denneys and I, among others, even had regular meetings at which we planned a magazine to be called *Vector*. Nothing came of the magazine; no one really expected anything to come of it, but it gave an ostensible excuse, at least, for getting together at more or less regular intervals. Reuel at this time was teaching in a Buffalo high school.

It was at the Denneys' rather than the library that I met Louis Untermeyer shortly after the New Directions volume appeared. I came home exhausted after an evening of returning Mr. U.'s fast serve.

Well, it's the day after, and I feel like it. Mr. Untermeyer is not what you'd call relaxing after a day's work. The only other guest was a young kid named John Harmon, who goes to Teacher's College here. I think he's an ex-student of Reuel's, nice boy, but no match for Louis. He mostly sat back and laughed heartily at quips, but said little. Mr. Abbott had said that Mr. U. was so self-conscious about what was expected of him in brilliance of wit and repartee that he was extremely fatiguing for at least the first half-day (as house-guest), but after that he relaxed and acted human. For one evening in company with two young poets, wife of one poet, and a college student, he remained on his company manners. Very talkative—you had to make your remarks pithy and to the point to get them in before he was off again, yet he managed always to leave openings for remarks, or ask direct questions, so that you felt it was up to you to contribute. Some famous men just monologue and if you don't say anything all the better. . . . He made some cracks about the poetry collection, and I smacked them back to him as smartly as I could. He's going to do a new complete five-star all-inclusive, etc. etc. anthology. Not just modern, but all English poetry—poetry in English that is, of course. We talked about that a good deal, about his lecturing, about hunting and fishing (which he doesn't care for), Breadloaf, the poetry collection, Randall Jarrell, Muriel Rukeyser. It was fast and furious, and was terminated when it was by the Denneys' having to pick up Dave Reisman at the station about 11:30—so they took me to the Main St. car, Mr. Untermeyer to the Statler, and that was that. I gathered that Mr. Untermeyer had not seen my poems; he asked me, when we parted, to send him something—I don't know what, or for what, but I don't quite see myself sending him the book. . . .

Later Mr. U. returned, stayed with the Abbotts, and was given a tour of the Collection. He immediately did an about-face and, far from ridiculing what we were doing, offered to give us his letters from Amy Lowell, Vachel Lindsay and Sara

Teasdale. He promptly did so. He saw the New Directions volume at the Abbotts', read some of my poetry, and complained that it was "nothing but imagism." I bore up.

In the spring of 1941 Reuel received a Guggenheim fellowship; the Denneys left the city soon after the school term ended, and I saw no more of them until much later in New York.

According to the arrangement under which I came to the Lockwood Library, I should have been leaving, myself, in August of 1941, but somehow or other the money was stretched, and my time extended, first for six months, then for a year, until finally I was put on the University payroll. A raise in salary, however, was too much to hope for. Soon after Louis Untermeyer's visit I described the situation:

> Afraid there's no chance of getting $1500. Mr. Abbott has tried, and has even been apologetic about not having better luck, but you see these people who give out funds for cultural purposes always specify how much is to go for salary, and they have explained to him that $1000 a year is as much as an artist is expected to have to live on (fellowships, etc.). I said, yes, but in that case you're supposed to have *all* your time for writing, and Mr. A. said yes, but they expected you to travel and absorb foreign atmosphere which cost more, and I said, yes, and they usually expect the artist's wife and family to live on it, too, so that was that.

While the pay remained the same, the deficiency in money was in part made up by an increase in free time. I was writing some poetry and publishing a few poems; I wrote a verse play; but of course that sort of writing brought in no money. The thing I needed to do with my free time was writing that would sell. I had long ago given up hope of anything more than pin-money from my poetry, but I thought perhaps I could supplement my salary with another form of writing.

The library published a little book-review bulletin circulated to Friends of the Lockwood Library, who were also privileged to withdraw the new books we reviewed from a special "Friends" shelf behind the main desk. I had been helping with these reviews, not very willingly, because I hate reviewing. To make matters worse, the books that came in for review while I was in Buffalo were of two sorts: books on the war, and escape reading, especially detective stories. I read both, but as many of the detective stories as I could decently remove from the shelf before someone else got to them. I had read a few before I left Vancouver, and had even started writing one, mainly in order to see whether I could handle a plot. When the first Maigret stories to be translated and published in America reached our office, I knew definitely what I wanted to do. I liked the short length. I wanted to use a small-town, middle-class background. There would be no tricky business with timetables, no literary quotations, but emphasis on plot growing out of character. I fell to and wrote one, which went off to Frank Morley at Harcourt Brace with that letter of introduction originally promised for my poems—if I needed it.

One of the first things editors learn to do is to say "no" in tones that sound almost as encouraging as "yes." In short, Mr. Morley wanted to be sure that I could follow up with more of the same. No publisher wants just *one* detective story from an author. Very well, I produced a second. He still made encouraging noises without actually saying "yes," and I began to think about a third, this time with a Buffalo setting.

While I still lived on the Pacific Coast, I thought the inclusion of Buffalo among the Midwestern cities was most amusing, but when I lived there, I found that it *was* Midwestern. It fronted on the Great Lakes, with its back to the Eastern seaboard. The point of view was Midwestern and the Midwest was strongly isolationist. In our Anglophile office, with letters arriving from poets now in uniform, and book packages from London booksellers who were doing business as usual with the walls falling around them, we had little peace of mind. However, life went on undisturbed until that December Sunday when I was listening to the Philharmonic broadcast and heard the announcer break in with news of the attack on Pearl Harbor. I was invited to a party that afternoon, and went off to it still shaking, still hardly believing my ears. At the party everyone seemed quite unconcerned. No one even mentioned the event until I brought it up; thereupon they nodded, gave me a serious glance, and afterwards went on talking about other things. I was made to feel that I had introduced an unsuitable subject into the conversation. I knew then that I would never, never understand Buffalo, but I thought it might make a good setting for a murder mystery.

The four years I spent there were made more tolerable by my long vacations at home—two weeks with pay and a month without—and by trips to New York that were not as frequent as I should have liked, but were combined with library business so that I had a little expense money and a longer time to stay. One segment of the collection that became my own particular domain was composed of little magazines: *The New Freewoman*, and its successor *The Egoist, transition, Broom, The Little Review, Others, Exile, Blast, This Quarter*, and a great many more. Some were intermittent, most were short-lived, and all our runs were gap-toothed. Filling in the gaps became my responsibility. I soon realized that if we attempted to supply the missing issues from book catalogues, the prices would bankrupt us. I suggested, therefore, that when I went to New York for a weekend, I might take an extra day and see what I could find on Fourth Avenue. My first tour of second-hand bookstores, though brief, was so profitable that from then on I combined magazine-hunting with pleasure every time I went to New York. It was dirty work, but fun. For the only time in my life I experienced the collector's itch. If we had six issues of a magazine that ran for seven issues, the thought of that missing number 4 or 5, or whatever it was, plagued me until the run was complete. On these expeditions I also kept an eye peeled for out-of-print books that were not precisely rarities, because no one else was collecting them; they were volumes of verse by half-forgotten poets, very cheap if plucked from the shelf, and very expensive if a search had to be made.

Gotham Book Mart was always one port-of-call, though because it was more expensive I bought less there than on Fourth Avenue. One day in the spring of 1941 when I dropped in (after lunch with Rex Arragon), Miss Steloff invited me to return on Monday afternoon, when there would be a little party in the garden behind the shop. I never did find out just what the occasion was, or who was being honored unless it was Christopher Morley. However, I decided that I ought to put in an appearance.

It was a beautiful May afternoon, ideal for an outdoor party. Mr. Morley, it seemed, had been the speaker at the dedication of the Lockwood Library. When Miss Steloff introduced me, he showed his big teeth in a terrifying smile, and roared, "How's Tom? And I don't mean, how's the gin—I mean, how's *Tom?*" He then covered me with confusion by introducing me to a native Buffalonian (I believe his secretary) as "Miss Lockwood." By the time I had extricated myself from that predicament, Marianne Moore had arrived. Although I had little chance to talk with her, my memory of her as she appeared that afternoon is one of those I most delight in. Wearing a suit with a long jacket and a tricorne hat, she stood in the middle of the little garden, her head and her color high, her eyes sparkling, talking animatedly with a circle of men like a queen with her courtiers. They had converged upon her as soon as she entered and completely surrounded her. Among them were Christopher Morley, Mr. Schuster of Simon and Schuster, Bennett Cerf, Marsden Hartley, Ivan Goll, and others whose names I never learned. I hadn't a chance. They were intent on keeping her at it and not missing a word. While I was biding my time in hope of speech with Miss Moore eventually, I found myself in conversation with Oscar Williams. He immediately asked me what I thought of Allen Tate's verdict on my work in the current *Partisan Review*. Now Mr. Tate had reviewed the four men at some length and dismissed me with the remark that if I would put as much effort into acquiring a metric as I put into avoiding one, I might do good work. I replied that I didn't agree with it. Oscar Williams seemed surprised. Apparently he had expected that I would agree. He did. He then invited me to a party that same evening. It was to be at the apartment of a Mrs. P., who was, it seemed, "a wealthy woman with a swank place overlooking the East River and a hankering after poets in general. She's at any rate willing to feed them sandwiches and scotch in order to have them around, I gathered." My first impulse was to say I couldn't make it (I had an invitation to dinner in the Columbia University district), but on second thought, I decided that this would be a good opportunity to see a number of poets and answer questions, if they had any, about the Collection. Accordingly, I did go for the first and last time to an Oscar Williams party.

> There were hordes of poets. Oscar Williams, Willard Maas (only one I knew), Lloyd Frankenberg (whom I liked), George Barker (Irish poet whom I didn't like), Alfred Hayes, Horace Gregory, Marya Zaturenska, Marshall Schact (spelling not guaranteed), Miss Steloff of Gotham Book Mart, Mr. Putnam of Macmillans, unidentified girl who has bookstore in Brooklyn. . . .

There were others, unidentified, with whom I had no conversation at all. I was still so green that I had not yet learned why people stand up at cocktail parties. I sat down and was immediately trapped by a woman poet who had had a bit too much scotch and wanted to tell me the story of her life. I left early, surfeited with poets. I doubt that I have been to more than a dozen literary parties in my life, and two in one day was too much.

As was to be expected, when I was in search of defunct little magazines, I was haunted by the thought of all those I had seen in Bill Williams' attic. We proposed to the doctor that he sell us the lot, but he said that he wanted to go through them and keep any issues in which he had published stories or poems, and he saw no hope of getting around to it soon. With the entry of the United States into the War and the mobilization of doctors, that hope receded still further. Finally a solution was found: *I* was to do the job. Naturally, I was delighted. I looked forward both to the work and the week-end I would spend at 9 Ridge Road.

One very hot Saturday afternoon in June of 1942 I went to Rutherford, taking my suitcase, and moved into one of the spare bedrooms. (Bill was in the Navy, in California, and Paul was working for Republic Steel in Canton, Ohio.) After I had washed up,

> we had a delicious dinner with chicken and trimmings, and sat out in the back yard admiring the roses until the mosquitoes got bad, and then came in and drank iced lemonade with stalks of mint in it until bedtime. It was terribly hot until morning, and I kept tossing around thinking how hot it would be in the attic, but a cool breeze blew up around seven o'clock. There were

windows in each end of the attic, with the breeze sweeping through, so I didn't suffer. . . . All day Sunday I worked in the attic. In the morning I sorted magazines and books. There's an enormous amount of material, and it was all scattered. Vol. I, No. 1 in a book case, Vol. I, No. 2 in a trunk, Vol. I, No. 3 in a desk drawer, another copy of Vol. I, No. 3 under a table, and so on and so on. I sorted one magazine from the other, books from magazines, and the things we were interested in from the things we weren't. It was dirty, but I had fun. After lunch the doctor came up with me, and we both sorted, and he began to get out letters. By that time I was down to making lists, so I wrote and he read letters to me. If the lists are right, it's a miracle, because I was so interested in the letters. As for giving them to us, first he would, and then he wouldn't, and then he didn't know. I think what finally threw a monkey wrench into the business, was Mrs. Williams' putting her foot down, with the result that I came away with only two letters, but very good ones, one from Pound about 1907, one from H. D. when she was working on the *Egoist* in 1916. We may get others later.

The magazines are less important, but I found a lot of things we need. The duplicates I know he'll let us have. Some of the others we may get, and in any case, I know about a lot of magazines I didn't know about before—what's in them, and what we need. That information in itself is so hard to get. Monday I finished my lists and did some more rooting around in the grime, turning up things I had missed the first time.

I worked at a big table by the window at the front end of the house. From that window I looked down to the sidewalk. On Monday, every time I glanced out I saw the same scene: a baby carriage, empty, was sitting in front of the house; another baby carriage (occupied) was approaching; another was just rolling away out of sight around the bend of the street. It went on all day long.

That morning the Williamses suggested that instead of going back to New York, I should remain in Rutherford and commute until time to return to Buffalo. "They were both so cordial, and I reflected that I'd already used the sheets, and my two pieces of toast for breakfast couldn't be *much* bother, and they said I could have a door key and come in any time I liked, so I stayed. They were both lovely to me."

After describing the crowded conditions on trains and buses, I added:

> I experienced my first blackout in New Jersey Monday night. It lasted about twenty minutes, I think. The doctor had to rush for the schoolhouse, which served as first aid station, and Mrs. Williams and I went upstairs and watched for a searchlight display which was omitted this time. The New York dimout is something. I came out of a subway a block from Times Square, and couldn't find the Square. Not a neon sign, not a theater marquee, no lights but street lights, and you have to get right under a street sign and squint at it to find out where you are. I suppose you know it's on account of the sky-glow silhouetting the convoys miles out at sea.

Finally, in this very long letter there was mention of a meeting with Muriel Rukeyser and another woman who was one of the "mulberry tree crowd." We had cocktails somewhere in Muriel's neighborhood, and I had a very good time. I preferred poets one or two at a time.

> Muriel has a new book, prose, coming out in August.★ She talked a great deal about it, and I was much interested. It was a very satisfactory little party. She has just got a job writing script for government files, on rationing, army work, etc., and asked me if I'd like one. I told her I'd see how my present job held out, though every time I come back to Buffalo I go through a mental crisis, and wonder if it's the thing to do, really.

The next day I learned that I had at last been put on the University payroll. I could stay if I wanted, which meant that I now had to make up my own mind about staying or leaving. The question would not be decided for me.

The following year was one of ups and downs, with more downs than ups. On the credit side, the Collection was taking firmer shape. Mr. Lockwood had been persuaded to give us tables, chairs, and book stacks to furnish the Poetry Room so that his fine bindings could be restored to the study bookcases. This was a great relief, because the study shelves were by that time two rows deep. My desk and the card catalogues went into

★ *Willard Gibbs*, a biography published in 1942.

the new room with the books and magazines, while the manuscripts and letters stayed in the strong room. With this development we seemed much more like a going concern, though we
still lacked customers. Only two appeared (together) during my
tenure. At Christmas time I paid a call on the Williamses and, to
my surprise, came back to Buffalo with a big carton full of letters:

> I think we now have most of the Williams letters. He said he
> might as well give them to us, because if he died, well, Flossie
> would be interested for a while, but then (so-and-so) or (so-
> and-so) might come around and carry them off, and he'd rather
> we had them. Besides, I think I've sold him on the idea that
> having his things in our library is just like having a private
> secretary. I've looked up and copied several things he couldn't
> find, have an order to do another one, and he is even thinking of
> sending us all his magazines, with poems he would like to an-
> thologize checked for me to copy and compile. It seems that's
> why he's holding them, and he'll *never* get around to it with-
> out help.

Iris Barry had sent us her Pound letters, and a Buffalo woman
had given us a set of D. H. Lawrence letters. Williams had also
filled two of our worst gaps in the book collection by selling us
his copy of Pound's first volume, *A Lume Spento* ("I'll buy a
War Bond!" he said), and finding a Rutherford friend who was
willing to sell us his copy of Bill's *Poems*, 1909. Of course none
of us had any idea of the fantastic prices these books would
some day bring.

The social situation improved during my last two years in
Buffalo because I was having dinner five nights a week with a
student named Charlotte Georgi and her mother. The first year
Charlotte was a senior majoring in English, the second year a
graduate assistant working on an M.A. thesis. I not only enjoyed her company, but through her I gradually infiltrated faculty territory. There was a cleavage I had not expected between
staff and faculty, and I was staff. Female staff wore hats to lunch
in Norton Union, and female faculty did not. I did not, and
Anne did not (she had only just ceased to be a student), but that
did not make us faculty. At any rate, things were much better
during after-office hours once I began to eat with the Georgis;

Charlotte, however, would be leaving soon; Anne, who was now married (and a mother), would also be leaving.

The war news was a little better; there were Allied victories in North Africa and the South Pacific, but D-Day was still more than a year away. The weather was not getting any better at all. In fact on January 20th I wrote:

> Everybody is saying this is the worst winter they can remember—started earliest, and there has been more snow, more zero weather, more dark days. And this, for a combination of cold, wind, *and* snow, is the worst we've had this winter.

Nobody talked about the wind-chill factor in those days; it would have sent Buffalo temperatures skidding. That winter the official temperature dropped to 17° below, the coldest we experienced while I lived there, and the winds reached seventy-two miles an hour (seventy-three was the highest ever recorded in Buffalo). I did not report on the humidity.

In April, with the snow again coming down steadily after a brief spell of mild weather, an epidemic struck the city. Some said it was intestinal flu, some blamed it on the city water, because Buffalo had had recent trouble with its water system. Whatever it was, it was not lethal, but it was painful and debilitating. Although most victims recovered quickly, some were so ill that they had to be hospitalized, and I was one of them. After two weeks in the hospital, I went to the Georgis' for a few days, while I got on my feet, then back to my apartment where I collected enough strength to travel.

While I was convalescing I received a letter from Bill Williams, dated May 22, 1943. It began:

> Dear Mary,
> You didn't tell me what was the matter with you nor how very sick you've been. Forget it. I understand now that you were very sick indeed and that it may prove your farewell to these parts. I hope that's not true.

Things were looking black for him, too:

> My book of poems, the one for which I wanted the two pieces you copied out for me, has been rejected by Simon & Schuster as it was rejected by our friend Jimmy (who never saw

it) because of an ostensible lack of paper. Now it goes to Duell, Sloan & Pearce because of Pearce who has always seemed friendly—but that may not carry beyond the lack of paper. After that, Random House, Harpers, and points south, east, north and west. It'll be published somehow, somewhere by fall, I hope. Keep me posted as to your address (which I think you gave me in your last letter) and you shall have a copy free, gratis, for nothing as soon as it appears.★

He was about to go to work on *Paterson* again, "a Mt. Everest" for him to surmount, then wanted to do his mother's biography, and then go on to his next play in verse. "I'm not permitting myself to think of anything else," he said. "I hope I live." The letter continued with news of his two sons, one in the southwest Pacific, the other about to enlist in the Navy. He concluded:

> So wags the world, my microscopic world. And the war is approaching a crisis and soon an end I confidently believe. Take care of yourself and write me when you will.

Although that illness did not prove my "farewell to these parts," if in that phrase he included New York City and Rutherford, it did mean my farewell to Buffalo. I never went back to work at the library again. When I was strong enough, I went home by train through Canada where wartime travel was less difficult. Edna Guck went with me and stayed a month, her first visit to the Pacific Northwest. I stayed three months while I completely recovered my strength and definitely decided not to go back to Buffalo. Vancouver at this time bore little resemblance to the town I grew up in. Trainloads of shipyard workers had been brought directly from New York City and the Deep South. Government housing developments sprawled over what had been wooded heights and farmland. The town had tripled in size. It seemed more congested, certainly more hectic than New York City, which was undergoing a wartime depression. My father was busier than he had ever been; as I said in my first chapter, his decision to keep on dealing almost exclusively with the little mills now paid off handsomely, while other lumber

★This was the collection eventually published as *The Wedge* by the Cummington Press.

wholesalers were crying hard times. Gas was rationed and we could not go anywhere except to sawmills, but that included trips to some of my favorite haunts. I enjoyed the summer, but I was still nowhere near ready to take up life in Vancouver again. In the fall I took a train back to Buffalo, collected the belongings I had left there, and moved to New York.

How much those four years in Buffalo did to boost me a little farther up the craggy slopes of Helicon, I do not know, especially if we consider the ascent in the sense Pound was using when he accused me of wanting to be carried up the mountain in an easy chair. At the very least, I had the money to live on; my reading, under sympathetic guidance and with a university library immediately accessible to me, was much extended. I had time for writing and I believe that I wrote a few of my best poems there. So far as my career as a poet was concerned, as distinguished from the development of the craft, my name and my work were much better known by the time I left Buffalo, thanks to the *Five Young American Poets*, which had been reviewed widely: by Tate in *Partisan Review*, by Blackmur in *Southern Review*, by Babette Deutsch in the *Herald Tribune Books*, and by Lloyd Frankenberg in *The Nation*. It is true that some of these reviewers, like Tate, were less than enthusiastic about my work, but the mail coming in from poets all over the country (in answer to my letters as Curator) contained so many appreciative comments that I suffered very little from the adverse reviews of established poets not of my school. As Victor Chittick said, the six pages Blackmur devoted to a discussion of my failings were as good as having my name in neon lights. Now all I needed to do was follow up.

Here, however, we come to the one aspect of my experience as Curator that perhaps had more influence than any other on my subsequent career. Whether or not I was any farther up the mountain in any sense at all, I had had a panoramic view of the terrain. It was not encouraging. I was depressed, not by the poets who had published one volume and then fallen by the wayside, but by the *successful* poets who issued a volume of poems regularly every three to five years, keeping their names always before the public by doing reviews, acting as poetry editors, publishing frequently in magazines, being included in anthologies, compiling anthologies themselves, and yet, within a few years after their deaths, were completely forgotten. We had shelves and shelves of these poets, rows of dusty names. Perhaps some day one of them would be rediscovered and find a place in the modern pantheon, but hardly more than one. I had come to the conclusion that a poet had to run very fast indeed to stay in the same place—that is, in the public eye and memory—faster than I would ever be able to run. I might as well save my breath. At the same time I became conscious that so far as my own work was concerned, the needle was beginning to go around in the groove. I wanted to do something quite different, something more concise, more concrete, simple in phrasing, almost palpable, but I could not find my way to it. I wrote a few poems during the first two years after my return to New York, but I had never been so dissatisfied with my work. I put most of them aside after much revision and never published them. I read no poetry at all. I had simply read too much. I knew I would write it again, but for the rest of that decade I concentrated on fiction.

Chapter 6

WHEN I returned to lay siege to New York for a second time, I had a bank account, a respectable wardrobe, and, within a few days, an apartment of my own. While Vancouver, in 1943, had tripled in size with the influx of shipyard workers, Manhattan was still in a slump. Apartments were plentiful and rents were reasonable. The apartment I found at 5 Minetta St. was a tiny room in a very old building entered from a courtyard. My living-room, whose dimensions were approximately eight by twelve, had a fireplace; the windows looked out on the courtyard and into the branches of an ailanthus tree. The back (bathroom) window looked down into the kitchen of Monte's Restaurant on MacDougall Street. With a studio couch and a few pieces of furniture from a second hand store I was all settled—for fourteen years, as it turned out.

This time, too, I thought I knew what I wanted in the way of a job. I was going to look for some kind of research work. Again, I started out by reading ads and going to the agencies, but there I was brushed off as unqualified because I had had no courses in statistics. I was hoping to find a job before I called Florence Codman, whom I had seen once or twice during the Buffalo years, but when a month passed without a nibble, I broke down and called her. She was most cordial, and full of enthusiasm for the research idea. She was, in fact, doing research herself for Earl Newsome and Company, a public relations firm. She pooh-poohed the notion that I needed statistics. Also, she was free-lancing, which was what I wanted to do. Through her I received a few little dribbles of work from Newsome and Company that fall, but there was no promise of a future there, and I continued to look for something else. In December of 1943 Florence left the city because of illness in her family, and I began to hear from Newsome more often; they called on me for odd jobs of research throughout all of 1944. Occasionally they gave me something big enough for me to get my teeth into, but for the most part, although I was well paid, the work was too intermittent and uncertain to live on.

For a time during the spring I combined Newsome research with work for the Educational Division of the War Prisoner's Aid organization. My experience there would make a chapter in itself, but would be irrelevant to my main theme, because it had nothing to do with writing or publishing. We were shipping textbooks (most of them specifically requested through the Red Cross) to American POW's in Germany and Italy. I found, however, that the job had been blatantly misrepresented. Instead of using either my writing or my typing skills, I was using only my muscles, as I moved stacks of heavy textbooks about in a sub-basement where the dust fogged into my sinuses. I also found myself between two warring personalities, who were using me to annoy each other. I believe I lasted about a month, and then quit.

There was nothing at the Museum of Modern Art. I considered applying at *Time* again, but Reuel Denney, who was now on the staff as a writer, discouraged me. Florence Codman was equally discouraging.

She said she had sent several girls there, and *Time* had reported that they weren't the "type." She said they had to be "well, you know, twenty-five and a little hard." I haven't seen them, but I can imagine—younger than I am, with the Eastern women's college veneer.

I was well aware, having just that week turned thirty-four, that I was nearing the outer limits of employability, for a woman, that is, with my sketchy work-record.

Meanwhile, I was seeing my Yaddo friends again, among them David Greenhood and his wife, Helen Gentry, who was a printer and book designer. Between the two of them they turned up several possibilities that faded before they turned into anything really tangible. Helen at this time was designing books for Simon and Schuster, and she wangled a temporary, part-time job for me there. That, again, amounted to very little, but I liked the idea that I was for once in my life behind the scenes in a publisher's office. I alternated this work, too, with the Newsome research. Then Helen took me in hand and showed me how to draw up an application letter that she suggested I send to a number of firms and individuals. My first nibble came from a public relations company that offered me a job answering letters of complaint about dog food. I would spend quite a lot of time visiting dog shows, the lady told me. While I like dogs—some dogs—I prefer to take them, like poets, singly or in pairs. The forty dollars a week I would have been paid was not enough to tempt me. I rather suspected, too, that I would find myself manning a booth at the dog shows, and passing out samples. I turned it down.

I sent another of these letters to Mark Van Doren. He knew Charles Abbott, who was my best reference, and had contributed to the Poetry Collection; he was teaching at Columbia, and while I did not expect that he would have work for me, I thought he might know someone who would. He replied promptly that I might hear soon from a friend of his who needed an assistant. Nothing happened until a month or so later, when Mark telephoned me.

He said he had a small job for me, just mechanical work, but if I would like to do it, would I come over and he would explain it to me. So I went to call on him at three o'clock. . . . The job is revising an index for a new edition of his critical book on Dryden. The paging is different in the new edition and all the page numbers in the index have to be changed. He expected me to take each number and hunt it down in the page proofs, but since he wanted the whole thing typed, anyway, I said I thought the best way would be to copy it off, read the book through, and fill in the numbers as I came to proper names, and then check it over for omissions. He seemed much impressed—thought that was a very good idea—just hadn't occurred to him at all. It seemed pretty elementary to me, but if he is impressed, that's just fine. Then I told him that I was afraid his friend hadn't been tempted, since I hadn't heard from him. He said, "Oh, no, not at all," I wasn't to think that, and I probably would hear, the person in question being his brother Carl, who has had an operation on his eyes, and doesn't know yet just what he will be able to do, but will probably need help. He has just come back to town, and hasn't got organized yet, which would be why he hadn't called me. Of course, he said, he couldn't promise anything, but he thought it quite likely. I wondered if this little job was also in the nature of a try-out. Could be.

I finished the index to Mark's satisfaction, and then, between Christmas and New Year's Day (1945), I had a phone call from Carl Van Doren, who wanted me to come out to his apartment next day.

He wanted me to start work right away, though we would get off to a gradual start because he isn't well enough organized yet, but he wanted to give me a check for two hundred fifty dollars as a retainer. . . . He is editing a volume of autobiographical writings by Franklin, a lot of it unpublished stuff which has turned up, or been made public since he wrote the biography. My work will be partly transcribing from photostats and probably from manuscripts, too, since he said I would need to go to Philadelphia to do some of it. Then there will be some research and he said he would ask me to check him on some of his research, and he said, "I'll probably stick you with the index, too, when it comes time for that." . . . He made an appointment with me to come out and see him yesterday afternoon at four. . . . He has an apartment on Central Park West, just above Columbus Circle, which makes it very convenient to my subway.
    Carl is very different from Mark, as I thought he would be. Mark is small and slender and quiet, and perhaps it's partly the

association in my own mind, but Carl reminds me more of Mr. Chittick, though he's more talkative. He is a big man, about Mr. Chittick's size, with close-cropped gray hair and horn-rimmed glasses and brown eyes. He was very nice, too, but I don't think as nice as Mark. He showed me the view over the park, which was very beautiful in the snow, proceeded to give me a brief topographical and geological history of Manhattan Island, and without drawing breath showed me into the study and started on Franklin. He said he needed help, and he thought I was the very person to do the job. I said I wouldn't be a quick typist on French (in which language a number of the manuscripts are), and he said, "Bless your heart, I'm not worried about that!" and said what he needed was not a typist, but somebody with the background to do an intelligent job on the work. By the way, when talking over the phone, he said Chittick mentioned me to him several years ago. I'm amazed that he remembered, unless he has checked with Chittick since he saw my application, but from what he said, I deduced that he hadn't.

When I left I took with me some of the photostats of letters that needed to be transcribed. It was the beginning of a very satisfactory relationship that lasted until his death in 1950.

Carl Van Doren, during the Twenties, Thirties, and Forties, was one of the best-known pillars of the literary establishment. The elevator boy said to me one day as we ascended to Carl's apartment, "Do you know that Mr. Van Doren's picture is in the *Saturday Review five times* this week?" He was on the board of the Literary Guild, wrote a weekly book-chat column anonymously, and had a finger in all kinds of literary pies. As a public personage he operated in what was to me alien territory, but I was to be working with the historian and biographer, who was the only Carl Van Doren I came to know. Charles Olson said to me once: "I detest what he stands for, but I think his books are actually very good." Olson mentioned especially *The Secret History of the American Revolution*, which was published before I joined forces with Carl. The book he was best known for, however, was his biography of Benjamin Franklin, which won the Pulitzer Prize for biography in 1938. He was planning a revision of this work incorporating new material; the present volume of Franklin's *Autobiographical Writings*, including letters, was a first step in that direction.

1. The author and her grandmother on the porch at Buxton. 1917.

2. The author wearing a beret. 1934. Photograph by Edris Morrison.

3. A sawmill at Silver Lake. Sketch by the author.

4. The Spokane, Portland and Seattle Railway passenger depot at Vancouver, point of many departures and as many returns. Photograph by Reid Blackburn.

5. The Mansion at Yaddo. The third-floor windows are those of the High Studio. Photograph by the author.

6. Muriel Rukeyser at Yaddo, 1938. Photograph by the author.

7. Guests at Yaddo, photographed on the terrace, Sunday, July 17, 1938. *Front row, left to right*: Leonard Ehrlich, writer; Muriel Parker, composer; Mrs. Waite, sister of Mrs. Ames; MB; Rebecca Pitts, writer; Muriel Rukeyser, poet; Edna Guck, painter and sculptor; Helene Magaret, poet; Elizabeth Worthington, painter; Mrs. Ames; Mrs. Thorp; Susie Fuchs; Dan Fuchs, writer; Willard Thorp, writer. *Back row*: Hubert Skidmore, writer; Kenneth Fearing, poet; Fred Miller, writer; Albert Frischia, painter; Wallace Stegner, writer; Anthony Martelli, painter; Joseph Vogel, writer; Charles Naginski, composer; Henry Roth, writer.

8. The New Directions office, Norfolk, Connecticut, 1938. Not a cow barn. Photograph by the author.

9. William Carlos Williams. "He is one of our realest people, and a most unmercurial friend" (Marianne Moore to MB, July 15, 1940). Photograph by John D. Schiff. Courtesy of New Directions.

13. Marianne Moore. Photograph by Marion Morehouse Cummings.

M   in a vicious world—to love virtue
A   in a craven world—to have courage
R   in a treacherous world—to prove loyal
I   in a wavering world—to stand firm

A   in a cruel world—to show mercy
N   in a biased world—to act justly
N   in a shameless world—to live nobly
E   in a hateful world—to forgive

M   in a venal world—to be honest
O   in a heartless world—to be human
O   in a killing world—to create
R   in a sick world—to be whole

E   in an epoch of UNself—to be ONEself

e. e. cummings

14. Ezra Pound at Rapallo, 1959. Photograph by the author.

15. Brunnenburg castle, Tirolo di Merano. Photograph by the author.

16. Mary de Rachewiltz in
the study at Brunnenburg,
1953. Photograph by the
author.

17. A window at Brunnenburg.
Photograph by the author.

18. The author, aged 72 and still writing. Photograph by
Mary Randlett.

By early March I was feeling disillusioned about my new job. There seemed to be much less to it than Carl had at first indicated. I had learned, from the experiences of my friends as well as my own misadventures, that if the job-hunter's résumé is occasionally rather wide of the truth, the employer's job-description can be equally misleading, especially if he mentions that it will "lead into" something better. I gave the following account of the situation as I then saw it in a letter of March 9, 1945:

I've been working for Van Doren again this week, but he has apparently just about finished the book, and the work is shaping up differently from what I expected. In the first place, of course, I haven't had as much on this part of the book as I thought I would have, though I imagine the index will take a lot of time. . . .

The other thing, a job for the future, came up when I went out to see Van Doren on Wednesday. He was feeling quite chatty, and we sat in his living room and talked for a long time about Buffalo and various other things. [He had just returned from a trip to Buffalo.] But first he told me of this project which is also connected with Franklin. The American Philosophical Society Museum in Philadelphia . . . has most of the important Franklin documents and large collections not only of his letters but of letters from all his family. Van Doren said that in an unguarded moment he made the statement that it was probably the biggest and best collection of family letters in existence, giving a picture of the family in adult life and into old age. Well, the Museum at once wrote and asked him, would he edit them. He said it was too big a job for him to take on, especially with his eyesight the way it was, that he wouldn't do more than supervise the editing and write an introduction, and would have to have a collaborator and that he knew just the person to do it. (Meaning me.) He said they seemed agreeable and he thought it would go through if I were interested. I said I would be. He said he thought they ought to give me enough money to live on comfortably for a year, or however long it took, and then added that they were simply crawling with money and there was no reason why they shouldn't spend it in a good cause and he would do the best he could for me. In other words, they would be paying me, he wouldn't, but he was undertaking to make the arrangements. I imagine he might do better for me than I would if I were to do the arranging, so that's all right. It would also mean that I would be doing the dirty work and he would be getting the glory, but that's all right with me, too. I would certainly need supervision for a job like that, and he knows all the Franklin history inside and out. It isn't just the kind of job I would have dreamed up—I seem to be retreating into the archives again—but one can't be too choosy, and it wouldn't last forever, and would, I should think, be impressive reference for future jobs. Might lead to something better, or as good, unlike the dog food. So if the money is good, I wouldn't hesitate. And Mr. Van Doren I still think is a very nice person to be supervised by, though he seems to see things that aren't there, judging by his outline of this job and what I've done. To be more explicit, I think he exaggerates the importance or onerousness either of what he's doing or what he asks other people to do—I thought there must be a lot of French, since he was so interested in my having a command of it—and there was only one manuscript. . . . Possibly, too, he didn't know how he would get along himself, on account of his eyes, and has found he could do more than he expected when he hired me. Some things he has turned over to me when they got too much for him.

One thing puzzles me about the above paragraph: I don't know how I expected to keep out of the archives while doing research. I continued:

Incidentally he was pleased as Punch that day because he had just been asked to take a part in the operetta version of *Liliom*,★ by the people who did *Oklahoma!*—the part of Mr. G., in other words, God, who lives in a bungalow with his wife, who polishes stars, one of which Liliom steals for a graduation present for his daughter, etc. He had to tell me all about what he would have been doing if he had accepted the part, which he did not. He said eight appearances a week no matter how you felt was too much for him, and besides he had said such things about authors who turned actors, like Woollcott and Benchley, that he didn't dare. He also had things to say about Buffalo, which has had just under nine feet of snow since the 18th of December, none of it melted, just packed down in sooty glaciers, some of the streets cleared only for one way driving. He said he never saw anything like it.

★*Carousel*, by Rodgers and Hammerstein.

At the end of this letter I returned again to my uncertainty about the work that was supposedly in prospect:

> He spoke pretty positively about the thing, but, as I said, I've concluded that he sees things that aren't there, and so am taking it with a grain of salt. . . . I was in on a piece of a conference with a protegé (apparently) of his one day this week, and I thought he was inclined to dispense intangible things with large and generous gestures to her, and his proposal about the family letters, following immediately, underlined the impression. When he followed that with the story of Oscar Hammerstein, who was one of his former students, wanting him to play Mr. G., I did wonder if O. H. had a similar impression and that was why he asked him!

When the page proofs of the *Autobiographical Writings of Benjamin Franklin* finally arrived, we worked together in Carl's apartment. He was a first-rate indexer, and taught me the art as we went along. Indexing is not something I would do just for the fun of it, but this task had bonuses that cause me to look back on it with pleasure. Although the weather was hot, Carl's apartment with its large rooms, tiled floors, and windows opening above Central Park always remained comfortable. Also, there was the food (again). Mabel, Carl's daily help, was delighted to find someone at her table whom she could stuff, and she was an excellent cook. Her popovers, soufflés, and the porgies she brought down from Harlem and cooked to perfection, figure largely in my letters. To add to my contentment, I knew now that there would be more work coming soon. The family letters were to wait while Van Doren edited the correspondence between Franklin and his English friend, Richard Jackson. The Franklin letters had turned up recently in England. I was to transcribe the letters from photostats, and presumably I would be working on the index, but so far I had done no research, which was what I wanted to do, and I had seen none in prospect. Then, one afternoon when I was to take the finished index to the Viking offices, Carl asked me to go to the New York Public Library and check on four names. Time was short; he doubted that I would find anything; I was to have a quick look for the first names of three people and check on the identity of a fourth. In case I found anything, I was to call him from the Viking offices.

The first name on my list was "Shermy," whose book on navigation Franklin mentioned in his *Autobiography*. There was no "Shermy" in the catalogue, so I looked under "Navigation" and found a book called *The Mariner's Magazine* by a man named Sturmy. The dates were right, and the book had gone through edition after edition. I made a note of that, and went on to Mrs. Howe.

Franklin referred to her as "Mrs. Howe," and also as Lord Howe's sister. One scholar had identified her as Sir William Howe's wife, but Van Doren said that was a mistake: she was a sister to both men, and the "Mrs." must have been a courtesy title sometimes given to women of a certain age whether married or not. He suggested that I look to see whether the Howes had more than one sister. If they had not, we could identify her. I looked in Debrett's *Peerage* for 1812 and saw at a glance that the Howes had four sisters; but when I read through the list, I found that one of them, Caroline, had married her cousin, John Howe.

I went on to the other two names, found them both, discovered that one was a person of some importance and the other had been wrongly identified in our index.

I phoned Van Doren from Viking, as he requested, to report my findings. He looked up the "Shermy" reference in his facsimile copy of the *Autobiography* and reported in great excitement that "Franklin *wrote* 'Sturmy.'" The Howe identification he accepted at once, saying that he should have realized from the context that Mrs. Howe had to be either a married woman or a widow. The other two items were less important, but at least I had answers (and more) to all the questions he had given me. In a letter written next day I admitted to a "feeling of satisfaction, not to say triumph, and if anything, it increased when I heard the words of gratitude and appreciation pouring over the telephone—I think my stock has gone up, and maybe he'll give me more of that kind of work to do."

He did. From then on, although I transcribed letters, typed manuscripts, and indexed the completed books, the most important part of my work with him was research, and I loved it.

2

With no little M.'s to look after in the evenings, enough money for an occasional theater or concert ticket, and a number of good friends around me, I was making the most of New York outside job-hunting and working hours. Soon after I arrived there in the fall of 1943 May Sarton organized a series of six poetry readings at the New York Public Library. This was the first such series of readings I ever attended, and so far as I know, it was the first held in New York. Interest in modern poets and poetry had quickened during the war years, whether because of the war or not, I don't know; perhaps nobody knows, but it is at least probable. Poetry is more easily portable, in the pocket or in the mind, than the novel; and the concentrated, more intense form suited the need of the times.

The noon concerts organized by Myra Hess as a gift to the people of London during the blitz were May's inspiration for the series of poetry readings. They took place on Tuesday evenings from eight to nine-thirty through six successive weeks. The poets donated their time and energy; admission was free. Two poets read each evening, beginning with Marianne Moore and William Rose Benét, who at that time was much better known than Marianne. I went with Edna Guck and another friend:

> We went to the library, arriving just at eight, and we got the surprise of our lives. The lecture room was jammed and the crowd was packed in the doorway and streamed out into the hall, more people arriving all the time. And May had been afraid nobody would come. I didn't see any publicity, and I don't know where all the people came from. Also we didn't know how many Benét drew, but quite a few people left after Marianne's reading, and she had much the biggest crowd around her afterwards. I wedged into the doorway and people inside who had given up getting seats and didn't want to stand began to leave, so I worked farther in. Finally a persistent woman behind me started pushing, and pushed me bodily into the room. . . . Fifty to a hundred people must have stood during the whole affair.
>
> After it was over, Muriel Rukeyser, May Sarton, a soldier

named Bill (otherwise unidentified) and Edna and I went out and had beer. Except for the jam, it was a very satisfactory evening.

The next reading, by William Carlos Williams and Horace Gregory, was on a stormy night of drenching rain and wind, with a gale off the coast. We thought on account of the bad weather that no one would be there, but we arrived at a quarter to eight to be on the safe side, and by eight o'clock the room, which seated 250, was completely full. On a night like that, I felt, "you couldn't hope for more. I talked to him [Williams, of course] a moment afterwards, and he said his next maternity case was November 27, and between now and then we'd get together."

On the third Tuesday Reuel Denney and Kenneth Patchen read. I had had a strenuous session with the dentist that day, and should have stayed home, but I wanted to hear Reuel's reading. Then friends of his invited me to dinner with the Denneys before the reading, and I accepted. That was a mistake. I had thought there might be six of us, but it was a buffet dinner for, I estimated, at least twenty-five guests, none of whom I knew.

> It might have been simpler not knowing them except that most of them turned out to be people I ought to know—critics, anthologists, etc. And poets. Some I never identified, and some I had long talks with and still don't know who they are—I mean, I got the last name all right, but I probably should have connected it with a first name which still escapes me. Somebody was editor of the N.Y. Times Index, and somebody was a German refugee who left Paris with a million and a half others on the eve of its fall, and somebody was a young man who had been out to Oregon taking pictures of convicts for True Detective Magazine, and somebody was a famous native Buffalonian—I've got that wrong, a Buffalonian of a famous family. The party was for Reuel, and if anybody did that to me before I had to get up and perform, I'd never speak to them again. What's more, only a few of the faithful like me, and the youngest young men, went up to the library and heard the reading.

This time, although neither Reuel nor Kenneth Patchen could be expected to draw a very large crowd—they were both younger and not nearly as well known as the four who had preceded them—the library had prepared a microphone hook-up so that the readings could be heard in the hall outside the lecture room. We arrived in time to get the last seats in the back of the room, and about fifty late-comers listened in the hall. One of the "youngest young men" who left the party for the reading was Howard Moss. If I had known he was going to grow up to be poetry editor of the *New Yorker*, I might have taken more notice of him. I said of him only that he "seemed nice," which probably meant that he neither barked at me nor snubbed me. He and his girl friend, the Denneys, May Sarton and I "and two unidentified very young people" went out for drinks. We discussed May's plans for a second series of readings. She was "determined that I should read on it, and I am equally determined that I shall not." The argument, I remember, continued in the taxi all the way back to the Village. The others went back to the party, still in progress, and I went home. Later, when the Denneys and I had a post-mortem conversation on the evening, I learned that I was not the only unhappy guest. One couple stayed twenty minutes, then told Reuel it was more than they could face, and left before dinner. Another man decided his host had insulted him, grabbed his wife and a friend, and departed in the middle of the meal. I also discovered the identity of a woman who exasperated me because, after helping herself to the salad at the end of the table, she stood over it, talking politics and international affairs nineteen to the dozen, with a man listening attentively on either side of her. Meanwhile traffic was blocked and no one else could get at the salad, which looked delicious. It was Dorothy Norman.

The readers on the fourth Tuesday were Auden and James Agee. Of all my own close contemporaries, that is, the writers born between, say, 1907 and 1917, those who began publishing about the same time my first poems appeared, Agee was the one I was watching most expectantly. My money, if I had had any, would have been on Agee rather than Schwartz as the writer with the greatest potential. Until his death, I continued to watch for what he would do, instead of realizing that he had done and was doing it: one volume of poetry, one novel, one volume of film criticism, that great, unclassifiable book, *Let Us Now Praise Famous Men*, and *The African Queen*—what more did I want, I wonder? This reading came at a time when the volume of poetry was out of print and almost forgotten; *Let Us Now Praise Famous Men* was being remaindered at Gotham Book Mart for half price. Agee was writing film criticism anonymously for *Time*. I had heard that he was still writing poetry, but never making any attempt to publish it. He lost the manuscripts or threw them away. I thought I could understand, and he interested me all the more. I had never met him, and I was looking forward to hearing him read, but on the whole I was disappointed.

Because Auden was reading, there was the biggest crowd yet:

> I got there at 7:30, and there was a crowd in the hall waiting for the doors to open. . . . By quarter to eight the room was packed. It seats 250, and Edna, who was out in the hall where they have put more chairs and a microphone, said there were about 300 out there and there wasn't even wall-space to lean against. The crowd is mostly young people, and nobody could deny their intense interest, at any rate, when they'll stand for an hour and a half to listen and then hang around in the hall for half an hour hoping for a glimpse of the poets. I was much interested in hearing James Agee, but his reading wasn't too successful. He read in a very low voice and too rapidly, but he read directly into the microphone, and Edna said it was fine outside. Auden was good in the lecture-room, but didn't read into the microphone, so they couldn't hear outside.

The truth was that during Agee's reading I had the uncomfortable feeling that I was eavesdropping on a man who was saying his prayers. Whether I had this impression because of the intimate nature of the poems, or because of his manner of reading, I can't say. Perhaps both. In either case or both cases, the disembodied voice heard in the hall would have pleased me better.

The readers on the fifth Tuesday were Muriel Rukeyser and Langston Hughes, on the sixth, Marya Zaturenska and Padraic Colum. I seem to have no account of these readings and may have missed them.

I did not see Williams again before the next maternity case, but I did call about that time, asking permission to bring an English friend to see them. She was an attractive young woman named Peggy, a friend of a friend of a friend who suggested that I look her up because she was interested in writing and wanted to meet more Americans. Peggy was in New York with the British Information Service, working exclusively with her own countrymen and having few opportunities to meet the natives. For a time I saw her frequently and introduced her to a number of other people. Thinking that Peggy and the Williamses would be interested in each other, and no doubt looking for a good excuse to go out to Rutherford myself, I proposed the little excursion. Of course we were invited, and Peggy made a great hit with them both, as I had believed she would. I have no account of the conversation, but I am sure it turned chiefly on life in London during the blitz, and the strange adventures of an English girl in the United States. We had turkey and mushrooms in patty shells and pomegranates (I never failed to mention the food if it was good).

The result of our visit was that in February of 1945 the Williamses asked Peggy to come again to Rutherford, this time to speak to a group of their friends about life in wartime England. Of course I was to come with her. This trip gave me one of my most cherished memories of Williams, as the Gotham Book Mart party gave me an equally cherished memory of Marianne Moore. But whereas Marianne was surrounded on that occasion by a gallery of admiring males, almost all of them celebrities of one sort or another, Bill Williams was surrounded by the people he lived and worked among, and had grown up with, who thought of him only as one of themselves, a competent small-town doctor who was "interested in poetry." The group was one that met monthly, I believe, in the home of a couple who also provided a speaker. There were about twenty couples there, most of them near the Williamses' age. Besides the members, young Bill was there with his wife and two children.

The club, Mrs. W. says, has been going for twenty-nine years, and they call it the Polytopic Club—just nice people, she said, who were interested in almost anything, except playing bridge. I talked to a contractor, a schoolman, a music teacher, and goodness only knows who the rest of them were. The daughter-in-law also had dinner with us, so it was quite a party—a tremendous big and luscious ham—the best I've had in months and months. Mrs. Williams was looking better and seemed less tired. Peggy was excited, I think, and talked so much at the dinner table and was so witty that I thought she would wear herself out and not have anything left over for the speech making.

Peggy had never done public speaking of any sort and loathed the idea, but felt that it was part of her job. She refused payment, saying that it was one of the things she was here to do.

Peggy started out on a rather serious level and didn't do so well at first. I think it was the English reticence when it comes to deep emotional feeling. . . . She talked about Dunkerque, D-Day and the robot bombs during that time, then went into the lighter and more personal side, and soon had everybody shouting with laughter and calling out questions and comments. She does have a way of expressing herself. And she looked very lovely in a rich red dress which was a recent splurge and everybody loved her, and told me how charming she was, etc. So I basked in reflected glory.

Once into her stride, Peggy seemed unable to stop, but the doctor finally called a halt and refreshments were served.

Individually, one at a time, they kept Peggy talking all through the refreshments. Nobody seemed at all inclined to go home, but finally they did, though by the time they had taken leave of all their friends one by one, and of Peggy and me, and of the Williamses, it was a long process. At a quarter of one, some were still there, but I inquired about bus schedules, and Peggy and I made a dive for it—the doctor drove us to the bus stop and we caught the one o'clock bus.

In March I had a letter from Williams in answer to a query of mine about poisons (I was still writing mysteries). Then, at Christmas time, I sent a note in which I accused the doctor of falling for a British accent. I knew that he had written twice to Peggy and not at all to me. In reply I received the following letter, dated December 28, 1945.

Dear Mary:
All right. So you're jealous. I'm glad. Beacause (skip the extra a) if you hadn't felt that way you wouldn't have confessed your love and I should have been the poorer.

Where the heck is Peggy anyhow? We had a Christmas card from her in Washington (I shd have said "from" not "in") Thank you for your card and the note as well as the unique and beautiful holly. Yes, it must be the British accent that caused me to write twice to her or perhaps just surprise and delight that a Britisher could be so much fun. I am so in the habit of despising the god-damned British attitude to American letters that I forget that they are a species worth paying attention to. But she is (being of a despised sex) as I have said, delightful.

Does that necessarily exclude . ?

My Paterson thing is in the page proof stage at the moment. Shd be out soon—I hope—if they can ever find Laughlin to OK the procedures.

Let's hope the ensuing months will disclose some means for my reducing my practice of medicine so that I may find my friends again. Happy New Year.

Bill

In saying that I had confessed my love, Bill was giving way to a flight of the imagination, or, more probably, simply teasing me. I was in love with someone else as he knew very well, but not because I told him; despite all his hints and leading questions, I held fast to the vow I made that first evening I met him: never, never to confide in him. I could not stop him from drawing his own conclusions, and even gossiping, but I did not intend to furnish straw for his bricks.

3

At the other end of the spectrum from the small-town doctor and the Polytopic Club there was Edward James. Perhaps he does not really belong in my narrative. He has never figured as a griffon in the forests of Helicon, rather as an elf with a pointed smile, sitting on a bag of gold. He is glimpsed here and there in the company of poets, but is never represented in any anthology or mentioned in any critical survey of twentieth-century poetry. However, Philip Purser, in his brief biography of Edward James, says: "He crops up in all sorts of memoirs, from Edith Sitwell's to Tom Driburg's," and if in theirs, why not in mine?

I first heard of him in the spring of 1945 when I came home one evening to find a telegram from Iris Barry stuck under my door. It informed me that a friend of hers, Edward James, was in desperate need of a secretary. She indicated that the work would be temporary—perhaps only a week—and asked me to call him at the Waldorf if I would be free to help out. As it happened, I was in that lull between the completion of the Franklin manuscript and the beginning of work on the index; Van Doren had gone to the country, and I was at loose ends. Accordingly, I called James and went out to the Waldorf for an interview.

James was a young Englishman of American ancestry on his father's side, slight in build and very restless. I told him I had no shorthand, but he waved that aside, saying that the best secretary he ever had did not use shorthand. He would prefer that I take dictation on the typewriter. With that, I sat down at the desk and he began to dictate. I found out within a few minutes why he was having difficulty with the Waldorf's public stenographer. She probably floundered over a name like Pavel Tchelitchev, and asked for the spelling. When I had spelled Tchelitchev and Klee correctly with no questions asked (he was pacing back and forth behind me and glancing over my shoulder), I knew I had the job.

The first thing he dictated was an autobiographical piece that told me quite a lot about his background; Iris told me more later, and recently Philip Purser's biography filled in the gaps. Briefly, his father's people were wealthy Americans who had settled in England; his mother was English, possibly the illegitimate daughter of Edward VII, who stood godfather to Edward James. He was at one time married to Tilly Losch. He collected paintings, especially surrealist paintings, commissioned theatrical and musical works (a ballet by Brecht and Weill, for instance, for Tilly), wrote poetry (sometimes bad and sometimes not bad at all), published his own poetry as well as John Betjeman's first book, painted with an airbrush (dreadful), and owned, at the time I knew him, an estate in England, a villa in Italy (at Ravello), a house in Hollywood and a house in Laguna Beach. He was living temporarily in a suite of two rooms at the

Waldorf, both full of paintings, and had at the same time a room or two at the Barbizon Plaza, also full of paintings.

In my first letter home after starting work, I described my new job as "the weirdest job of my entire career, I think—though remembering Anita Browne, maybe not." I began work on a Wednesday.

I expected to be fired on Thursday, but we got along fine, and I'm still going—maybe for a week, maybe longer. The dictation and typing are not the weird part of the job. The weird part is Mr. James himself and the kind of personal secretary and *alter ego* I'm expected to be. . . . He is thirty-eight [he looked younger] and little and fidgety, but also agreeable and not at all high-handed or overbearing—not so far, anyway. I thought I wouldn't last two days as secretary because I never learned how to be self-effacing as rich people expect their secretaries to be. But I didn't care too much, so I acted like myself, including giving him advice or cracking wise as I felt like it, for two days, and he seems to take it and like it, and I'm still on the job. Apparently I'm not supposed to type only, but to manage him, and it certainly needs doing. A more erratic guy I never came across. Thursday we spent running around town—first to Saks where I won his admiration by being able to read his saleschecks. Also by pointing out that I could deliver his check to the office while he bought his gloves and save him the trouble of mailing it—I think he was about to send me to buy an envelope.

Then we walked to the Plaza Hotel, parted and met again at the Museum of Modern Art, parted and met again at the Barbizon Plaza, etc. . . .

Life went on in this fashion for a little over two weeks. On May 6th, I wrote:

My typewriter is at the Barbizon Plaza. I'm not sure why, but there it is, and I have to write with a pen. I'm still working for Edward James, who continues as scatter-brained as ever. I take dictation, pay bills, type, run errands, and sit in the Waldorf or the Barbizon lobby. He has taken another room, adjoining the first, at the Waldorf, and I work in it, which is simpler all around and much better. I've worked fairly long hours—longer than at first, usually not starting until eleven, but working until six or seven some days. I've got him a passage on a stratoliner leaving for California the last of next week, and about time to save my sanity, but I couldn't bear to quit, out of curiosity as to what he will do next. Thursday he lunched with the Marquise de Mont-ferrier and brought her back to the Barbizon Plaza with him, where I was sitting in the lobby, and we, the Marquise and I, helped him move paintings out of the room he has had there, over to the Waldorf. It's all I can do to keep from bursting into laughter sometimes—I'm pretty sure he knows I think he's crazy, but he seems to think so, too.

When we had got ourselves and the paintings into the cab and were on our way back to the Waldorf, he suddenly re-marked: "I don't know how I ever came to have that room at the Barbizon Plaza, anyway." And then, cheerfully: "Mad as a hat-ter! Mad as a hatter!" The bills were paid with Waldorf counter checks, no stubs, no receipts. Small wonder I thought he was mad. I remember the dubious reception I got at the airline offices when I tried to pay for his ticket with one of those counter checks. "But what does he *do*?" they asked me. I forget how I eventually persuaded them to take it; perhaps they called the Waldorf and were assured that he was solvent. Small won-der, too, that he sometimes suspected secretaries or other people with whom he dealt, of cheating him. They probably were.

On Sunday, May 13th, I was able to report an end to the Jacobean interlude. Perhaps I should explain that Iris was now divorced from John Abbott and living alone on East Fiftieth.

The principal news is that E. J. got off for California Friday
night, or rather early Saturday morning, the plane having been
delayed three hours by the grace of God, or he never would have
made it. He called me at quarter to eleven in a great frenzy and
said he was going to have to leave this, that and the other—some
I already knew about; so I spent yesterday afternoon clearing the
debris out of the Waldorf, some of it in the parcel check, and
some in his room. . . . The room looked rather as though an
explosion had taken place, and E. J. is rather like an explosion
especially when he is getting off for somewhere. There was a
suitcase, packed, thank goodness, two pairs of shoes that
wouldn't go in, three pictures still on the walls, and an airbrush
motor in a carton. All that had to go to Iris Barry's. I delivered
four small pictures by cab to a framer's, two large pictures by

cab to Nierendorf gallery, got a bell hop for the stuff in the room, and another cab, and departed for I. B.'s. . . . She gave me a drink of iced rum and coca cola which I was desperately needing by that time, and we had a heart-to-heart on Edward James. She said she felt some compunction about recommending me, because she could guess what I would be getting into, but after all it was for only a little while at the most, and she thought I might be glad to have it. I was glad to have it, and we both agreed that we liked him in spite of finding him very, very difficult in spots. Maybe it was good for me to work for a boss I find difficult, for a change. Sometimes he got irritable and at first I took it personally and was slightly, but not very, unhappy about it. Then I realized that there was nothing personal in it— he simply got all tied up inside himself and started slashing out in all directions. It never lasted long, and when I realized the nature of the irritation, I understood better how to handle him, and we got along pretty well. Not that he was ever really un- pleasant, or that his manners failed him, but he was, as Iris put it—"waspish." She knew him in London, first, and she said, to my relief, that she had never known anybody like him. I had been wondering how many of him there might be in the world.

Anyway, we got him off all in one piece except for his sus- penders which he unaccountably left behind him in one of Iris's chairs. She had found them behind a cushion, and said that if she hadn't found them, and the guests she had invited to tea Sunday *had* found them, she would never have lived it down; also she was wondering however he was keeping his pants up, English trousers being absolutely dependent on suspenders.

We parted on good terms, but possibly just in time.

In a letter he left for me with the floor clerk, he said, "Thank you so very much for everything. I am in a frantic hurry or else I would write more fully my appreciation of your kindness and patience with me during the last two weeks. It has been a great priviledge to have known you"—I told you, didn't I, that he can't spell? In either French or English.

The Monday before Edward James left was V–E day. He said that when he woke and looked out the window, he saw bursts of paper scraps from windows high in the skyscrapers. He knew that must mean that peace had been signed, so he dressed and went out for a look around. What he saw was the same thing I saw as I approached the Waldorf that morning, and later when I went out at noon: there was no sign of jubilation, only streams of people, grave-faced, converging on St. Patrick's Cathedral. James was so impressed by the sight that he went into St. Patrick's himself and while there wrote a little poem that he asked me to copy for him. It was one of his not-bad-at-all poems. I wish I had asked him for a copy of it.

I had two or three letters from Edward James after he returned to California, then heard no more from him or of him. In the years that followed I often wondered where he was and what he was doing. Finally, about fifteen years after I had last heard from him, I came across the stanzas from John Betjeman's *Summoned by Bells* that tell of his friendship with James at Oxford, and I found that Betjeman was asking the same questions:

> The sun that shines on Edward James
>   Shines also down on me:
> It's strange that two such simple names
>   Should spell such mystery.
> The air he breathes, I breathe it too—
> But where's he now? What does he do?

After a few stanzas about their Oxford days, I found:

> They tell me he's in Mexico,
>   They will not give me his address. . . .

I decided that if John Betjeman did not know and could not find out where James was and what he was doing, I would probably never know. I was sure of only one thing: he was not lying on the beach at Acapulco. He was up to something, and it would be a waste of time to try to imagine what that was.

Then, another eighteen years later, Philip Purser's *Where Is He Now?*, subtitled *The Extraordinary Worlds of Edward James*, appeared, and I found out what he is doing, or at least was doing in 1978. He has retired from the world, driven partly by the conviction that people who seem to care for him live only to rob him. Gray-bearded, portly, wearing a poncho, he is designing and building, tower by tower as the fancy takes him, a fantastic, uninhabitable palace in the jungles near Tampico. Unfortunately, the tourists and hotel-keepers have discovered him, and may drive him into some further, deeper retreat.

Before my work for James came to an end, I had decided that he needed a secretary chiefly in order to ensure that he would not find himself alone. Purser also pictures him as a man so desperately in need of society that, recognizing his obsession, he first made sporadic attempts to put himself out of reach of his friends, and, finally, withdrew into the jungle. Purser described, too, the "ever more frequent, ever more tortuous, ever more speculative process of finding a secretary—no, not just a secretary; the *right* secretary." And later: "The secretaries were a saga in themselves. Should he find some promising young writer and give him this opportunity of earning a living, and perhaps even learning a thing or two, while having plenty of time for his own work?" He tried one and then another and another. "Alternating with them were business-like women, including—improbably—Lauren Bacall's mother." And also, even more improbably, me.

4

From the time I returned to New York in the fall of 1943, through all of 1944 and 1945, I was writing. By January of 1946 my unpublished work included four mysteries (two written after I left Buffalo), three short stories, and fifteen poems. I had not had a poem accepted for over two years.

In the fall of 1944 I sent the third mystery to Harcourt Brace. The response this time was a letter from Frank Morley suggesting that I come out to the office for an interview, so that we could talk things over. We talked for an hour. He was pleased that instead of re-working the first story when he rejected it, I immediately wrote another, and then another. He was pleased that I was in New York; it was so much easier to discuss changes than to write about them. He was also pleased that I was doing research and expected to go on working instead of living off mystery-writing. He went into details of publishing, pointing out how desirable it would be for me to publish with Harcourt Brace. He wanted to re-read the earlier mysteries if I would bring the manuscripts in again, so that he could make notes on possible revisions. Then he and I and Miss Cudahy, who had also read the stories, would have lunch together and we could both beat him over the head if we didn't like his suggestions. In any case, he felt it was now time to stop and revise. This all seemed to me most promising. An ominous note was struck only at the end of the interview:

> He talked a good deal of hoping we could "collaborate"; I hope he means as author and publisher, not as co-authors, because he went into the routine that all mystery writers say all acquaintances go into as soon as introduced—about having some ideas for detective stories, and always thinking if he had the time and ability, he would like to do one himself, etc. He seemed to want to make me a present of two or three ideas on the spot, which may be flattering, but is also alarming. I was astonished and amused at his doing it word for word, the way it has been recounted so many times, but it made me feel as though I had "arrived" and was now one of the brotherhood.

All these marks of interest, with a great deal more about how much fun the stories were to read, and the like, filled me with such excitement that I could hardly sleep. On the other hand, I knew that publishers were not to be trusted. They might be most encouraging and not mean a word of it. But *why*, in my case, should he encourage me if he didn't mean it? I decided to ask Helen Gentry to lunch and see what she thought. She and David both had lunch with me, and both dashed cold water over me. However, although they thought all the encouragement was probably just publisher's palaver, they were emphatic about the prestige Harcourt Brace enjoyed. I had had it impressed upon me years ago that the best way to get a volume of poetry published was to get a foot in the door first with a novel. Harcourt Brace would be a good publisher for my poetry or the serious prose I was now writing, but if I let the mysteries go to Dodd, Mead or Morrow, for instance, my goose would be cooked as far as poetry was concerned. I continued, for another twelve months, to dangle on Frank Morley's hook.

During the interview I had told Morley that I was toying with an idea for a fourth mystery. Now, while I was waiting to hear what changes he would propose in the three he was supposed to be re-reading, I went ahead and wrote the fourth one. Probably because I find it easier to live with even a shred of hope than with a definite rejection, I postpone putting a publisher on the spot, and demanding a yes or no answer. In June, however, with a rough draft of the fourth mystery completed and no word from Morley, I called him, and he asked me to come to see him the next day. I went, prepared to collect my manuscripts and take them elsewhere. This time the cat jumped out of the bag at last. He seemed to have an idea that I might collaborate with his niece, Blythe Morley, Christopher's daughter. To cap it, he said that he thought she had the ability to do serious writing, and should not be wasting her time on detective stories, but she had some very good ideas (she had published at least one mystery), and, in short, she could supply the ideas and I could write them up. I controlled my tongue, but I think my face gave me away. I wrote:

> My impulse was to walk out with the stories, but I thought maybe my temper was getting the best of me and I was being unreasonable, so I left them. I still wish I hadn't. Of course I can refuse collaboration if offered, but with things as they are, I haven't the impetus to do the necessary revision on this fourth story. It's the same old tale, as the Greenhoods warned me, of the publisher not being able to make up his mind to accept, but being totally unwilling to let go of the author he won't publish. I am disgusted.

Later, I told Carl Van Doren about Morley's proposal.

> He exhorted me to be FIRM and NOT to give in to any idea of collaboration, and pointed out that if I collaborated with my publisher's niece and Christopher Morley's daughter, I would be in an absolutely helpless position.

He also offered to do anything he could for me if Frank Morley turned me down.

I cannot understand now how Morley persuaded me to leave the three manuscripts there for his niece to read and report on, and, after I had read the report, to take the fourth story to him when I had finished typing it. This was an especially stupid thing to do, because by that time I had received two letters from Diarmuid Russell, the literary agent, asking me to let him see my work. Peggy, my English friend, returned home after V-E day, but during the spring she had placed a story with the *New*

Yorker, and had become one of Diarmuid Russell's clients. She mentioned me to him before she left, and he wrote to me immediately, saying that he was especially interested in detective stories. I put him off, hoping to hear from Morley, yes or no, before I had any dealings with an agent. Talk I had heard at Yaddo about agents was discouraging. They were always wanting changes made. If the author made the changes and the manuscript did not sell, the author blamed the agent, saying that it would have sold in its original form. If the author refused to make the changes, and it did not sell, he still blamed the agent, saying the agent did not *try* to sell the manuscript, in case he should be proved wrong. I was to learn that Diarmuid was a different breed of agent. He offered no criticism, suggested no changes. If he liked it he tried to sell it; if not, he sent it back.

However, like a dunce, I put Russell off, took the fourth mystery to Harcourt Brace in late September, and waited. In mid-January of 1946, still waiting, I received a third note from Diarmuid. He had had a letter from Peggy, asking whether I had ever been in to see him. That same week I learned from Charles Abbott, who was in town on business, that Frank Morley had been in Europe for the last three and a half months and was now on his way home—by freighter. That did it. Someone, I thought, could have told me. I wrote to Diarmuid explaining everything, and he took over.

Peggy had told me something about Diarmuid when she asked if I would like her to mention me as a possible client. About all I got out of her description was that he was the son of the Irish poet, George William Russell (who signed himself Æ), and that he was in some way rather odd, perhaps a bit pixilated, because she kept saying, "Of course, he's *Irish*," as though that explained everything. The result of this conversation was that I went to his office expecting to find a leprechaun, or at least a James Stephens type, small, dark, whimsical, and rather other-worldish. Instead I found a tall, fair, business-like man, younger than I expected, and apparently as preoccupied with money as any American I could imagine. I never did, in all the years of our association, make out what Peggy could have been talking about. I had to assume that the Irish appear stranger to the English than they do to Americans. Throughout our first interview, I had the feeling that I must be talking to the wrong man.

At the time, the carbon copies of the first three mysteries were in Buffalo, but I had brought with me the carbon copy of the fourth, as well as the shorter prose pieces, and some poetry. "He seemed quite uninterested in anything but the detective stories, not that I said much about the other things, but I pointed out that I had brought them along. From the questions he asked and the calculating look in his eye, I could almost hear a cash register chiming in the background." His attitude dismayed me. I could not imagine that he would want to take me on, and, if he did, wouldn't I wind up with Dodd, Mead? I went home in low spirits, blown on a bitter January wind.

Diarmuid Russell was not a man to let grass grow under his feet. He telephoned next morning:

> He had read the detective story and liked it and wanted to act for me. He wanted to know whether the others were as good, and couldn't I get the carbons for him so that he could read them before Morley came to the point, whatever point he was going to come to, the idea being that if the others were as good, it would be a shame to let Morley accept the last one and reject the first three, because he would have an option on my next book, and, having seen the first three, they wouldn't count, and I would be held up on publication of them indefinitely. Besides, the carbons would have to be on hand to send around to the magazines for possible serial publication while the first copies went to the publishers. That is, if he liked them, and if I wanted him to act for me.

He had not yet read the shorter fiction. I promised to send for the carbon copies, but told him that I was reluctant to let him handle the mysteries if he would not handle the other things as well. He seemed dubious, but said he would let me know tomorrow.

The next morning he called again to say that he liked everything, but thought we should have lunch sometime and talk matters over. I agreed. Today? I agreed. We had lunch at a French restaurant somewhere east of Lexington Avenue.

We talked business and got acquainted, and whether it was the American cocktail, the French food, or the Irish charm, I succumbed completely, although he said he just could not handle poetry. He said he had tried and invariably lost money on it, because it took as much secretarial work as a novel manuscript, and he might send the poem out ten times and finally sell it for five dollars. . . . He said it wasn't because he didn't like it, but he just couldn't do it. About the other prose, he was doubtful whether it was saleable, but said it was so good, he would want to send it around and have a try at selling it, anyway. . . . If he had refused to do anything about it, I doubt whether even the drink, the lunch, and the Irish charm would have availed. This time I liked him very much, even if he did give me the impression every now and then that he was giving me a little shake to hear the gold chinking—even that can be a pleasant sensation once you get used to the idea—and not too used to it. It certainly is a new feeling to me.

My account of our first interviews now strikes me as very strange indeed, because Diarmuid labored for years in my behalf and can hardly have got enough in commissions to cover his postage. It is true that he sometimes said rather plaintively that he wished I would get interested sometime in writing something that had money in it, but he constantly tried to place work that, even if he succeeded in selling it, could make very little money for either of us.

At the same time, he had no illusions about the publishing world. He was continually having to explain the facts of life to me. A talk with him, on the telephone or in his office, usually left me feeling at once buoyed up by his appreciation of my work, and depressed by his pessimistic view of the literary scene, highbrow or lowbrow.

5

Now, to get back to Ezra.

For six years, from the time of my move to Buffalo, which coincided with the beginning of the war in Europe, until the winter of 1945–46, I had no correspondence with Pound, and, in fact, all I knew of him was what I read in the papers.

Then, in December of 1945, after he had been committed to St. Elizabeth's Hospital, I received a letter about him from Viola Baxter Jordan.

All his life Pound kept up a correspondence with two women whom he had known before he went to Europe to live. One was "Mary Moore of Trenton," to whom he dedicated *Personae*, and the other was Viola Baxter Jordan. When he was in the United States in 1939, he mentioned me to both of them. "Mary Moore" tried to reach me, I learned only recently, but I had already left the city. Viola was the woman in Tenafly with whom I was supposed to get in touch when I came back to New York in the fall of 1939. Because I went to Buffalo instead of returning to New York, I did not meet her until 1942, although we had exchanged a few letters in the meantime. Unfortunately I paid my first visit to Tenafly about two days before I went to Rutherford to clean up the Williams attic. The letter I wrote home after I returned to Buffalo is entirely taken up with the Rutherford visit; of Tenafly I said only that it was a long story; I waited to tell it until I went home later that month. My next visit was similarly passed over because I was more interested in writing about my interview with Frank Morley. I remember Viola vividly, but my first impressions are overlaid by subsequent memories.

She had been a great beauty in her youth, and, although the beauty was gone, she clung to the hair style she must have adopted in the Twenties, with her long, still dark hair braided and wound into buns over her ears, bangs, and a black velvet ribbon across the top of her head. She was opinionated, and completely outspoken, haphazard in her housekeeping, casual in her relations with her three children. She was always ready to tell them off, but not as though it really mattered to her what they did. At the time of my first visit the two girls were still in their teens; her son was with the Air Force in the South Pacific. Her marriage had ended in divorce when the children were still small.

Pound not only corresponded with Viola from the time of their first acquaintance, when he was at Hamilton College, but he sent her all his books, beginning with *A Lume Spento*. They were mouldering in the attic, nibbled by mice. She once read me a long passage from *Marpessa* by Stephen Phillips to show me the kind of poetry *she* liked. She also knew Williams and H. D., but naturally did not read their poetry. The diary she kept in this period before her marriage, written in German, is now being translated by her daughter, Barbara. If she was in her youth the same sort of woman I knew, the diary should be a gem.

Viola numbered among her overseas correspondents H. D., Bryher, Dorothy Pound, Olga Rudge, and Mary Rudge, the daughter of Olga and Ezra Pound. During the war and postwar years she sent Care packages to them, and later she was always posting off little gifts to Ezra at St. Elizabeth's, perhaps jars of jam that broke in transit, or candy that melted on the way. He never hesitated to let her know when her gifts were a nuisance, but she cared nothing for that. She would light-heartedly post another package destined to meet with the same fate. Her means were, I think, barely adequate, but she was unrestrainedly generous, as she was unrestrained about most things. I was half terrified of her ("Ezra tells me you are very shy," she wrote in her first letter to me), but she amused and interested me so much that I went out to Tenafly many times. And then she fed me so well!

Shortly before Christmas of 1945 I had a note from Viola saying that she had had two letters from Ezra. I summed up what she told me:

> The only thing he seemed to want was for food to be sent to his family. Apparently both his parents, or at least his mother, are in Italy still, as well as his wife and daughter, and the food situation is pretty desperate. Viola said she was going to make up a package as soon as her financial condition permitted, and I thought I would send her a contribution—financial—to help her make it up. She quoted him as saying a number of people had written to him, and she said she thought he would like hearing from me. I think I'll write, though it will be a harder letter to compose than the first one I wrote him. She says H. D. is coming over in February to lecture at Bryn Mawr.

I did write, but had no reply until March of 1946. In a letter written on the 29th, I said:

About the only interesting news, and that isn't what you would call very jolly news, is that I had a letter from Ezra. It showed, as Viola put it about her letters from him "the old restless Ez looking for intellectual excitement"—the only personal note was in the first line: "Did I thank you? I forget." And it went on from there in a penciled scrawl to inquire in several different forms whether *no*body was doing *any*thing—not about him, about poetry. I had to confess, no, so far as I knew, not. The fact is, I think we are in a pretty low state, and I think we miss ole Ezra-Diogenes looking for a self-respecting poet. I didn't tell him that, but I told him quite a bit, and sent him a copy of the poetry issue of the *Saturday Review*, which I thought was really AWFUL. I thought it likely that both my letter and the magazine would throw him into a perfect passion, but then I couldn't think of anything that would be a more normal state, or one likely to do him more good, so I let fly with both. We shall see. The only signs in the letter of breakdown in mind or spirit were that all the words were correctly spelled and he signed his name legibly "Ezra," just like that. Maybe the censors were responsible for that—for both—since if he wrote in his usual style, they would probably think it was some kind of black-shirt code. The letter was obviously censored. And I was rather touched by the fact that under the scrawled "St. Elizabeth's Hospital," at the top, he had carefully printed "Elizabeth's" again, which was an indication he was anxious for a reply and was afraid I might not be able to read the address. I also offered to send him some of the quarterlies if he wanted them, and I enclosed some recent poems of my own, and told him what I knew of our mutual acquaintance—that part answering questions Viola relayed to me. . . . The letter came Tuesday, and I couldn't get it off my mind until I got it answered on Wednesday, and it still rather haunts me. The whole thing seems to be just resting, and whether it's a friendly gesture on the part of somebody, who thinks he is better off locked up on an insanity charge than on trial, or whether they still lack enough evidence to start a trial (which has been indicated by a couple of news reports) and are therefore keeping him shut up on an insanity verdict, I wouldn't be able to guess. Or maybe they really do believe he is insane. Maybe he is. I shall be interested to see what reaction my letter provokes, anyhow, and if my writing to him keeps him slightly amused, I'll go ahead and write.

By April 5 I had had two more letters from Pound and one from Viola:

I'm going to have to stop going down for my mail before breakfast—every time I pull one of Ezra's letters out of the box my stomach turns over and I think I can't eat a bite—which is very bad before breakfast. I forget whether I had the second letter before I wrote last. I think perhaps I hadn't? Anyway, it was just another scrawled invective against the literary situation— nothing to do with either him or me, though it was in a way an answer to what I had told him. I didn't answer it, though I thought I would write again when I could think of anything to say. Meantime I had another letter from Viola which threw new light on his condition—she hadn't given me any hint of this before, and I had gathered from what she had said and what the papers had said, that he was being pretty nonchalant about the charges against him. But she said in this letter that he was apparently really in a serious condition, and quoted one of his letters as saying, "Exhaustion, m'deah, it's a day's work to write this." And she said that he was apparently famished for news from outside, but couldn't get his mind off his situation and who could blame him? That sounded more normal—I had thought that if he was taking it as casually as he seemed to, that he *must* be crazy.

This morning I got another letter with the copies of the poems I sent him returned all marked up, with marginal comment—the first time in all our correspondence that he has done that. I sent him four—one he didn't touch, and the others he slashed into, but with such point, that it did me a world of good. I haven't had any criticism at all for a long time, the truth being that I feel sure enough of myself now that there are few people I would take it from, or ask it from; and of the poets I respect, he's the only one, I think, whose direction is close enough to my own to criticize my poem and leave it still my poem. Anyhow, while I probably won't revise them as drastically as his slashes indicate, I intend to study them very carefully. And pull myself into line in the future, I hope. And the letter was sweet. It was, really. He suggests I send a group of poems to H. D., who has had an attack of meningitis and is going to Switzerland to recuperate, advises me how to approach her, and says to "ask her opinion (whether you want it or not) & ask if wd be any use trying 'Life & Letters'" (English magazine), gives me addresses for both H. D. and the magazine, indicates what poems to send, or what kind, and says: "She shd appreciate the neat work," which is about as close to a compliment as I ever got out of him. That was not correctly expressed. It is a compliment—as enthusiastic an opinion as I ever got out of him, I suppose. One thing that makes taking his advice a little awkward is that Viola sent her a copy of the "Five," and never got a syllable out of her about it. However, if I approached her in the manner he suggests, I might produce results. Viola isn't long on tact.

I have to write to her today, too. She is in a great to-do. She received a letter from Dorothy Pound thanking us for the food, a very nice note, and saying that she planned to come over as soon as she could get transportation, but didn't know what to do about Ezra's mother, who is eighty-six, and has no relatives, and no place to go when she got here, though she is terribly anxious to come over to be near him. Viola, bless her heart, went into a tailspin over the whole affair and wrote me a frantic letter saying she wanted to invite Ezra's mother to stay in her house—that is, she wanted to and she didn't want to, etc. etc., and what did I think and what should she do? Naturally, I am not going to tell her what to do, but I do want to answer the letter, and I may advise caution. I think it's a very generous gesture, especially for the jilted girl-friend of thirty or forty years ago, but she is like that. But it is certainly a gesture that should be considered carefully.

This was the beginning of our post-war correspondence, which continued until about the time of Pound's release from St. Elizabeth's. For at least ten years the penciled scrawls turned up in my mailbox regularly. People also turned up. Pound believed strongly in the value of cross-fertilization, exchange of ideas, the stimulation to be had from talk with another writer even if it was quarrelsome. Digging one's own little burrow and crawling in with a book or one's own manuscript was not enough. The English, he said, at least had sense enough to eat once a week or once a month with people they didn't particularly like in order that life and letters might persist. When people went to see him or wrote to him in Washington, he would suggest that they get in touch with so-and-so. I have no idea how many people I met because he suggested they look me up, but they were a varied lot, from young hopefuls just out of high school to college professors. Some were an embarrassment, some I got rid of as soon as possible—or they got rid of me—and one, at least, did me an inestimable service. Occasionally I think I was able to be of use to someone.

The first person I met in this way was Charles Olson. On April 24, 1946, I wrote:

> The phone call Ezra wanted me to make was to a man at the Commodore Hotel. I had seen a piece of his in a magazine, and the magazine said he lived in Washington, and E. P. said in his letter, "I shd like you to meet him," so I thought maybe the phone call was partly a piece of strategy . . .

Apparently this was the case. The message I was to give him made no sense to me, and seemed to baffle Olson. I decided that it was simply a device to get me to call him, because Pound was afraid that he would not get around to calling me, and he wanted us to meet. So far as I know, neither of us benefited in the least from this meeting except that several years later I put the Olsons up overnight when they were roughing it on the West Coast, and I think they were glad of a bed. However, my account of the meeting may be worth quoting because there seems to be some controversy over Olson's relationship with and attitude towards Pound at this time. The letter I quote was written three days after the meeting. Once I was on the phone, Olson seemed to recollect that Pound had said he should look me up, and we settled on my apartment as a meeting place on Sunday afternoon. If I had known his dimensions, I would never have invited him to my tiny apartment. However, he appeared to enjoy the afternoon enough to stay two hours, and told me all about Ezra:

> Olson has been visiting him as regularly as the authorities will allow—never knew him before, but sent a piece about him to Laughlin, who sent it back, but said, "If you're interested in him, why don't you go to see him?" I was a little dubious before they came, wondering if Mr. O. would turn out to be pro-fascist, in which case things might be awkward, but it turned out quite the contrary. He said, "I just can't get excited about his politics—" meaning he couldn't condemn E. P. for them—"to

me, he's simply the first gentleman of our time." Then we told each other with much enthusiasm all he'd done for us—he has written to Eliot about something of Olson's, and to some other people in England. I'll try to cut this short and tell you all of it when I get home, but Olson says the new poems which Ezra got back recently from Laughlin in typescript are tops [this would have been the *Pisan Cantos*] and that the return of the typescript copy was what really brought him round—he took a decided turn for the better. That was just about the time I got my first letter. He's terribly lonesome, of course. Two of his most regular visitors were the Misses Maple aged about eighty, friends of his parents, who bring their sewing and mend his clothes. The doctor who has been in charge of him was a very nice young man—couldn't have been a better person for the job, says Olson, but he is leaving and the older doctor who was his subordinate is, Olson thinks, just waiting for a chance to crack down—particularly on Olson's visits . . .

After that came the breach between them; but while Pound made it clear that he had turned against Olson, he gave me no inkling of the reason.

6

The shorter fiction I took to Diarmuid Russell in early 1946 was of two kinds. One piece was a black cat story, a conventional tale with overtones of the supernatural. It was a low-brow story I thought he should have no difficulty in selling. The others were not stories at all in the conventional sense; each was rather an exploration of a single theme through the experience of a fictional character. The first dealt with names, the second with possessions. They were too short for book publication, too long for the literary reviews, but I planned to do at least five in the hope that they would make a book-length manuscript altogether. I called them "Boundaries." Although Diarmuid was willing to handle all these pieces, he was discouraging about their prospects. To my surprise he said that most magazines would not touch stories dealing with the supernatural. The two "Boundaries" were an awkward length, as I knew, but

I was prepared to do some cutting if necessary. He was much more optimistic about the mysteries. However, I wrote,

> he obviously yearns for me to do a straight novel. Well, maybe I will—I dunno. But I told him that the more I thought about it, the more it seemed to me that the detective story was the only artistic form of the novel. He laughed very hard, and said I wouldn't get him to disagree with me on that, and of course you could only write what you wanted to write, but what he meant to say was that there was no reason why I shouldn't write a straight novel any time I felt like it—the principal interest in my mysteries being the setting, characters, humor, etc., and the mystery being a mere side-issue. I agree with that, and it's possible that the reason I don't want to write a novel is that I'm afraid of some hard work, but most novels are so bad—just frightfully bad, in my opinion, mainly because they are so sloppy, and I'm determined that whenever I do one, it won't be a sloppy job. I think probably writing a detective story is as good practice as anybody could have for discipline in novel writing, and maybe by now I could do a good one. One of the biggest troubles is my conscience—the themes that would interest me would be drawn from life, and I can't do them because they would hurt somebody—I think I have discussed this in my letters before.

I had also discussed the problem with Bill Williams. I said, "It isn't fiction that interests me—it's what really happened." He said he agreed. What really happened was the interesting thing, and that was why he was in hot water all the time, because he drew his material from life. But I not only had no desire to be in hot water, I could not face the idea that I might hurt someone. I have had the experience of reading fiction obviously based on the personalities and experiences of certain of my friends, and I hate it. People say that you can "change things," but I have never found this to be possible. By the time I have changed the character and the situation, the thing that was to be the crux of the story is lost.

A week after this conversation about novel writing, Diarmuid called again to say that Frank Morley had turned down the mysteries and was sending the manuscripts back. This occasioned an outburst:

He told Russell that they were better for atmosphere and characterization than as mysteries—a little weak on that end. . . . I was doubly disgusted to think back to my conversations with Morley, when he said, "Don't bother too much about the detective plot, the atmosphere and characterizations are the important things"; and I said, "Yes, but it bothers me when the plot creaks too much"; and he said, "Yes, of course that's true. That's what's the matter with Blythe's. She knows her plots creak a bit, and that is what has put her off doing any more for a while." That was my first conversation with him, and in the second one he suggested I should collaborate with Blythe so she could remedy my defects. Which certainly goes to prove that he is either crazy or a liar. Maybe he was trying to keep me dangling till I would produce a straight novel, but he didn't even hint that he thought I could write one—only that I could write Blythe's ideas while *she* wrote a highbrow novel. I am incensed.

During the spring of 1946 while Diarmuid was sending my manuscripts around, I wrote the third and last "Boundary" and began the fifth and last mystery. In May *Harper's Bazaar* accepted the second "Boundary." During the summer I finished the last mystery at Ocean Park, and took it to Diarmuid when I returned to New York in September. Although he had felt that the biggest difficulty with the others was the short length, and this last one was book length, he was not hopeful. Apparently it was too somber. Again he started talking about a straight novel. Shortly afterwards, to his own surprise, he sold the black cat story to *Today's Woman*. With three hundred dollars from *Harper's Bazaar* and six hundred from *Today's Woman*, I felt that I was launched. I might even be about to make some of those chinking noises that Diarmuid had been listening for.

Meantime, although there would be little money in it, I was much gratified that John Crowe Ransom had written to Diarmuid offering to publish the first "Boundary" in *Kenyon Review* if I would be willing to cut it. Diarmuid forwarded the letter to me (I was on vacation, up at the head of Lake Chelan), and I wrote Ransom that I would cut it myself, either by taking out certain sections, or by shortening each section, whichever he preferred, or I would give him permission to cut it himself. By

Columbus Day I had still not had a reply to my letter, and was waiting to hear what I should do, when I stopped by Diarmuid's office to speak with him about another matter. I found him on the phone trying to reach me to tell me that he had heard from Ransom, who was returning my story.

He showed me the letter, which started out by saying that he (Ransom) had said he would take the story if I would cut it. Then he said, "This she declined to do." I had to read it over four times and couldn't believe my eyes then. Of course I hit the ceiling and Russell was wearily philosophic about it. My first reaction was that I should write back and set Ransom straight, but then I realized that it was impossible that he had misunderstood me. It was just an out and out lie, putting his refusal off on me. He went on to say that he himself felt that probably I was right—I was in such a tearing rage, and reading through such a red fog that I don't remember the exact phrasing of any but the one sentence about my declining to cut the story, but this was the gist of it. . . . Russell's only explanation was that some other editor might have dropped in on him and read it, and said no. Whatever it was, I think it irresponsible, low, and downright treacherous to write like that to Russell. If I had been in Vancouver instead of Russell's office, I might never have known about it, and Russell might have thought I did refuse to cut it. Oh, I could howl! . . . I don't need to go into detail about how I felt, since you probably know only too well how I reacted. I would have written a letter to Ransom and told him to go to blazes and burned that bridge to the reading public forever if I had been acting on my own, no doubt. However, I knew Russell wouldn't approve, and I do want to stay in his good graces and not be so exasperating he throws me out (more reasons why it's a good idea for me to have an agent). So I asked him hopelessly if he thought it would do any good for me to write Ransom and say that I'd said I would cut the story; and he said he couldn't see that there would be any possible advantage in it, since Ransom undoubtedly knew that he was doing me dirt. And that it might be to our advantage to leave it like that, since we might have to "use" him later—there being only about four possible outlets for this kind of thing, which I seemed to go on writing—and that we were more likely to be able to "use" him if he had a guilty conscience about me.

By January of 1947 Diarmuid had given up on the third "Boundary" and returned it, but Helen MacAfee of *Yale Review* was nibbling at the first, the one Ransom had returned. Also, I was trying a new departure. Completely spontaneously and without any forethought at all, I was writing fables. Diarmuid was delighted with them, but could think of only one or two possibilities for publication. "These editors are a pretty conventional crew," he said.

At this point my black cat story appeared, and I received the second shock of that season. The story had been inspired by the adventures of a friend of mine, a lingerie designer who had owned, and lost, a black cat. I wrote it as much for her entertainment as for publication, but I made the principal character in the story a gift-shop owner rather than a lingerie designer, just in case. I called both the cat and the story "Edward." The editors took me out to lunch, but made no mention of any change to make in the story. I don't know how I had lived so long in such a state of innocence, but I did not realize that editors did not need to ask permission to make changes. They had every right to go ahead and do anything they liked. I was not very much surprised to find that the story had a new title, "The Cat." I was more surprised at some of the internal changes, which I listed in a letter:

> They gave the narrator a first name, Meg, dropped entirely a
> very minor character I had named, changed the color of the cat's
> eyes (probably the illustrator drew a green-eyed cat and it was
> easier to change the story than the picture), changed the profes-
> sion of the heroine (I did not want Leonie to be a lingerie de-
> signer, just because Marq is), dropped phrases and changed
> phrases, none of which were really important, though I writhed
> to find "us" changed to "us girls." Practically all the changes
> were on the first page or page and a half, but by that time I was
> in a state I leave to your imagination, and went racing through
> to find out whether they had dropped the fire incident and per-
> haps changed Edward into a fairy prince and married Leonie to
> him happily in the end.

The editors of *Harper's Bazaar* had asked me to cut the story they used, and I had complied, but had not done quite as much cutting as they wanted. They had hinted, I realized later, that they might have to prune it a little themselves, and when the story appeared I saw that they had done so. I felt that it made the end a little choppy, but I was not especially unhappy. "Edward" was no great matter, either. When I had had lunch with the editors they had asked me whether some real life incident had inspired the story. Thinking that they were simply making conversation, I opened up and told them about my friend the lingerie designer, never dreaming that they would make that change. Luckily, she was a good sport (even when she received marked copies of the magazine with notes saying, "This sounds like you"), but the possibilities were frightening. The thing that most alarmed me, however, was the thought of what might happen to the fables I was writing:

> These fables are so condensed and so freighted with implications that the changing of a word or a phrase could throw the whole thing off. Not only that, but the style is certainly peculiarly my own—colloquial, but with just enough variation (I think) to give it a special tang and twist, and I will NOT have it worked over by anybody else. They could drop a phrase and drop the whole idea down the drain.

I copied two new fables and took them out to Diarmuid the next day. I wanted to know what an author's rights were, if any. He explained.

> When a magazine buys editorial rights, it buys the right to do any revision it considers advisable without the author's permission, and if there is a contract, that clause is in the contract. There are no exceptions. There is, however, a difference in the policy of the different magazines about consulting the author, and so on. He said he wouldn't dare mention it when sending things in, but after something was accepted, he could sometimes suggest that the author was sensitive about changes and would prefer to be consulted. He talked at some length, and I had the feeling that the little lecture had been many times rehearsed— that I wasn't the first who had blown in, all up in arms. He said that nobody had more prestige right now in the short story field than Eudora Welty, and on that account, he had suggested that her stories ought to be published as written, but nobody would even hear of such an agreement. Sometimes, he said, it's a case

of the thing not coming out even, when in print, and the printer saying at the last minute—seventeen lines have got to come out of this, and whoever is in the office at the moment does the cutting, and there isn't even time to consult the author. . . . I explained that I was particularly worried about the fables, and he seemed to think I hadn't much occasion to worry about them since it was doubtful anybody would publish them anyway. That, of course, didn't make me a lot happier.

He also told me of one case he had been involved in where the *New Yorker*, which had strict styling rules, insisted that one word be changed, the author refused, and the *New Yorker* rejected the story. That seemed to me permissible, so long as the author was consulted. He also admitted that he knew of some "fantastic cases," including one where a whole character was changed by the dropping of a few phrases.

Perhaps my trouble was that until now I had published only poetry. Granted, many poetry editors like to meddle, too, but I have never known one to revise a poem without permission. Helen MacAfee of *Yale Review* once offered to take one of my poems if I would remove the last four lines. I refused, because that amputation would have removed the point of the poem. She then returned the poem, but that was her privilege. She did not accept the poem and remove the final lines without a word to me.

At some point in our discussion Diarmuid said: "One thing you *could* do would be to write a novel. Authors always get to read proof on books." Of course book manuscripts are also revised by editors. Many would be unpublishable if they were not edited, but at least the author can put up a fight. When Viking made changes in Carl Van Doren's text, he changed it back on the proof, and pointed out in a note that he was not to be charged for the changes, because he was changing it back to the original. His view was that editors "have to show they are earning their salaries."

So far as "Edward" was concerned, I had very little to complain about. That same week I came upon our building superintendent's wife, whose first published story had just appeared in a popular magazine. She was all but sobbing with rage. A good half of her story had been cut, and the title changed from

"Shabby Genteel" to "Fugitives from Paradise." She had had no more idea of editors' rights than I had had. Most short-story writers, our agents informed us, put up with this treatment in the hope of having a book published eventually in which the stories will appear as they were written. Without magazine publication first, a volume of short stories is out of the question.

I did not cease from this moment to write short fiction, but the impetus seemed to be gone. I wrote no more "Boundaries" and only one more fable, which was never published. Every time I found myself struggling to get a paragraph or a sentence right, I would wonder, but won't they cut it, anyway? I understand that some esteemed *New Yorker* writers hand in a batch of scribbled notes, which are then "edited" into a story. Why not? Perhaps editors prefer their authors to be simply "idea men."

After almost six months of negotiation *Yale Review* at last accepted the first "Boundary," "A Character Must Have a Name," in an abbreviated form. Diarmuid sent my three fables to *Kenyon Review*. Whether Ransom's conscience was pricking him or not, I shall never know, but he took them and published them without changing a letter. Ironically, Diarmuid had by now sold all but one of the shorter things he had thought would be so difficult to place, but had to give up on the mysteries, for which he had had high hopes. He returned the last one, *Swamp Lake*, in October of 1947. I felt little pain, because by that time I had begun work on a novel. It had occurred to me that the turn my writing was taking in the fables could be extended into the novel form. When Russell called, I was "so deep in the new story that I could just manage to reach out and grab the telephone."

> Russell said for the umteenth time that the reports all said more or less the same thing: "This woman is a very good writer, but she should be writing straight novels." I said, "Well, as a matter of fact, I am." After expressing some surprise and satisfaction, he said in a depressed voice, "When we get to sending it around, I hope they don't report that you are a very good writer, but should be writing mystery stories."

Diarmuid then went on to tell me a horror story about an author whose publisher accidentally remaindered his book at five cents a copy *before* it was published. The publication date had been postponed because of serialization, and the book forgotten until someone noticed thousands of copies in the warehouse and remaindered them. Sometimes, I said, I feared that Diarmuid would "give up literary-agenting for good and retire to the cultivation of peonies even if his family has to live on them, fried, boiled, or in salad."

During all that winter and spring I did little but work on my novel, *Ashe Knoll*. I put off work for Van Doren with his permission, and turned down an opportunity to do a subject index of Harold Laski's eight-hundred-page *magnum opus* for Viking. ("Good God!" said Carl at the mere thought of it. "Good God!") I found the novel-writing very exciting, and did not regret the time and effort expended on the mysteries because the work I had done on them had been good experience. I was handling my material easily, with very little fumbling.

When I estimated that I had finished one third of the book, I took a copy of the completed chapters to Diarmuid, who left them on his commuter train. He said that he had done that before, and always the manuscript had turned up eventually, but mine never did. ("What a thing it must be to have an Irishman for an agent," Carl said when I told him.) I had made a single carbon copy, and of course Russell and Volkening offered to pay for the re-typing, but I was nervous about letting it out of my hands. My apprehension was justified; I should have re-typed it myself. (It is to be remembered that there were no Xerox machines in those days.) Instead, I took it to a young woman typist, who, after promising me not to let it out of the apartment, farmed it out to an inexperienced friend who lived at the other end of Long Island. This friend took forever to do the work, and then, when she started to bring it back to Manhattan, was in a taxicab accident. The new manuscript was ruined, and my original was a mess, but legible. She re-copied it after a fashion, skipping a paragraph here and there as she neared the end.

Meanwhile I was going on with the writing although I was on tenterhooks until I had the original manuscript back in my own hands; after that I had to re-copy all the last part of it. I was not letting it out of my apartment again. I finished a corrected draft before I went home for vacation in July, copied the manuscript there, and mailed it back to Diarmuid. His reply was more positive than I had dared hope for. He said he was fascinated with it and called it a most astonishingly dexterous and clever job. Later, he said to me, "You have no idea what a pleasure it is to have an *odd* book come in." He was even "sure" that there would be a publisher. I never knew him to be so optimistic about anything, before or since, but he was mistaken. He was unable to find a publisher who liked *odd* books as much as he did.

7

In his after-Christmas letter of 1945, Williams had spoken of his hope of reducing his practice so that he could see his friends again, but the practice still remained heavy, and, worse, the physical difficulties that were to beset him for the rest of his life were beginning. I did not see him again until December of 1946, when a bookshop in my neighborhood gave a party for him. The occasion was the publication of a Williams issue of *The Briarcliffe Quarterly*. I stopped in and found the shop fairly packed with poets. There were friends from my pre-Buffalo days, whom I hadn't seen since my return to New York, like Ted Wilson and Babette Deutsch. There were poets I had corresponded with and never met, like Weldon Kees and Theodore Roethke; and besides the poets, I found the whole Williams clan, including Paul and his wife and Bill's brother, Edgar. Even Auden was there, seen dimly through the haze of cigarette smoke, and, of course, Oscar Williams. Despite the din, which was awful, I managed to have a little conversation with Bill and Florence. He looked very frail to me. Surgery performed the previous May had been unsuccessful, and was to be repeated in a few days.

During 1947 I neither saw nor heard from him, but one result of the publication of my "Three Fables" in *Kenyon Review* was that he was moved to write to me again. On January 16, 1948, he wrote expressing his appreciation of my new work (for Partisan read Kenyon):

I read your pieces in Partisan Review with the greatest pleasure and admiration, they are as interesting in detail, word freshness, as in general conception and overall quality of composition. It's wonderful to me to see the writer go ahead perfecting his work. This is something really distinguished, I'm glad it was you.

Floss and I often speak of you (I know that's an old device for putting off a friend) we'd like to see you but we practically never get to New York any more and this place might as well be in Greenland as far as New York City is concerned—at least that's the way we have come to feel about it in recent years. It's much closer to California or New Mexico or even Washington, DC than 14th Street.

Floss will write you a note in the near future asking you to come out some Sunday, I hope you will be able to make it.

About a week later I received another note, this one inviting me to Rutherford on Sunday, February 22nd, with two of my young friends. "Come out then if you can and we are all alive," he wrote. When Bill made the invitation conditional on all of us being alive, he spoke as if with premonition. Before the date set, he suffered his first heart attack, and although he was of course still alive, the dinner date had to be canceled. He recovered slowly, and the next time I saw him was in May of 1948, when he read from *Paterson* at the Y.M.H.A. Describing this reading in a letter, I said:

Williams looked fairly good, but I thought he got tired, and the discussion afterwards went on and on. He did very well and I thought he went over well, but there was a small crowd. He always draws a bad night, and that one was no exception—rain had been pouring all day, and the evening, though not so stormy, was still wet enough to discourage people.

He wrote again, on May 18th, soon after the reading. This time he renewed the invitation to Rutherford that had been canceled because of the heart attack. Again, I was to bring my young friends:

Won't you come? Any time after three in the afternoon. We can bat along, one way or another, as long as we like. I won't ask Floss to make supper. But we can have beer and ham sandwiches or what not and regale ourselves accordingly.

Scotch, rye, bourbon, gin, courvoisier: as you may desire. Bring Auden with you if you can find him and shd care to do so. Or water or ginger ale. Or nuthin.

Quelle rotten weather! We are sick over it! As one of my patients said yesterday: We're having an early fall, aren't we, this year?

Best,
Bill

This time everything worked out as planned. The three of us went over by bus. We did not take Auden with us. At that time I had never met him, and had no intention of calling him to suggest that he join us, nor do I suppose that Bill thought for a moment that I would. The next day I wrote home about the latest excursion to Rutherford:

Yesterday was sunny but very windy. . . . When we arrived we sat out in the back yard under the trees and looked at the flowers, and talked. And then we went inside and had supper. Bill had said he wouldn't ask Flossie to fix supper, but we would have beer and sandwiches, or something. We had more than that. We had heaps of sandwiches and tea and enormous, delicious olives, and then ice cream with strawberries and layer cake. Jim has a growing-boy appetite and made away with everything anybody else didn't eat. Bill seems pretty well. He is tired, and acts and talks tired, but he did before the heart attack. I think it has discouraged him, though. He is invited to the Northwest Writer's Conference next (this) summer at Seattle, and plans to go, but they intend to fly there and return directly it's over . . .

They had other news to tell us. The honors were coming to Bill finally, but late, when he was almost too tired to care. He had just received the Russell Loines Award of one thousand dollars given by the National Academy of Arts and Sciences. Marianne Moore had introduced him at the presentation ceremonies. He had also been asked to fill the Chair of Poetry at the Library of Congress for a year. He told us that he would receive some money and not have to do too much work.

Bill had also paid a visit to St. Elizabeth's since I saw him last. It was a surprise visit, and he said that as he approached, Pound jumped up from his chair and cried, "We have no agenda, but we'll find plenty to talk about!" And Bill said to us, "You see, that *proves* he's crazy." I found nothing irrational in Pound's remark, because I knew that whenever Pound learned that a visitor was coming, he prepared a list, which he called his agenda, of the things he wanted to discuss. The English magazine *Agenda* takes its name from those lists. My own conclusion, drawn from Bill's comment, was that he was trying to convince himself that Pound was insane. However, he seems to have told someone else that he found Pound just as crazy as he always had been, which (if one allows for the stress induced by the two years he had spent in a ward for the mentally ill) was my own view.

The epilogue to this Sunday afternoon excursion to Rutherford was a letter of June 1st, 1948, in which Bill enclosed a letter and manuscripts sent to him by an admirer. He began:

> God forgive me for doing this to you but after one look at the gentleman's orthography—its overpowering vigor and Olympian self assurance I had to run to cover. Read the enclosed letter and, if you will, please, answer it for me as you may. I have written to Mr. Polychronopsulos telling him that I just haven't the time for his project but that if you would be willing to talk with him you might bring him some assistance. I did not give him your address but said you would write to him if you thought well of his proposal.
>
> I also gave him Finley's name. Maybe they'll strangle each other!
>
> At that the boy does have something interesting to present and you just might want to take him up. He sounds like an able person.
>
> It was a delight to see you again. I never saw you in better form. Kitty Hoagland told me, when I saw her the other day that if I had read about you in the New Directions 5 young poets I would have known that you were a Greek student. But, alas, I suppose I skimmed through the book as usual—reading here and there—and so missed finding out what I should have known earlier.
>
> However my neglect had a silver lining for it left the pleasure of the discovery to these days. We'll see more of each other as time goes on—if we go on. For both Floss and I love you very much and admire you tremendously for the way you have battled it through in that God forsaken city without bitterness,

in fact with a generosity of heart which shows you to be . I can't quite finish the sentence. I mean to say that we find you to be a distinguished person of great gentleness in a world not very much to be admired.

So with that "he hands me this Grick!" sez you. Don't take him on if you don't want to.

Our best
Bill

Not even that heartwarming tribute (which I still cherish) could persuade me to take on his Greek admirer. Our correspondence then lapsed for more than two years, until a proposed visit to Portland and Reed College reminded him to write to me.

Chapter 7

THE THREE years 1949, 1950 and 1951 were clearly, as I look back, the watershed years. During those years I topped a ridge, took a long look and a new course. Six things taken in chronological order influenced my change of direction.

First, in the spring of 1949 I went to Italy for three months.

Second, my father sold his business that same year and invested his money, one third of it in my name, so that I might feel more independent.

Third, at the end of 1949 Diarmuid returned *Ashe Knoll*.

Fourth, in that same month I turned forty.

Fifth, Carl Van Doren died suddenly in the summer of 1950.

Sixth, in the early spring of 1951 I fell seriously ill, not with just one potentially fatal virus, but with two, one following on the other, and spent several weeks in two different hospitals and month upon month in bed. By the time I was on my feet again I was on my new course.

First, about Italy.

In 1928 when I entered college, I was indulging in day dreams of a European trip, perhaps in the mid-1930's when I would have been out of college two or three years. By the mid-1930's New York was as much as I dared dream of, and once I was in the East, where Europe might have been more accessible to me, war broke out. Foreign travel was postponed for another ten years. In fact, I had even given up thinking of it. Europe had been for so long associated in my mind with war and its attendant horrors that it had lost its appeal. Then, on the first of February, 1949, in Philadelphia where I had gone to do some research for Van Doren, I received a letter from my father offering me a trip to Europe in the summer if I would prefer that instead of making the usual trip west. Immediately I knew exactly what I wanted to do: I wanted to go to Italy, and I wanted to go in the spring. I spent the next two months in a frenzy of preparation, including finishing up work for Van Doren, and sailed the first day of April.

During the Forties I had continued to attend poetry readings, which were now more frequent. One evening I heard Allen Tate, who read, besides his own poetry, a passage from Dante in Italian. The effect on me was like that made by the Homer I heard during my freshman year in college, except that in this case my curiosity had already been whetted by the Italian I heard spoken in my neighborhood shops on Bleecker and MacDougal. Deciding to do something about it, I bought a *Teach Yourself Italian* grammar and pitched in. With my Latin and French to help me along, I made good headway, and was soon in love with the language. I bought the three Temple Classics volumes of the *Divine Comedy*, read them, and with them background reading on Italy in the Middle Ages. That led me into Renaissance Italy. I had also been doing a good bit of reading on the classical period. By the time my father's proposal reached me, a desire to see Florence and Rome had superseded my earlier desire to see London and Paris.

My choice of Italy as a destination was not a result of Pound's influence so much as Allen Tate's, but I naturally wrote to Ezra as soon as I knew I was going, and asked whether he had any advice or exhortations. Immediately I received a page covered with scrawled queries:

Problm:
> how long for?
> how much to spend?
> licherchoor, kulcher
> or wot? . . .

and on the verso:

> in short
> bizniz
> or
> pleasure?

I replied that I was staying three months; my aim was pleasure, but if I didn't have a good time, I would have to chalk it up to education. I then received from St. Elizabeth's an itinerary that covered three typed pages. Mary de Rachewiltz in *Discretions* referred to my 1949 trip as a "*Cantos* tour of Europe." Not precisely. The three months were spent entirely in Italy, and if the trip turned into a "*Cantos* tour," it was not by my design. The itinerary was too attractive to ignore, and because Pound had drawn it up, of course I touched a number of cities that were off the beaten track in those days, but figure largely in the *Cantos*, such as Rimini, Mantua, and especially Ferrara, where I went to see the frescoes in the Schifanoia Palace. When I signed the visitors' book, the custodian said with an air of satisfaction: "We had an American here *last* week, too."

Pound wanted to see me before I left, and Dorothy Pound, who was now living in Washington, offered to put me up overnight if I would come. One Saturday in late March I took a morning train to Washington, found a cab, and went directly to St. Elizabeth's. Writers who did not visit Pound while he was behind bars sometimes seem to be perplexed by the differing reports from those who did. It is necessary to remember that he was there for twelve years, that he was subject, like the rest of us, to different moods, reacted differently to different visitors, and of course made a different impression on each visitor according to the visitor's own expectations. I give my impression exactly as I put it down at the time, unmodified by subsequent impressions or inevitable changes in my viewpoint as I became better acquainted with the situation, some parts of which I still do not understand and probably never shall.

In the first place I was even more nervous on this occasion than I had been at our first meeting. I had never before visited either a prison or an institution for the insane, and as I waited alone on the stairs outside the door of the ward while the guard unlocked and unbolted—I could hear the rattling of keys, chains, and bolts—my knees were ready to fold. Once I was inside—locked inside, of course—I gradually recovered. I had had to present a letter from Dr. Overholser first in order to gain admittance. My account is as follows:

> I presented my letter and was admitted with a minimum of fuss, and got an enthusiastic welcome. He grabbed me and kissed me and leapt around getting a chair for me while I said how de do to Mrs. Pound, and then we sat down in a neat little circle behind a screen (a special dispensation for a distinguished inmate) to discuss "Miss Barnard's invasion of Europe." I planned the two visits because I knew I would be upset the first day, and probably unable to do any talking myself, and not even able to follow him all the time, and I was awfully glad I did arrange it that way. I was upset not only by the background, which is enough, but I had to get used to his personality, which must surely be something never seen before. Certainly never seen by me, anyhow. He just isn't like anybody, and I can't describe him—like a bird looping the loops far away in the blue sky and suddenly darting past your ear close enough to touch it—and I had the uncanny feeling that one of those swoops was enough to enable him to find out everything about me worth knowing. Anyway, the first day I was fairly tense, but he went over the list of people I should look up, telling me something about them, and suggesting others, and suggesting to Mrs. P. that perhaps she should write a letter of introduction for me to Max Beerbohm, who is at Rapallo—I nearly fell off my chair at that, since the extraordinary Max is almost as much of a legend as E. P. or G. B. S. The Paiges are also in Rapallo. He is still editing letters. I did come into the conversation at that point, to express my disapproval of Paige's editing, and incidentally, I told him what you pointed out about the letter where there was a passing reference to Marianne

Moore followed by: "127 words omitted" or whatever number it was. You should have heard him laugh. When he stopped laughing he said, well, he thought Marianne had it coming to her, and then we went on talking about something else.

Douglass Paige had sent me a sample of his work on the letters, and I had protested vehemently. I felt that the editing was so awkward that the letters became unreadable. The style he eventually used, in the 1951 *Selected Letters of Ezra Pound*, was a great improvement over the first sample. Pound also asked me whether I would like to have an introduction to George Santayana in Rome. I wondered what I would find to say to George Santayana, and came up with a complete blank. Accordingly I said no, and have regretted it ever since, wondering what Santayana might have found to say to me. To continue:

> When we left, the guard who unlocked the door to let us out said, by the way, he saw in the paper that Mrs. Longworth broke her arm. I thought, this is Washington D.C. for you—where Mrs. Longworth's broken arm is a topic for conversation between the guards and the patients' visitors at an insane asylum; but he went on to add that probably that was why she hadn't been in lately, and I realized that she was one of E. P.'s visitors. Thornton Wilder was there on last Wednesday and they had a fine visit—met only once before in Europe years and years ago. A good many people come strictly on the q.t. and don't want anybody to know they come. So of course I don't know who they are, but I suspect university people, for some, and maybe some with government jobs. I learned that there has been more uproar over the Bollingen Award [for the *Pisan Cantos*] than I was aware of—somebody wrote an article saying that everyone on the jury should be tried for treason; and one of the jurors wrote and said he would be *glad* to be tried under such circumstances.
>
> When we got outside, Mrs. P. pointed out his window and said he always came there to wave goodby (we had to visit in a large public room, but behind the screen). I think it was when he appeared to wave to us that I realized the complete incongruity of the situation: that I felt as though I had got a shot in the arm, and that probably everybody who comes feels that way, and that's why they come—to take life away instead of to bring

it. Not that they don't bring it, too, but it's the exchange that is important—one certainly doesn't come away depleted. I feel as though I have almost as much to assimilate as I'll have after two or three weeks in Italy.

Mrs. P. is a good-looking woman in her late fifties, I suppose, tall, rather slender, with quite English looks and charm and style, but pretty well on the ragged edge herself. I thought time and again she would break down when we talked about him, but I felt it was very important to get some facts straight, and I've heard so many rumors. I certainly can't go into all the background in a letter. Some of the rumors were false, as that the charges against him had been dropped—she nearly had a fit when she heard that. Some were true, particularly one I hadn't written you about, concerning the treatment he got in the prison camp at Pisa—an account was published in an English magazine, but never over here. It was so bad both physically and mentally that eventually he blacked out and she thinks possibly had sunstroke—at any rate, the officials realizing that he would either go insane or die if they didn't relax a bit, did relax (some), and there's a theory that one reason the case wasn't brought to trial was that they didn't want the story to come out, or anyway, that they thought he could have got off on a plea of insanity, hands down, if the story *had* come out. So they preferred to chuck him in St. Elizabeth's without the story being published. The officers in the camp said they didn't know where their instructions originated, all they could do was obey orders. As nearly as I can work it out, probably Rome was using him in a slightly different way from the way he thought he was being used—I mean he thought he was using Rome, and Rome was using him, though Mrs. P. said he frequently gave the Italians the jitters by the things he said. With his fixed ideas about economics and his enthusiasm and militant attitude, combined with the apparently calculated cruelty with which he was treated at Pisa, he wouldn't have needed a loose screw to convince himself that he was being martyred to his economic convictions (not meaning Fascism) and is where he is because he is too dangerous to be loose, and perhaps that's one thing that keeps him going.

Dorothy Pound also confirmed a news dispatch concerning their thwarted attempt to return to the United States immediately after the Pearl Harbor attack. I had read the report in a

Buffalo newspaper at the time, but had not the sense to clip it, and nobody would believe me.

Mrs. P. is leading a dedicated and pretty sad existence, I'm afraid. She impressed me very favourably while we were in the hospital, but as soon as we were alone together, she seemed to stiffen up. That only lasted a short while, and gradually she relaxed and became very friendly. I think she did like me, but she is very tense over Olga. . . . You would have thought that in the last twenty years one of those women would have thrown him over for good, or else that one or both of them would have got resigned to the situation, but no. Added to that, his mail is all censored by psychiatrists, and he's trying to keep Olga out of the picture, I think. On the second day, after about an hour, Mrs. P. withdrew to go over some proofs, ostensibly, but I'm sure she had been told to give us a private interlude, where I got some further briefing on what to say and what not to say to Olga—what to say being mainly "Patience and fortitude" as the Little Flower used to say . . .

At this point I departed from the main theme of the letter to relate news of a friend in Washington, took time off to go to Van Doren's, and returned to my story again in the evening:

So to continue: One thing I particularly wanted to add was that during our tête à tête yesterday Pound suddenly asked, "What about the novel?" I shook my head and shrugged my shoulders (I had already written him that it was being turned down). He said, "Well, do you want me to read it, or would you rather wait until you've put it over?" I said whichever he liked. He asked did I have an extra carbon, and I said I did. So he asked me to send it to him and he would read it and if he liked it, he might recommend it to Eliot for Faber and Faber, not, of course, that that would necessarily do any good, but it would be worth trying—all of course, depending on whether he liked it. I told him that Diarmuid, who wasn't stupid, said he had never read anything quite like it, whereupon E. P. rolled his eyes and said, "Good God! If it isn't like anything they've ever read, it will have to be *clandestinely* circulated!"

About this point the area behind the screen was invaded by a very smartly dressed and effusive bit of femininity who had known him in Europe years ago, and who came bearing gifts in the shape of the *Sat. Rev. Lit.* She drew up a chair and chattered away gaily for a couple of minutes, and then said she had better go, she felt she was interrupting something here, and he politely rose and politely ushered her to the door. When he came back, I said I could have gone, but I didn't know whether he was through with his briefing, and he said that I was leaving the city and leaving the country, and she could come any time—which was true enough but she had apparently made a long trip by bus to get there, and it seemed a pity she had to turn straight around and go home—which indicates the sort of topsy-turvy way things are—the privilege is more in visiting than in being visited, or so it seems.

I didn't know about these invasions of smart femininity into the ward of unaesthetic males (I suppose Mrs. Longworth is smart), but I started out Saturday morning with the thermometer standing at nineteen degrees in my black coat instead of my fur coat just because (well, maybe a little vanity, but mainly because) I thought, poor thing, he always liked to see good-looking well-dressed women, and few enough he sees these days, and I can't do much in that line, but I'm going to do what I can. I wore my new black hat over one eye, and with my new shoulder bag and my hatbox for luggage, the outfit was snappy enough to call forth admiration in Penn Station last night, so I think I didn't do too badly despite the unexpected competition. E. P. admired the coat, and said, "Dorothy, maybe Mary could help you with your shopping." So I felt repaid.

I stayed with Mrs. Pound, as she had suggested, and I described her quarters also:

Mrs. P. has an attic room—the whole attic, with the stairs coming up in the middle of the floor, and the ceiling sloping almost to the baseboard in all directions. The bathroom she uses is in the basement two flights below, and my bedroom was a kind of playhouse room walled off from the oil burner and clothes lines—both her room and mine fitted with an electric heater, without which they were devilish cold. There is one day a week when E. P. has regular callers, and she usually uses that for errands downtown (mainly for him, I think) and all the other days she goes to visit him and stays the full time, and I don't know what she does the rest of the time, but she certainly can't have much fun. She gets breakfast and supper in the landlady's kitchen, and I fear supper is usually something out of a can. I don't think the trouble is actually so much lack of money as it is the housing shortage plus the fact that she wants to be near St. Elizabeth's—which is way out on the outskirts.

By the time I left St. Elizabeth's the second afternoon I had several more pages of notes including hotels and pensiones to stay at (if they were still standing), dishes to try, even a wine list. Pound showed me some postcards, including views of the waterfront at Rapallo and Brunnenburg castle at Merano. His daughter Mary was now the wife of Prince Boris de Rachewiltz. The young couple had acquired a Tyrolean castle that was falling into ruin and were beginning its restoration. Although Pound warned me that he could not guarantee that it yet had a roof, one look at the postcard was enough to persuade me that I should by all means visit Mary, roof or no roof. It looked like the fairy-tale castle of my childhood dreams, and the lack of a roof made it sound all the more romantic. He approved of my hatbox, saying that it was exactly the right amount of luggage to take to Europe. As I told him good-bye I thought for one moment that he was going to break down, but he recovered himself quickly to wish me *buon viaggio*. I returned to New York that evening and wrote the letter the next day.

2

Although I was excited about going to Italy, and much intrigued by that postcard picture of the castle, my expectations were toned down by middle age. I had already had my fair share of disappointments and disillusionments, and I approached Europe now with a strong suspicion that it would turn out to be not so wonderful after all. I assumed that I would be often uncomfortable, unhappy, displeased, or disappointed, but I hoped the pluses would equal the minuses. What actually happened was that my three months of travel exceeded all I could have hoped for even if I had let myself go and hoped for heaven. No other three months of my life left a deeper impression, and no travel anywhere since then can compete with that first *giro* from Genoa to Rapallo, to Florence, to Siena, Perugia, Assisi, Rome, and back up the peninsula to Ravenna, Rimini, Ferrara, Venice,

Vicenza, Verona, Mantua, Merano, Sirmione, Milan and so again to Genoa. I stayed two weeks each in Florence, Rome, and Venice. The other six weeks were spread among the smaller towns, with one week in Perugia and almost a week with Mary at the castle.

Sometimes I envy those who had, or are having, the European experience in their youth; and then again it seems to me that too often they are not even aware of what is happening to them, and so miss half the fun. To go for the first time at the age of thirty-nine, when one knows exactly what one wants, and why, is a tremendous experience. I had been half-persuaded that Europe was not, after all, necessary; but I found that for me it was absolutely essential. Some of the people who make light of that necessity have had Europe early (like Bill Williams) and absorbed it without knowing what they were doing. All their lives they have been able to take for granted a reservoir of impressions and memories that they never thank God for, because they have no way of knowing what the intellectual life is like without them.

I have no desire to turn this narrative into a travel book; I shall neither regale the reader with lyrical passages from my letters, nor detail the churches, palaces and museums I visited, but I must give some account of my first week in Italy. I arrived, after a stormy crossing in a small, overcrowded Polish ship, to find northern Italy enjoying its first taste of real spring weather. Wisteria was in bloom and fountains glittered in the sunshine. I spent the first night ashore in Genoa, where the Paiges, having been alerted by a letter from Dorothy, found me at my hotel and showed me where to get a bus for Rapallo next day. When I arrived the following morning I was dizzy with the beauties of the Italian Riviera, and already, after one dinner and one breakfast, looking forward with great anticipation to three months of eating in Italy.

It seemed to me that I must be starting my trip with the best the country had to offer, but the Paiges assured me that that was not so. There was better to come. They spent the next several days initiating me into the Italian ways of doing things, an invaluable service. The fine weather held. We took a picnic lunch to Portofino, sat in cafés, and climbed the *salitas* around Rapallo. Olga Rudge, who had written to Ezra that she would be pleased to see me, was expected daily; she finally arrived just before I left for Florence.

At Olga's suggestion I met her on the terrace of the Albergo Rapallo. I described her as "good-looking, with fine features, a springy stride, clear grey eyes, and a fair complexion." Her hair, which had recently turned grey, was worn in a French roll. I had brought a gift from Ezra that was intended, at least in part, "to smooth my way," but it seemed rather to work against me. I characterized her in my letter as "fiery," but "electric" might have been a better word. She gave off sparks, it seemed to me, and she met me with bared teeth. After the first quarter of an hour I decided that I had nothing to lose; this was none of my affair, anyway. Let her hate me if she would, I might as well relax and speak bluntly.

God knows she had enough to try her nerves and temper. If wild rumors were circulating in the States, by the time they reached her they were even wilder. One correspondent, who should have known better, had written her that Dorothy did not want Pound to be released. Naturally she was beside herself. And none of them, I felt, understood the first thing about America. Olga was born in the United States of American parents, but had grown up in Europe. Dorothy was English. Mary had an American passport, but had never set foot in the country. Pound's America was the one he left in 1910. After we had talked for a while she began to relax and even to listen to me, but she refused to let me take her to dinner at Portofino as Ezra had suggested. Instead, she insisted that I come up to her villa, where she fixed a supper for both of us—spaghetti and Spam out of a Care package sent by T. S. Eliot. At 1:30 we stumbled down the *salita* in the starlight, or rather I stumbled, and she held me up.

The next morning before my bus left for Florence we met again on the seafront. When I caught sight of her, I saw to my surprise that she was laughing. She called me to come and see: Sir Max Beerbohm, wearing a Panama hat, was sitting on a bench in the sunshine, "spats, cane and all." His housekeeper had told the Paiges that the Beerbohms were "away," not explaining that they were "away" at a hotel in Rapallo while their

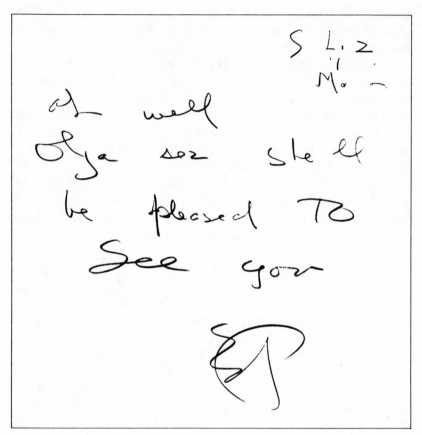

Letter from Ezra Pound, March 7, 1949.

villa was being redecorated. As soon as Olga learned that a letter of introduction to the Beerbohms had preceded me, she insisted that I go speak to him. We had a very brief conversation during which he inquired about Dorothy, shook his head over Ezra, and asked about my travel plans. Ah yes, he said, I would go to Florence, and there I would see Michelangelo's David "looking rather more like Hercules." The remark stayed with me. When I saw the original, I thought he was quite right. Donatello's David looks like David, but Michelangelo's looks like a young Hercules.

On shipboard I had made a friend of my own age, who was awaiting my arrival in Florence. Of American parentage, like Olga Rudge, she had grown up in the Anglo-American colony there and married an Italian. She reserved a room for me at a pensione next door, where her mother was also staying temporarily. By the time I left Florence, I was primed with still more useful information, and was able to manage very well on my own.

Until I landed in Italy I had never had the experience of actually having to *use* a foreign language. Like most people under similar circumstances, I became tongue-tied when I tried to speak, but I soon discovered that it is much more important to understand than to speak, and I could at least understand with little difficulty. I had a few phrases, also, that I could produce to get things started, and the Italians, of course, always told me that I spoke it beautifully, a bare-faced lie that made us all feel happy and pleased with one another. It was not true, as I had been told repeatedly, that "everyone spoke English." In the smaller towns and the cheaper hotels, everyone definitely did not. Tourists were still a rarity in places like Siena and Mantua, and tourists who tried to speak Italian were rarer still. Whether my smattering of the language had something to do with it or not, I can't say, but it seemed to me that I met with more kindness and consideration than I have ever encountered before or since, anywhere. I was accustomed to snarling taxi-drivers and porters who felt it was beneath them to carry bags that were not matched cowhide. The Italian porters seemed to like me better because I had only two small bags and asked them to take me to an inexpensive hotel.

Rebuilding had only just begun. The medieval towers rose formidably from the rubble along the Arno. The bridges were not yet rebuilt. Hotels that had stood too near the railway lines were gone. However, the thing that amazed me most was how much Italian art and architecture had survived. It seemed to me that after four or five more such wars, which God forbid, it might just be reduced to manageable size. I realized that in the three months I had allowed myself I was only skimming a little cream off the top. In succeeding trips I have got to Naples, Paestum, Amalfi, Sicily, Bari, Bergamo, Tarquinia, Gubbio, Urbino, Orvieto, Pisa, Lucca, Parma, Piacenza, Pavia, Asolo, Castelfranco, besides the resort towns of Cortina d'Ampezzo, Menaggio, Lerici, Riva, and the like, but I still feel that I am skimming the cream from the top of the pail.

To help me skim, and come at some of the best butterfat, I had not only a selected list of specific things to look for, drawn up by Pound, but also much practical advice of a more general nature, such as the recommendation that I take buses through the mountains because the trains would be in tunnels most of the time, and I would see nothing; or the comment: "Rome is an *outside* city," and a warning against trying to see the interiors of all its churches. John Drummond, who had edited the English section of the *Westminster* anthology, and was now living in Rome, spent two days guiding me, not to the Vatican and the Forum, which I could perfectly well find by myelf, but to lesser known or outlying points of interest. In Venice, which I reached in early June, I was on my own, but I soon learned to plunge into the labyrinth of *calles* and canals, knowing I would be lost after the second turn, but that there would always be someone to direct me to Santa Maria dei Miracoli, or the Scuola di S. Giorgio degli Schiavoni (or whatever I might be looking for) and back to the Piazza San Marco eventually. After Venice, it seemed to me that I must have rung all the changes possible so far as Italian cities were concerned, but Vicenza with its Palladian architecture was still different, and Verona turned out to be one of my favorites. There I boarded the Brenner Pass train, traveled up the Adige, changed at Bolzano, and went on up the Adige into the incredible mountains of the South Tyrol. Mary met me at the Merano station and took me to Brunnenburg castle, where I began just a year ago to write this narrative.

At that time Mary and her husband had restored only a few rooms: two bedrooms in the tower, one above the other, the kitchen, the study, and a little room where we had tea in the late afternoons. The rest of the castle, which can now house as many as sixty people, was a ruin. She took me on a conducted tour, telling me what she hoped to do with each part of it; I lost my bearings immediately, and when we returned to the habitable portion I had no notion where we had been. The setting, however, was more impressive than the castle itself. I thought I knew mountains, but I was staggered by the view from every window, in every direction, looking down the river towards Verona, or up the river towards Switzerland, or simply towards the mountains rearing immediately before and behind us. The stillness of the night, as I emptied my washbasin out of the window in the top of the tower, is one of the things I remember best, the immense hush that continued unbroken for a long, long moment, before I heard the faint splash of water on the stones far below.

Still more impressive than either the castle or the setting was the twenty-four-year-old girl who was living there with her three-year-old son. Boris was in Rome, and I did not meet him. I had no need to say "Patience and fortitude," to Mary. She had both. Over our afternoon teas I heard about her childhood in Geis, and the rest of the story she has told in *Discretions*. Or she listened and I talked; I was the second visitor to Brunnenburg, and the first to bring news of her father since he had been taken to America. I also talked about *my* mountains. Ever since that week of late June, Mary and Brunnenburg have been a lodestone drawing me back to the South Tyrol again and again—eight times in all. As she says herself, "People who come to Brunnenburg usually come back."

When I returned to New York in mid-July I found the city appalling, revolting, unendurable. No doubt I was suffering from culture-shock, but there were other difficulties as well. We were having the worst heat wave I could remember. Almost everyone I knew was out of town, including Carl Van Doren, who said he would not be needing my services before Labor Day. I was not only at loose ends so far as my own work was concerned, with no writing projects in view, but I was so discouraged about the fate of my novel that I no longer wanted to think of fiction. I stopped in to see Diarmuid Russell, who told me that although *Ashe Knoll* had been rejected by ten publishers, he would go on trying to place it. Then, surveying my wilted state (the heat was ferocious), he suggested that I had better go home "and get used to being in this country gradually." I took his advice and went out to the West Coast for a month.

As I traveled across the plains and through the Rockies I was looking out the train window with new eyes. Although the junky little Main Street towns that lay along our route seemed to me cruder than ever, I exulted as never before in the empty rolling miles of country, the almost unbelievably uninhabited spaciousness of all that western mid-section. Also, I really saw the barns for the first time; that is, I saw the American barn as a satisfying architectural form, and, besides that, as a symbol of plenty. I wanted to travel around the country taking photographs of barns. As for Vancouver, it seemed spacious, too, and smelled of flowers and newly-mown, watered lawns, very different from both New York and Italy, but pleasant and a relaxing place to be, now that the war was over, the shipyards closed, and the town emptied of half its wartime population.

I returned to New York again in September, and in early October I made another trip to Washington D.C. This time I stayed with friends who lived on the other side of the city. I had not used a camera in Italy, but I brought home a large collection of black-and-white postcards and a few commercial photographs of paintings, some of which I took with me when I went to St. Elizabeth's. The weather was fine, and this time I found the Pounds on the lawn just outside the ward, instead of behind a screen in a public room. Mrs. Pound, it seemed, had been "constituted special deputy or something," and was allowed to take her husband out on the lawn during visiting hours when the weather was good enough, even if the other inmates were not allowed out.

I can't say the conversation on Saturday was very satisfactory. It was a lovely day and the grounds were beautiful, with a view of the Capitol dome framed in the trees, and the squirrels romping around (both the Pounds feeding them nuts from time to time), but the hospital is near the Navy Yard, and the Navy Yard is having some kind of celebration—centennial it seems to me I heard—and we had planes zooming over, sometimes very low, sometimes sixteen together, sometimes jet planes, every few minutes so that we kept getting interrupted in the middle of a sentence. By the time the roar finally died down you would forget what you wanted to say. Then since Mrs. Pound was there I thought I couldn't talk about Olga, and he didn't mention her, so I didn't either. And while we did talk about Mary, we didn't talk much.

Viola Jordan had written Pound that I was bursting at the seams. He obviously wanted me to talk about the trip and what I had got out of it; but I felt exactly as I had felt during tutorial conferences with Victor Chittick long ago. I could no more tell Ezra about Venice than I could tell Victor about Keats. However, when we were looking at pictures, I said that just once I had wished for a movie camera, so that I could record the motions of the gondoliers (there were many more gondolas and man-powered freight boats in 1949 than there are now, and very few motor boats). Then I showed him a photograph I had brought back, a detail of Carpaccio's "The Healing of a Man Possessed by a Devil," in which a number of gondoliers are shown, each in a different position, so that they suggest, as the eye travels among them, the completed motion of a gondolier propelling his boat.

Pound agreed that it was so, and was struck with wonder that he had never noticed it although he must have seen the painting, which hangs in the Accademia, dozens (or did he say hundreds?) of times. He then told me with great gusto of the time he apprenticed himself briefly to a gondolier. When I was ready to go, he asked if he might keep the pictures until I returned on Monday. Of course I left them with him; if I had not, I doubt that I would have gone back. I have seldom felt more inadequate. It seemed to me that I had nothing to say to him, and I doubted that he had anything more to say to me.

Not going would have been a mistake for two reasons. On the second afternoon, as I approached across the lawn, he pulled some typed papers from his pocket and greeted me with the news that he had a project for me. (His exact words were: "Have you ever thought of the art racket?") Of course Pound was always thinking up projects for people, most of them completely unsuitable, and I may as well say at once that nothing came of this one, so far as publication went, but it was a godsend to me at the moment, when the impetus that had carried me through several years of fiction-writing had failed, and the impetus towards poetry had not returned. The project was, in brief, a guide book to certain Italian paintings, mainly frescoes, still *in situ*. As I worked out the plan of the book in the following months, there were to be about ten essays, each devoted to a different painter, all but one about a series of paintings, each series located in a different city, and still to be found on the walls for which they were painted, *not* in museums. Chronologically they would fall in the period 1450 to 1525, which would allow me to include Fra Angelico at one end and Carpaccio at the other. My text would avoid art criticism, but give information (briefly) on the history of the city, the biography of the painter, and a more detailed discussion of what was going on in the paintings. For the Camera degli Sposi in Mantua this would include Gonzaga family history because members of the family are portrayed in the frescoes. In other cases I might be dealing with lives of the saints or with medieval legends. In addition, the book was to contain practical information. (It is to be remembered that postwar guidebooks were still unobtainable.) Obviously, I could not carry the project through without returning to Italy, but that was part of the point. What I would have to do would be to work up an outline and write two or three chapters in the hope of finding a publisher and getting an advance that would enable me to go back. When I expressed diffidence, saying that the idea fascinated me, but I would never have the courage to attempt it without being pushed, Ezra replied: "Well, it's a hole you can't CRAWL through, I'm sure of THAT."

We had been discussing this project for about an hour when

Dorothy gave a cry of welcome, and I saw a stately figure in a large hat advancing across the lawn in the bright sunshine. She was wearing something dark, navy blue or black, and carrying an ear-trumpet. It was Edith Hamilton. A folding chair was quickly produced, and she joined our circle. She had brought Ezra a new translation of a Greek play done by some young man whose name I did not recognize. Apparently it was a first effort. He had spent many months laboring in a garret to produce his translation, which had been sent to Miss Hamilton for review, and she did not like it at all! She felt most unhappy about her inability to give it a good review, and she was bringing it to Pound because she thought that he would be more likely than she to find merit in it, and if he did, perhaps he could write the young man a letter and tell him so. The trouble with the translation, she said, was that it had no *dignity*, and she added that in her opinion the very best translations from the Greek were Gilbert Murray's. They had *dignity*.

I jumped, and looked at Pound in apprehension, thinking, "He'll eat her alive!" At the very least, I expected him to rear up and bellow, but no, he was lying back in his chair with a blissful smile in his beard. If I have a favorite glimpse of Pound to place beside my view of Marianne Moore at the Gotham Book Mart party and Bill Williams at the Polytopic Club meeting, it is this one. I wished not only for a movie camera, then, but a tape-recorder. Miss Hamilton sat there *lecturing* Ezra Pound for a good quarter of an hour on the beauties of Gilbert Murray's translations from the Greek, while he uttered not a syllable and looked more delighted every minute. Presently time was up, and we had to take our leave. Miss Hamilton gave me a lift back downtown in her chauffeur-driven limousine. On the way, she said something about Pound—I forget what, but I said in my letter that she seemed devoted to him—and then she added: "Of course I have never read his poetry." No, I thought, nor his criticism; and I keep wondering what she would have made of *The Women of Trachis*.

3

My postwar correspondence with Pound was entirely different from our correspondence of the Thirties. For one thing, the penciled scrawls from St. Elizabeth's were written in what Hemingway called "an Unknown Tongue," or simply "U.T." For another, because I was writing prose rather than poetry, I was not sending poems to him for criticism. I am quoting only a few of the one hundred or more postwar missives I received from him for both reasons: they would be unintelligible to the general reader without extensive footnotes, and they do not bear on the theme of my book except in so far as they kept me in touch with other poets and introduced me to some I had not met before.

I did send him my fiction as it was published. The cat story, "Edward," seemed to interest him most. His project for me, before the fresco book, was to "Ring and Book 'Edward.'" I refused to consider writing a series of "Edward" stories, but Pound simply would not give up. Newspaper clippings about the strange doings of cats kept turning up in my mailbox with a scrawl attached, saying: "Edward again!" or "Edward, without a doubt!" After the trip to Italy, the clippings about cats changed to brief articles, usually in Italian, on some aspect of Italian art. In one mail I would receive instructions to read Pausanius, and in another the baffling news that H. D. was coming to my rescue with Gozzoli, and so on. When I saw him after my return from Italy, he urged me—or ordered me—to see Marianne. In explanation of this command, which I was more than willing to obey, I said:

> E. P. wanted me to see Marianne just on general principles, I think. She had written the Pounds that she had settled into hibernation for the winter, or something of the sort, and that seemed to alarm him. You know her mother died, and he said that while Mrs. Moore was a terrific burden in some ways, she did criticize Marianne's work and sort of spur her on, and naturally Marianne misses her in more ways than one.

I had not seen her since my return to New York except at a public reading. She had been much occupied, I knew, in caring for her mother in her last illness, and I had not wanted to intrude. Now I wrote to her, and on November 10 had a reply inviting me to come over to Brooklyn the following afternoon about four o'clock, and suggesting that we might have supper together. Of course I went, and afterwards wrote a full account of the visit:

We talked till about six and went out to dinner at a little restaurant near by, and then returned to her apartment and talked some more. It was very interesting talk to me, and she seemed interested, too, but somehow, though she expresses admiration for me, which makes me uncomfortable because I don't think I deserve it, I don't think she takes to me much. She talks as though she just never sees anybody, or goes any place, but that isn't true, because she continually mentioned people that she does see. It's true that she doesn't have very good health, and wants to limit her social life, which she has a perfect right to do, and I feel that the limits leave me out. I think she has given Pound a wrong impression of her life—as though she just weren't seeing anybody—because she didn't want to see the people he wanted to send to her. I took over a small batch of Italian postcards to show to her. She was much interested in them— said she had never seen such good ones. She has a remarkable eye for detail, and kept me as interested as she was, by the things she picked out in them. I told her about my project and said that when I got it a little further along, I would very much like to show her the reproductions, to see what interested her in the pictures. She agreed to that—quite gladly, I thought—so I do expect to see her again, but certainly not often. She did seem sad, I thought, as Pound told me, and as one would expect.

Since her mother's death she has been working at translating the fables of LaFontaine—it was a good project for her when she couldn't very well settle down to anything else—rather as this one I'm working on is good for me at the moment. She said Auden put her up to it. . . . She had a contract with Reynal and Hitchcock to publish them, and then they disbanded and reorganized, etc., and she was out in the cold. She took them to Macmillan and after six months, when they still hadn't made up their minds, she asked for their return and meanwhile Monroe Engle at Viking had heard about them, and asked to see them. Viking gave her a contract and an advance (she has almost no money, and her brother is paying the rent). She likes Engle very much. I've dealt with him only on the indexing business, but she thinks he is a very intelligent editor. Anyhow, she had sent some of the translations to Ezra and he apparently liked them and urged her to go on. Later she sent some more (after the deal with Viking went through) and he didn't like them. He wrote back that she had to throw out this French syntax—"The proper order of a sentence in English is subject, verb, object," etc. She went to work and did them all over and took them to Engle. He said, "*What* has happened? It seems incredible that there could be as great an improvement as this in two versions done in such a short space of time. What happened to you?" . . . She told me other stories about Pound's help . . .

Here we seem to have got into a discussion of the attack launched by Robert Hillyer in *The Saturday Review of Literature*, not against Pound alone, but against the Bollingen Award jury, C. G. Jung, The Pantheon Press, T. S. Eliot, The New Criticism, and the whole modernist movement in literature.

She also told me that the *Sat. Rev. Lit.* sent her proofs of Hillyer's articles before they came out, and asked for comment, implying that they expected comment agreeing with him, and also implying that the editors agreed. She wrote back and said what she thought, taking the opposite side, though she certainly must have written mildly compared to the way some other people would have done. She wouldn't be in the least violent or insulting—and her letter was not published. . . . Considering that Hillyer launched his attack against the whole modern movement in literature, I can't think what the editors were thinking of, writing to a person like Marianne and expecting her to agree. She has been up to her neck in it all her life, even editor of *The Dial* for years.

Apparently I was mistaken in thinking that Miss Moore had certain reservations about me or my work or my intelligence. Ezra wrote me saying that Marianne was impressed ("!!!"), and before the end of the year I had heard from her that she had taken two steps intended to assist me, although neither of them came to anything. I was astounded to learn that she had suggested me for the Chair of Poetry at the Library of Congress, "but I infer that I was perhaps precipitate!" she said. "I don't expect anything to come of it." She also spoke to Monroe

Wheeler of the Museum of Modern Art about my fresco project, and reported that he was "really excited when I spoke of it, and said he would like to know what it comprises as you work the plan out." I believe that Marianne asked me every time she saw me from then until the end of her life about that project. She seemed to think that it was little short of tragic that I gave it up, and always hoped that some day I would complete the book. It was one that *she* wanted to read.

The project, for as long as it lasted, was not only a stop-gap while I recovered from my disappointment about *Ashe Knoll*, but it has been of great benefit in another way. While my Italian experiences were still fresh in my mind, I was reading intensively about the towns I had visited and the painters whose work I had seen, so that, with life and literature reinforcing one another, both became well-fixed in my mind, a foundation for all subsequent travel in Italy. I collected notes for the whole book, provisionally entitled *A Pagan's Guide to Italian Frescoes*, and wrote two chapters, one on Pisanello, his "St. George" in Verona, and the *condottieri*; the other on Mantegna, the Camera degli Sposi in Mantua, and the Gonzagas. I also wrote a preface and a synopsis. With this much done, I submitted the manuscript to both Diarmuid Russell and Pound. I heard immediately from Ezra, whose comment was: "OK. This seems to be it." Coming from him, I felt, that was "good enough to be inscribed in gold on parchment, especially since he cooked up the idea himself." Diarmuid was even more pessimistic than usual. Illustrations—black and white only—would be absolutely essential, and publishers habitually blenched at the thought of including them because of the extra expense. A publisher would be unlikely to undertake such a book except as a prestige publication, and since my name was virtually unknown and I had no credentials as a scholar there would be no prestige involved. Diarmuid was willing to try—he noted that he had been wrong before—but he seriously doubted that any publisher would offer me a contract, let alone an advance. I had already written to my parents that I would not gamble on this one; too much expense was involved. I turned to other things while Diarmuid circulated the manuscript to the only publishing firms he thought might be willing to consider it. The verdict was that it was not a work that would be of interest to scholars, because it would contain no new, heretofore unpublished material, and the general public was not interested in frescoes. Finis. Ezra kept throwing it up to me that I failed to carry the book to a conclusion, but I was firm. No contract, no book.

Meantime Pound had been up to his old tricks: he had sent a manuscript (not his own) to Cummings for an opinion. He wanted me to pick it up at the Cummingses' and read it, and take it to Marianne. Accordingly, I wrote to them asking when I might call for it, and Marion Cummings telephoned to invite me to tea on Sunday, January 15th. I went, of course, taking the book on the Schifanoia frescoes that Pound had lent me. Cummings was almost a recluse, or at least had that reputation. He never attended literary cocktail parties and seldom made public appearances of any kind. A reading he gave that same winter was a literary event; the place was mobbed, and the crowd (mostly young people, naturally) was enthusiastic. They loved him. He read well, and his personality came across in a quietly dramatic way. Close up, in their rather small living room, he seemed even more magnetic. I liked them both, and thoroughly enjoyed my evening with them; I felt no constraint at all—too little, perhaps, because afterwards I was dismayed to realize that they had kept *me* talking all evening. I had expected to gather pearls, and instead had monopolized the conversation. My excuse is that when they learned I had seen Olga and Mary last spring, and visited Ezra at St. Elizabeth's, they wanted to hear all I could tell them about everybody. As I left, with the manuscript I had ostensibly come for, I explained that the errand was, I felt sure, one of Ezra's subterfuges. "He thinks I don't see enough people, and Marianne doesn't see enough people," I said, "so he arranges for me to pick up a manuscript and deliver it to Marianne. That way I pay two visits and Marianne receives one caller." It was a cold, clear evening, and Cummings had stepped out the door with me as I left. His delighted laugh rang out in the stillness of Patchin Place, and he called after me: "Come again and bring Marianne!" Perhaps I might have done it; the possibility was certainly tantalizing, but my life was about to change. I did not even deliver the manuscript to Miss Moore. The weather was bitter, and I was ill half the time with afflictions of one sort or another, especially sinus infection, and a virus popularly known that year as "the green death." While I delayed, hoping for better weather and better health, Ezra sent another of his correspondents to pick it up and take it to her. Marianne still received one caller, and I also received one, but I was too busy with work for Van Doren and too miserable to be very gracious. I'm afraid I simply gave him the manuscript and sent him packing.

In the last five years I had worked with Carl on five books: *The Autobiographical Writings of Benjamin Franklin, The Letters and Papers of Benjamin Franklin and Richard Jackson, 1753–1785, The Great Rehearsal, The Letters of Benjamin Franklin and Jane Mecom*, and a biography of Jane Mecom. When Carl had questions for me to work on, he mailed them to me on loose-leaf notebook paper, leaving space for my answer below. Sometimes there was only one question at the top of the page; sometimes there were two or three to a page. His queries were informally phrased, and my replies also; the exchange was almost like a recorded conversation. He might begin, for instance: "You're going to love this one!" And after I found that the mother of Franklin's cousin Kezian Coffin was named Mary Barnard, he invariably referred to that controversial female as "your kinswoman Kezian." He was assembling all these pages of questions and answers in a notebook in preparation for the planned revision of the Franklin biography, but time ran out. The notebook went with his other papers to the Princeton University Library.

The biggest job we did together, and the most interesting to me, was the correspondence between Franklin and his sister, Jane Mecom, who lived all her life in Boston. We found that while Franklin's life in Philadelphia, London and Paris had been well-researched, surprisingly little had been done on his Boston background. I had a great deal of sleuthing to do, and I found it fascinating. As soon as the manuscript of that book was ready to go to Princeton University Press, which was publishing it for the American Philosophical Society, Carl began the biography of Jane Mecom, to be published by Viking. He mailed it to me, chapter by chapter, and I mailed the final copy back to him. For a while, he was writing faster than I could type. I finished the typing in the spring of 1950. In early July we were still waiting for page proofs of both books, so that we could do the indexes. I was impatient, because I wanted my usual month at home before summer was over; and then I learned that Carl was in a hospital in Torrington, Connecticut. I knew he had had some trouble with his heart; this was apparently more of the same, but not serious. Then on July 18th one of the Viking Press editors called to tell me of his death. I was not wholly unprepared for the news. Aside from the knowledge of his heart condition, I had been conscious for some time that he had become very forgetful, and that worried me. He called me three or four times to tell me the same thing, and he allowed some shocking errors to creep into his notes on the Jane Mecom correspondence. (When I came to do the index, I found them, and called Princeton, but apparently I was too late; they were not corrected.) I had once remarked in a letter that one of the things I liked about working for Carl was that I never felt I was wasting my time or his. There was no backtracking and doing things over, or digging up of information that was never used. When he began to slip, the slippage was perceptible, to me at least, and I had already been wondering how long my job would go on.

Although I was in a way prepared for the news of Carl's death, it was still a sad blow. I liked him, I liked working for him, and I had no idea where I could find similar work. I made the two indexes when the time came, and then I was unemployed again. The curious thing was that several people, reading of his death, wrote to me later asking whether it made any difference in my job. I told my parents that apparently most people thought of Carl as part of an institution or corporation, not an individual, "and of course some ornery critters like EP would say he was." Pound did in fact imply something of the sort in his letter of condolence, if it could be called that.

To be sure, I had been doing free-lance indexing, and I could probably have gone on with it. I rather like indexing a book I have been working on, but the thought of doing one index after another, all for books I cared nothing about, was blood-curdling; the pay was low, and the pressure under which I worked, with the publisher calling at least once a day to know when I would finish, was tolerable only at fairly long intervals. To make matters worse, I had turned forty at the end of the previous year, and I found when I began to read the classified ads again that all employers were looking for a woman "under forty." Furthermore, although I was no longer without work-experience, all I had (except the social work fifteen years before) was in jobs so unusual that I was unlikely to find another of the same sort. I did a little work on an academic project, poorly paid and frustrating, and had not quite finished it when my health gave way completely.

In the spring, while Diarmuid was circulating the fresco book, I had written a novelette that he thought he could not only place, but get a "solid sum of money" for. It was inspired by my stay at the castle in the Tyrol, had suspense, a romantic setting, everything (it seemed to me) to make it acceptable. Two months after Carl's death Diarmuid gave up on both the novelette and the fresco book, and sent them back to me.

I became more and more depressed, probably because I was already ill, although I did not yet know that there was anything seriously wrong. Many people might say that the illness was caused by the depression, rather than the other way around, but hope usually springs eternal in my breast, and I invariably re-bound with new ideas and new interests so long as my health holds up. This time I did not rebound. In January, when my landlord decided to put in a new boiler during a cold snap, it was the last straw. I thought of moving to a hotel over the week-end, then decided that I might as well go to a hotel in Washington D.C. as in New York. I was confused and low, and I thought that a good shaking-up might help me to put my mind in order. The person most likely to do that for me hap-pened to be in what he referred to as the loony-bin (otherwise "S. Liz"), so to the loony-bin I went. I stayed at the YWCA, which had been highly recommended, instead of a hotel. Doro-thy Pound had moved, and no longer had room for overnight guests.

I just hoped I was arriving on a week-end when it would be convenient for me to visit Pound—when he wasn't having more important visitors he wanted to see alone—and I also considered that he might be ill, but I chanced it. As it turned out the week-end *was* a convenient one, he was well—quite in the pink of condition, I should say—seemed less nervous than before, and more contented—he said if one must exist on this planet at this moment, a bughouse is about as good a place to be as any.

Dorothy Pound was there, of course, and also other visitors on both Saturday and Sunday, none of them people I knew or ever saw again. I took two or three rejected short stories with me, and left them with him on Saturday. The next day he gave them back "and took me apart and scattered the fragments around, which is what I expected and really rather hoped for." Apparently that sentence aroused alarm at home, because I replied to their comments in a later letter: "If Pound thought the organism was too feeble to snap back together and go on with renewed vigor, he wouldn't bother taking it apart."

> I told Pound that I didn't much like the YW—that my father had always told me to stay away from them, and he was right. EP seemed to appreciate that. Next day, Sunday, he presented me as soon as I arrived with the enclosed cartoon from a recent *New Yorker* [I have not found the cartoon] . . . I had a long letter from Paige, partly about Christmas with Basil Bunting . . . I was able to give Pound a little news out of that, but mostly, as he told somebody Sunday, he had been trying to pry news out of me with no success. I said I didn't know why he would expect news from me, and he said he didn't *expect* it, he was only trying, only *attempting*—"the fascination of the difficult, as Yeats says," he went on, and proceeded again to scold me for sitting up on the fifth floor at Minetta St. taking no interest in the world about me and never going to see anybody. I said it was only the second floor, and I heard a good bit that went on, on the stairs. Well, anyhow, he laughed at me a good deal, and he seemed to enjoy that.

Query: did anyone ever manage to take a picture of Pound when he was laughing? He did laugh quite a lot, but I can remember no photographs taken when he was laughing. Usually he directed a gimlet gaze at the camera. The letter I wrote in answer to the next letter from home contained some amplification of the above paragraph:

> Pound's point about my getting out more was that "Miss Jane Austen went to the picture galleries, not to look at the pictures, but to look at the fauna." And "If you want to be the feminine

Flaubert," he said, "you have to study the human animal on the HOOF." Thinking of what I might spin out of my insides, I suppose, he added that the tape-worm school of literature had never interested him.

Of course I was seeing people, but few literary people. My letters are full of character sketches of situations that might have been developed into short stories or novelettes if, as I said earlier, I had been willing to invade the privacy of my friends to that extent.

I think it was on this visit, too, that I demanded to know what it was he had against Florence (Italy). In my itinerary he slashed away at the time I had planned to spend in Florence. In his letters about the fresco book he continually fulminated against Florence. Of course I knew that the Medici were bankers, and bankers were anathema, but I felt there must be something more. When I asked him, he reared up out of his chair, and exclaimed: "There's no place to SIT DOWN." Well, it's true. I had to grant him that.

A day or two after I returned to New York I came down with the Bug-of-the-Year. My friends assured me that it would hang on for at least a week, but after almost a month I had still not recovered. In late February I entered Lenox Hill Hospital for a long stay. I weighed in at 105 pounds.

4

After my trip to Italy in 1949, I had made no move to go out to Rutherford; I did not want to talk about Olga and Mary and their affairs, and I was afraid I would be pumped. In October of 1950 I heard from Bill that he was about to head west. After telling me that he was to speak at Reed, he said:

> I've had a disturbed year over some differences of opinion with my old pal Laughlin but, finally, we have come to an understanding. He will do my verse and Random House the prose—at least this will hold until 1952 when I shall be on the brink of my 70th year, perhaps.
>
> After that I'm a free man!$&(★) or whatever. Dregs.

This was followed by a postcard from Portland showing a picture of Mt. Hood and telling me that he was very enthusiastic about Reed. According to his *Autobiography* it was at Reed that Bill finally learned to relax and stop fighting his audience. Three fledgling poets were among the students then—Gary Snyder, Philip Whalen, and Lew Welch. He is said to have sat up all night talking with them. I should like to have heard about that visit, but before I had a chance to see him again, I was in Lenox Hill Hospital. He was giving a reading in New York that I had planned to attend, and, being unable to go, I asked a friend to speak to Bill afterwards and explain why I was absent. Immediately I received a very sympathetic letter written on St. Patrick's Day.

> Dear Mary,
> You're always in the backs of our minds, year in year out. That's a hell of a place to be. Now it's the hospital. I'm just in the process of writing of the "City of the Hospital" in my autobiography. We've been to Portland. And still we don't see you. I don't know why. I wish you'd been at the New School the other evening. The young lady who spoke of you to me was very appealing. I was attracted to her. She said you were ill but didn't go into details that I remember. I know it's a good hospital, I hope you'll do well.
> Floss sends her love. When you're out again you must come out here for a little rest. We'll speak of that later.

He went on to tell me of the difficulties he was having with the autobiography:

> . . . I've been in hot water from the start. The result is that I feel at this later moment, all tightened up, obsessed with the thought that what I'm putting down is both empty and dull, dull as all hell. A failure, in short. It stinks. (I don't quite believe this but fear that it may be true.)

He closed the letter with the surprising news that he had developed an admiration for Auden's work:

> Yesterday, having been invited by him at the Patchen reading, to have tea or luncheon with him I had a nice visit with Auden at his room 7 Cornelia Street in New York. He's on his

way to India for a "conference" of some sort. I have been much impressed by his recent book of poems *Nones* published by Random House, a very good piece of work very different from anything I could do but outstanding as skill and, I'm happy to say, as feeling. A definite development in Auden's attitude to the world, adult, warm. Would you like to see the book? Drop me a card, I'll have it sent to you.

Must cut this short. Love from us both.

Bill

This was followed by a second letter written six days later. It began:

Happy Easter! (Happy hell, sez you) Can you be used? Could you run over a script and give an opinion on it? I ask you, that's all. Or wd it be too disturbing to you. I wuz just thinking, mebbe, when the autobiog reaches a certain stage you might like to spill some spleen on it, might relieve you. . . .

Bill did not send the manuscript of the autobiography, and no doubt that was just as well, because it is a book I wish he had not written. At least, if he had to write it, he ought not to have written it to order and under pressure. If I had read it in manuscript I should certainly have called him on all those references to "poor old" So-and-so (Charlie, Bob, or whoever)—and threatened to pay him back if and whenever I wrote my own autobiography by sprinkling it with "poor old Bills." I don't know what else I could have said except that I might have corrected his confused geography of Oregon state. Also, I might have disillusioned him about those American grapes, whose root-stock grafted on that of the European varieties, saved the vineyards of the Old World from destruction. My understanding is that the reason the American grapes were immune to the blight that was killing French and German grapes was that the blight itself was American in origin, therefore the European grapes had no immunity to it. If Bill could have been persuaded to believe that a blight had spread from America to Europe (which I doubt), it would have made him very unhappy.

5

When I shakily emerged from Lenox Hill Hospital, I spent one month convalescing in the care of a long-suffering friend, and then traveled home only to come down as soon as I arrived with a prime case of serum hepatitis. I was soon in a Vancouver hospital, hooked up to a glucose bottle. This time I was really deathly ill, and my doctor became exceedingly cautious. I suppose it must have been sometime in June that I reported to him by telephone and heard him say: "That's fine. Stay in bed another month."

He had been saying, "Stay in bed another week," and I had been patient. When he said, "Stay in bed another month," I protested vehemently, but he remained firm. I went back to bed and thought things over. I could see that it would be not just one month, but many months, before I would be able to live a normal life again. (I was quite right about that; when I was permitted to sit up, it was for fifteen minutes a day for one month, and half an hour a day for the next month.) I felt that I must do something to make this catastrophe *pay*, to move it somehow from the loss column to the profit column, to make it turn out to be, like all the disasters in English history since 1066 and all that, "A Good Thing." I wanted to feel, when at last I was able to be active again, that I had accomplished something; the way to bring about that result, I thought, was to do something I would *not* have done if I had been on my feet. At the same time, it had to be something I could do comfortably while propped on pillows. There are other ways of dealing with a stone wall besides trying to climb over it or bash a hole in it or dig a tunnel under it. One can follow it to find out where it leads. Mine led me to Greek. I finally remembered that I had thought and said repeatedly that if I ever had time I would like to take up my Greek again. During my summer vacations at home I had occasionally taken my Homer out into the garden and read a bit, but the tools were definitely rusty. This was my chance to do something about it.

Once I had my answer, I went to work immediately. Since I had two beginner's grammars in the house, I began by working my way through both of them. I then read twelve books of the *Iliad*, but because I was unable at that time to get the text of the last twelve books, I switched to the *Odyssey*, which happened to be available, and read twelve books of that. If you have to be in bed for weeks at a time, there is nobody better to be in bed with than Homer—in the original. I wrote to the Paiges, who were still in Rapallo, told them about my illness, and mentioned that I was reading Greek. They sent me in return a copy of Quasimodo's little volume *Lirici Greci*, containing poems by Sappho and other Greek lyricists in the original, with Italian translations. In order to explain what that little book meant to me, I must say something about the problems of translation.

In the first place it should be said that the perfect translator of poetry would presumably be someone who was completely bi-lingual, having grown up speaking both languages *in* the countries to which they belong, one who was equally well-read in the literature of both languages, a contemporary of the poet to be translated and a poet of genius in his own right. If he were temperamentally akin to the original poet, that would be a help, too. Whether there have ever been any such translators is doubtful, but obviously there has been no such translator of ancient Greek since Roman times. The translator who does not speak the original language like a native is willy-nilly dependent upon lexicons and cribs, which are, in the case of ancient Greek, compiled and composed by classical scholars, usually late-Victorians. They often erect another barrier, as T. S. Eliot said of Gilbert Murray's translations, between the reader and the original text. I had tried to read Sappho in the original, but I needed a crib, or notes, or a lexicon, and my efforts only left me wondering what all the fuss was about. The first thing Quasimodo's translations did for me was show me the text through the medium of a language that was not English, living or dead, leaving my mind free to balance between the Greek phrase and the Italian phrase while I searched for the truly equivalent phrase in living, not lexicon English. This little book removed one of the chief obstacles to translation, so far as I was concerned, by showing me how to use a third language as a bridge.

In addition, I found the Italian translations very beautiful and wanted to match them, if I could, in my own language. Most important of all, however, I found here in Sappho's Greek, as revealed to me now through the medium of the Italian, the style I had been groping toward, or perhaps merely hungering for, when I ceased to write poetry a number of years before. It was spare but musical, and had, besides, the sound of the speaking voice making a simple but emotionally loaded statement. It is never "tinkling" as Bill Williams's friend A. P. characterized it. Neither is it "strident" as Rexroth described it. It is resonant although unmistakably in the female register.

Hesitantly, I tried to put a few of the fragments and one of the longer poems into English. I sent some of them off to Pound, whose reply was: "Yuz—vurry nize—only grump iz yu didn't git to it 20 years ago."

This was followed by a typewritten letter that accompanied my manuscripts, which he now returned.

> AN ADVANCE, so far aZi kno on earlier trans/ of S/ BUTTT
> yu mix two languages, the LIVE
>   as in first line/
> and the dead / on delicate neck by me.
> Waal gorrdammit / what is the time lag / 25 years / but better now than never. / no, time lag 16 years. not bad for murka.
>
> Now as fer the sittin-on-the-tree bird, that wd/ be german order.
>
> Can't perfect simply by deleting useless words and words NOT in the speech of line 1.
>
> BUT there are other good lines. Job not wholly wasted by any means. The circled words can't simply be cut out
>
> merely energy gets lost.

In a postscript he added:

> THE JOB of the writer of verse is to get the LIVE language AND the prosody simultaneously. Prosody : articulation of the total sound of a poem (not bits of certain shapes gummed together.)

A marginal note on the manuscript said:

> crit cannnotttt consist in mere

excision. ergo this is NOT definite
  some stickum and/ or stitches must replace jaboutz

Obviously, although I knew what I was after, I was not yet achieving the effect I wanted. I kept on revising and after Christmas sent him new versions. I give the reply in full:

        *Frankly I
Yes, it* is better. That is to say, my first impression is that it is better.

          NOTE that what grampaw canNOTTT do is come out of wherever, AND concentrate on anything tother whatsoDAM.

I can STILL see rewrite / I do NOT spose yu want ME to rewrite it.

it is now more homegene / it is purrhapz a bit lax /
whether one emend that occurs wd/ lax it still more ???
it still reads a bit like a translation /

what is the maximum abruptness you can get it TO ?
Fordie: "40 ways to say anything"

          I spose real exercise would consist in trying them ALL.

for wot good it did / old Sternberg made Antheil do a fugue a week for a year, *on the SAME theme.* One fug/ NO exercise.

52 on *SAME* theme : some training.

Cleis: bout time "fair" was ousted fr/ poetik jarg/
utility of syntax ? waaal the chink does without a damLot

I kept on trying. Eventually I think most of the fragments and each stanza of the longer poems did go through about forty versions. The fragments, especially, were great pillow-work. I could lie there rolling them around and around in my mind, trying different words and different arrangements of words, asking myself over and over: what did she *mean*? why did she say gold *sandals*? is she speaking or is someone else speaking? why would peace be difficult to endure? When I sat up for my allotted hour or two, I typed the versions I had been trying in my head; usually the fragment went through many more typed revisions; often I would work in one direction, then backtrack and start off in another. If I had been leading an active life, I would never have had the patience to work so long over each fragment, or if I had, the job would have taken me ten years. As it was, I worked for a year or more on the one hundred poems and fragments, although the last things I did came more easily.

I made no attempt to translate into the original meter. Greek normally has more syllables than English. I have never been able to see any way of rendering a Greek stanza in the equivalent number of English syllables without padding. The padding may take several forms: the embroidering of an image, repetition, or the introduction of unnecessary words ("I really believe"), all of which contribute to make the poem lax, to use Pound's word for the effect. One may also use a great many words of Latin derivation, or follow the Greek syntax slavishly; either of these dodges might work for Pindar—I don't know Pindar well enough to form an opinion, but they are out of place in translations of Homer and Sappho. Underlying the stanzaic form there is, I swear (in the teeth of those who have said otherwise) a cadence that belongs to the speaking voice. That underlying cadence is what I tried to find an equivalent for, because, so far as I knew, no English translation had yet conveyed it.

6

In the fall of 1951, while I was still half in, half out of bed, I wrote to Williams again and received a reply dated October 26th. He had also been ill. The letter began:

Dear Mary,
    So you're getting fat! I remember that crossing of the Columbia (was it the Columbia?) river south of Vancouver and just before we got to Portland. The train was held up by the open bridge. There we were, some lumber mill of enormous proportions stretching off to the west and I wondering where your old man might live, he liked White Mule I remember and so I thought of him. Now you're back home—and one of the holly berries you inadvertently sent us one year has sprouted and the resulting seedling is ten inches high in our yard. I hope it continues to survive . . .

I hope you're as well as your gain in weight indicates. I've been ill too, as you may have heard, had a "stroke" on March 28th, not a bad one but—it reminds me of something one of my boys told me: he served on a "tincan" on Atlantic patrol. The hull was made of ¼ in metal so that when a fish of any size hit it you could distinctly hear the thud next to your ear as you lay in your bunk at night. A mild stroke is like that.

Keep writing. That's the only hope there is for any of us, poor scriveners that we are. We're a sad lot even the best of us with our silly hopes and sillier disappointments . . .

Bill's description of the DuBois–Matlack mill as "a lumber mill of enormous proportions" caused much merriment around the lunch table. The next letter I had from him was written in December of 1952, after I had returned to New York. This was a thank-you for a privately printed pamphlet of my poems.

While I was working on the Sappho, I had begun to write a few poems of my own again. This, in turn, set me to thinking of the uncollected poems I had written since 1940. For several reasons I wanted to collect about a dozen, published and unpublished, in a pamphlet. Lloyd Reynolds, who had recently organized a Graphic Arts department in an attic at Reed College, made *A Few Poems* possible. A printer friend of mine hand-set most of the type, and he and Lloyd ran off three hundred copies. I paid for the paper, the printing was done out of friendship alone, and I bound the booklets myself. I sold a few copies, but sent none out for review. I wanted them to give to my friends, especially to one friend, and to new acquaintances who asked where they could find some of my poetry. The New Directions volume had been remaindered years ago.

When I returned to New York in November of 1952 I had an added thirty-five pounds of flesh on my bones, a half-finished translation of Sappho's poems, and my little pamphlet that I called *A Few Poems* (there were twelve of them). I hoped that perhaps the pamphlet would help me to get a larger collection of my poetry published, not as a section in an anthology, and not in a pamphlet, but in a real book, all my own. For that, as it turned out, I had to wait until 1979, when Breitenbush published my *Collected Poems*.

Of course I sent a copy of the pamphlet to Williams, who had suffered a more serious stroke in August of 1952. His answering letter showed the effects of the stroke in its typography and its quavery signature, but also showed that he could be as enthusiastic as ever about new work by his friends. This letter was written on New Year's Eve.

Dear Mary,

When I think of what you have been through and survived it gives me courage. Nuff said.

These poems in A FEW POEMS are distinguished, by far the best you have ever done. I was thrilled at the reading of them. I am sure that they will be remembered. They have a profundity of feeling which reaches the heart. I am impressed and rewarded.

It is all there; the new is all there. I have only this to say. Not yet has it been recognized for what it is: a recognition that what we have been about for all these years is a change from, away from, accented verse to a verse that takes as its unit elapsed time. When this is recognized, all the experiments in free verse, such beautiful verses as your present ones with their regularity, will be recognized for what they are: a new way of measuring verse according to the expanded requirements of the age.

But we require, what free verse has never had, regularity. Without a means of MEASURING THE MEASURE, we are lost. I have found one means of measuring the measure which may not be satisfactory to you but which if worked with can serve; see the recent issue of POETRY, it contains food for thought—at least so I think.

WITH MY LEFT HAND (I didn't mean to italicize this), this is the best I can do.

Happy New Year!

Love. And from Floss as well.

Bill

The importance of elapsed time, rather than stress, was of course what Pound had been dinning into my ears in the Thirties. I had worked then, and was working now in my Sappho translations with the principle of a balanced line that I had found in the Laurencie and Lavignac volume recommended (and sent to me) by Pound at that time. I once tried to talk to Williams about this line with its variable feet that nevertheless balance one another, but got nowhere. My impression was that the mere fact that my balanced line was related to Greek metric turned him against it. He was determined that Greek rhythms were as alien to American speech patterns as the well-worn English version of iambic pentameter. I agreed with him about iambic pentameter, and I knew that Dr. Rouse had believed that the Anglicization of Greek metrical patterns using both stress and quantity was impossible, but I was still convinced that Greek cadences were not so alien as Bill thought. I had once heard a dining car waiter chanting in perfectly recognizable dactylic hexameter:

> Luncheon is now bein' served / in the dining car five cars
>   forward.
>
> Please take your seat checks with you!

I could not quite make out what Bill was after any more than he could understand what I was doing. We went our separate ways. At any rate, it was a satisfaction that for once he found my poems not wanting in emotional intensity.

Chapter 8

AFTER MY return to New York in November of 1952, I ceased to look for work, freelance or otherwise. I also ceased to write with an idea lurking in the back of my mind that what I was writing might bring in money. I was no longer thinking even in terms of my future career as a writer. The change in my perspective derived in part from the fact that I had passed my fortieth birthday, in part from the long illness. The paramount consideration became the question of how I wanted to spend my time *now*. More money would have been nice to have, and in our society it can be difficult to hold up one's head when one is neither gainfully employed nor publishing regularly, but economic necessity had been removed. If Carl Van Doren had lived, I should probably have gone on working for him, but I could see no reason to waste my time hunting for or doing low-paid literary hack-work. Also, I was no longer going to waste my time writing fiction that nobody wanted.

During the first winter I finished the Sappho translation and did research for my introduction, which became a Footnote when the publishers asked Dudley Fitts to write an introduction. My research led me into a merry maze from which I extricated myself, eventually, more than ten years later. By the summer of 1953, however, I had managed to pull the introduction together and finish the translation. Before I left for Europe in August I delivered the manuscript to Diarmuid Russell, who agreed to handle it for me, much against his better judgment, I am sure. I then sailed for Plymouth on my way to Greece via London, Paris, Brunnenburg and Venice. I remained in Greece through the winter, returned to southern Italy and Sicily, traveled up the Italian Peninsula and back to Paris via Dordogne (so as to visit Lascaux, which had not yet been closed to the public), and sailed for home from England in June of 1954.

By the time I returned to New York I knew that Diarmuid was giving up on the Sappho translation. In Greece I had had a letter from him saying that Viking had turned it back because "while it seemed well done, there just wasn't a chance of any sale whatsoever." He had talked to other trade publishers who told him not to send it, or looked at it in his office and said: impossible. He then tried two small presses, Grove and Noonday. The only nibble came from Grove; they said they might at some later date want to bring it out, but they would have to do it in a limited edition. I was willing to consider that solution only if all else failed. What I really wanted was a paperback. The quality paperbacks that were beginning to appear seemed to me an ideal form for my translation. Anchor Books, especially, was bringing out attractive paperbacks, some of them translations. After Diarmuid had returned my manuscript, Harvey Shapiro told me that he was sure Anchor Books would be interested. They were even *commissioning* translations from the classics. At my request, he wrote a letter commending my manuscript to the attention of Nathan Glazer, who was then editor at Anchor Books, and I took the manuscript around to them. It was the usual story. They liked the poems, or so they said, but Sappho would never sell.

Next I tried to publish a sizable collection of the poems in a periodical. Reading over my letters, I have been surprised that so many people were trying to help me get the translation into print. Richard Eberhart sent a selection to *New World Writing*, but they reported after six months and quite a bit of prodding that they had no room for it. Douglass Paige, now in New York, spoke to Ted Weiss about it, but he said *The Quarterly Review of Literature* had recently published a Sappho translation and could not do two. I even tried, through another intermediary, to get them into *Mademoiselle*. Several people assured me that Meridian would be interested, but the publisher, I learned, had told someone else that he wanted *no* poetry.

It seemed to me that one of the obstacles to publication was that too few people were qualified to judge the poems both as poetry and as translation. Only Greek scholars would know what I had done with the Greek, and Greek scholars as a rule were hostile to modern poetry, like that famous Greek scholar, Edith Hamilton. I needed to find one whose taste in verse embraced the post-Tennysonian mode.

Among the people Pound sent around to Minetta Street was John Edwards, one of the editors of the *Annotated Index to the Cantos* soon to be published by the University of California Press. In November of 1955 he stopped over in New York on his way home from Europe, took me out to dinner and asked what I had been doing. I told him about the project I was currently working on, and mentioned that I was feeling despondent about the Sappho. John was at that time teaching at the University of California, and he proposed that I let him take the manuscript back to Berkeley with him. He would show it to his friend, Dr. Peachy of the Classics Department; if Peachy liked it, he might recommend it to the Press. This seemed a wonderful idea; I had no real hope that California would publish the book, but I wanted to know Frederic Peachy's opinion of my work. I knew that he had identified and translated all the classical quotations in the *Cantos* for the *Annotated Index*, which would indicate that his taste in poetry was, to say the least, not stuffy. The next day I left a selection of the poems at John's hotel. In due time I heard from him that the manuscript had been delivered to Frederic Peachy and another member of the Classics Department. On December 8 John wrote me that their response was all we had hoped for; the letter concluded: "Congratulations on arousing such energy, shaking the dust off academic shelves and revealing depths of emotion I had not suspected in my colleagues." I quickly forwarded the rest of the manuscript, and received another report from John, saying that before the poems went to the Press, one of the Classics professors would write to me concerning certain changes he would like me to consider.

Patience is the watchword when dealing with any publisher, as I had learned long ago, and when publishers and professors are both involved, one needs patience doubled and redoubled. By May of 1956 I had heard nothing from either the professor or the Press. I wrote to John and asked what had happened, if anything. He investigated and found that the manuscript was still on the desk of the professor who still wanted to make those notes on changes to be considered. In October John wrote saying that he had at last removed the manuscript from the Classics Department, apparently by main force, and would submit it to the Press himself, within the hour. In January of 1957, over a year after John had carried the translation out to Berkeley, I heard from the Press at last; and after several months of negotiation and revision (of the Introduction rather than the poems), I was offered a contract.

I was delighted that the Press proposed to do the book as a quality paperback in the new series they had just launched. It finally appeared in February of 1958, five years after it started its rounds. Now, almost twenty-five years after publication, it is still in print, and, I am happy to say, currently ninth on California's list of best-selling paperbacks. Typically, the trade publishers decided, once my *Sappho* had appeared and started selling, that what they needed on their lists was a Sappho translation; imitations began to appear on all sides, one of them published by Anchor Books.

Of course I sent copies of the published translation to both Pound and Williams as soon as it appeared. The contrast between the two poets as mentors is nowhere better illustrated than in their letters responding to my little book.

In the spring of 1953, when I was completing the manuscript, I had sent Bill some copies of the fragments. Certain that he would like them, I waited in happy anticipation of an enthusiastic response, but I received instead a brief note dated June 3, 1953, in which he mentioned that he had had a stroke involving his "right hand, speech, and eyes—a little." In conclusion he said only, "Congratulations on what you evidently feel is a magnum opus." To say that I was disconcerted is an understatement. I have only recently discovered that my manuscript must have reached him as he was emerging from the darkest period of his life. Following a serious stroke the previous August, he had been involved in a maddening hassle with the Library of Congress over his appointment there as Consultant in Poetry, an appointment withdrawn not because of his health, but on grounds that he had both fascist and communist sympathies, the first because he had studied medicine in Germany before World War I, and was a friend of Ezra Pound; the second because he had published in *Partisan Review* and *New Masses*, and signed petitions circulated by left-wing organizations. Like the rumpus over Pound's Bollingen Award, this whole affair, which was both appalling and ridiculous, was set in motion by conservative poets who hated modernism in literature worse than they hated any political -ism whatever.

The emotional tension he suffered from at this time was followed by a severe depression for which he was hospitalized. I had been out of touch, and knew nothing of any of this. At the time, I was acutely disappointed by his reply, but I can now see that the amazing thing is the fact that he answered at all, typing the little note with his left hand and concluding with the usual invitation to come and see them when I could. By the time the *Sappho* was published, however, Williams himself had struggled to translate one of her poems and was ready to respond with all his old enthusiasm. His letters about the book are a little incoherent, filled with the strange Williams mystique about women, and rapturous about the fragments: ". . . sometimes their brilliance fills the air about them with an answering brilliance which justifies everything you have done. What an example they are, in exactly the way you have handled them, for all subsequent poets." A check was enclosed in one of the letters with a request for four more copies of the book, which he called "one of the most remarkable and informative and most satisfying and most beautiful books I have ever read—and at the same time the saddest when you think how much of Sappho we have lost."

In contrast, Ezra's response which was dated March 3, six weeks before his release from St. Elizabeth's, began abruptly:

> It is now to be pointed out that there is no decent translation of Callimachus "Delos" or of the old bogie Bion "Adonis" / both of which give something to get one's teeth into and a sustained body of verse, that needs an idiom AND a swing etc.

In other words, no pat on the head, no pat on the back, certainly no raptures, just a crack of the whip!

But as Marianne Moore had said twenty-five years earlier, "One's reward is not praise. . . ." Especially not when it gushed forth as easily and indiscriminately as it did in Bill's case. Ezra's brusque admonition to get on with it, although momentarily frustrating, probably meant more to me in the end. As for other rewards, the steady dribble of money from royalties is a meager reward for so much hard work, even after twenty-five years. Then why do we do it? Mainly, I suppose, because we are driven; if the reward is not in the doing, we are likely to go without payment. But every time someone says to me, "Thank you for the *Sappho*," as though I had conferred a personal gift, there surely is a bonus.

2

About the time the Sappho manuscript was accepted I moved back to Vancouver. Although I had been feeling better than ever before in my life, thanks to added weight and the discovery of anti-histamines, trouble developed in another quarter. I discovered soon after my return from Greece that cataracts were forming on both eyes. I have no idea why I should have developed cataracts in my early forties, or why they thickened so rapidly, but by 1957 I could no longer read the sign on a bus until it stopped in front of me. I had had enough of New York hospitals. My ophthalmologist was in Portland, and I preferred to have the surgery done there. Much as I hated to do it, I decided to pull up stakes and move home. My parents were in their mid-seventies, and it seemed probable that they would be needing me before long. In the early summer I gave up my apartment, sold my furniture, and moved back to the West Coast. I still had every intention of returning to New York when my parents no longer needed me, but, as it turned out, twenty years elapsed before I was free to return, and by that time I had no desire to do so. In the first place, New York had changed; my friends were either leaving the city or talking of leaving. In the second place, Vancouver had changed; it had become a small city with a community college and a much more cosmopolitan outlook. In the Twenties I knew no more than three or four people who had ever set foot in Europe, or in New York for that matter; "Back East" was Iowa, Michigan or even Utah. In the late Seventies, my neighbors were coming and going from Tokyo and Katmandu, Egypt and the Balkans, as they once went to San Francisco or Seattle. And I had enough money to travel if I wanted. Even more important, I had changed. I was now twenty years older. A life that seems deadly at twenty-eight or even forty-eight can seem delightfully peaceful at sixty-eight.

In 1957, however, I was far from happy about the move. Having made up my mind that the time had come, I simply gritted my teeth and carried it through, bringing home with me a much re-worked manuscript. During the years when I was trying to get the Sappho translation published, I had been working hard on my next book, *The Mythmakers*. The poems of Sappho had raised questions in my mind concerning her religion. If, as it appeared, she was a priestess of Aphrodite, I felt that I should explain something about her cult in the essay that ultimately became a Footnote to my translation. Accordingly, I looked in the obvious source books on Greek mythology and religion. Now one can believe almost anything about some abstraction called "primitive man," but Sappho to me was no abstraction, and certainly not "primitive man." She was a civilized, sophisticated woman, and furthermore the poems themselves had given me certain ideas about the cult—its probable origin in Crete, the importance of the moon, the possible use of a drug in its ceremonies—but everything I read contradicted my conclusions. I kept on reading, becoming more and more determined to do something to correct the picture. I worked some of my ideas into my Footnote, but the Press asked me to remove that part of the essay, and I obliged. By that time, I was deep in my maze. While I was in Greece I was carrying on my investigations. Because this kind of research was new to me, I went off the rails from time to time and had to make a new start. I drafted a few chapters and showed them to Rex Arragon, who said simply: "You can't do this, you know. You are writing for the experts, and the experts won't read you because they won't believe you have anything to tell them. You have got to put your material into a form that will appeal to a literary audience." I argued, but eventually made a new start, the first of several.

I should make clear, however, that while I knew that the anthropologists would consider me an interloper trespassing on their territory, I thought that I had a better right to the territory than they had. Whatever a myth is, it was not put together originally by anthropologists, but by a poet, or poet-priest, or priest-scenarist, and it seemed to me that the anthropologists had very little understanding of the way poets make use of the world around them, very little understanding of metaphors and their function. As for those schools of mythology that reach into the unconscious mind of a man who died during the Ice Age, in order to formulate a system of mythology, I could not see how anyone could fall for it. What was worse, the findings of this school were being expanded to form a system of literary criticism. I knew that writing a book whose argument ran counter to the teachings of Freud, Frazer, Jung, and Lévi-Strauss was probably a futile exercise, but so much of my writing had fallen into that category that I hardly gave it a thought.

The move to Vancouver, by putting me out of reach of the New York Public Library, forced me to concentrate, willy-nilly, more on writing and less on research. However, I was loathe to conclude the research, and the initial adjustment to life at home was difficult. When Radcliffe announced its new fellowships for women who were doing scholarly or creative work, but were not associated with any academic institution, I thought I saw a possible solution to several of my problems. If I could only have one of those fellowships, I should have access to one of the finest university libraries, I should be better able to approach some of the people I needed to consult, and I should have a feather in my cap, or at least a badge to wear on my lapel when the time came to look for a publisher. Lining up my references carefully, I applied, but was turned down. From that time forward, research was for the most part limited to a few weeks in New York each year and one ten-day stay in Berkeley where I worked at the University of California Library.

In the case of *The Mythmakers* my greatest difficulty lay not in the attempt to publish, as it turned out, but in finding someone to talk to in one or another of the fields I was invading as an outsider and an amateur. Archaeoastronomy and ethnoastronomy are hardly respectable even now. Twenty to twenty-five years ago anyone who dared mention astronomy in connection with mythology was asking for either a snub or a sneer. One astronomer told me that *no* astronomer was interested in ancient astronomy. One anthropologist told me that we did not know and could not know the origin of any myth. This seemed to me a circular definition; if it is a myth, we cannot know its origin; if we know its origin, it is not a myth.

Finally I wrote two letters that paid off. I wrote as I had written to Pound, quite out of the blue, and presented my case. One letter went to Maud W. Makemson, an astronomer teaching at Vassar College, who had published a book on Polynesian astronomy. The other went to R. Gordon Wasson, the Wall Street banker whose publications on the hallucinogenic mushrooms of Mexico supported some of my hypotheses. I chose well. They were both most helpful. They not only discussed my problems with me by the hour, on several occasions, but both read, not just one version of the manuscript, but two or three, including the final version.

I discarded several beginnings and two almost book-length manuscripts. Finally, when I thought I was on the right track at last, and had the book about one-third to one-half completed, I lost my only copy at the Portland Airport. This may sound incredible; the explanation of how I happened to have only one copy, how I happened to have it at the Airport, and the rest of it, is too complicated to go into here. The manuscript was in a manila envelope, plainly labeled with my name and address. Why do people who find envelopes full of typescript put them into the rubbish bin instead of taking them to the Lost and

Found? I shall never understand. I knew I could not rewrite the book; I should have to take a whole new approach. This time I organized the material into separate essays on different themes in the hope that some of them might be published individually in periodicals, as actually happened. Diarmuid sold two of the essays to *American Scholar*, and the editor's interest in them led to the eventual sale of the book to Ohio University Press. With time out for cataract surgery and three more trips to Europe, I spent about ten years on *The Mythmakers*, which was published in 1966. There is not one word in it about Sappho, but it was she who beckoned me into the maze.

The Mythmakers was the last manuscript that Diarmuid Russell handled for me. In October of 1972 I received word that he was in a Westchester hospital; a lung tumor had been diagnosed, malignant and inoperable. I had only one more communication from him, a form letter saying that the agency had been sold. His death followed soon after.

In the Introduction to her *Collected Stories*, Eudora Welty says: "Diarmuid Russell's integrity was a clear stream proceeding undeflected and without a ripple on its own way through the fields of publishing. On his quick perception, his acute and steady judgment in regard to my own work, as well as on his friendship, I relied without reservation." His belief in her was justified. His faith in me was one of the things that kept me going when the rejections piled up; but the reader may ask, was that a good thing? In the end, what did all my effort amount to? For that matter, what did his amount to? He failed to place my Sappho translation, which has been my most successful publication, and I fizzled out as a writer of fiction in a very few years. His pessimism concerning possible publication for *The Mythmakers* turned out to be mistaken. It has not been a best-seller in anybody's terms, but it is in its second printing as a hardcover book, and a paperback edition was issued in 1979. The important thing is that, despite his pessimism, he was willing to handle it, and did succeed in finding a publisher for it when I should almost certainly have failed. He told me one time that while some agents refused to take on any author who had not proved his ability to make money from his writing, he (Diarmuid) would read anything brought to him, even by someone who walked in off the street. He would not handle the work unless he liked it himself, but so far as he was concerned, the fun was in gambling on unknowns whose work he did like. He gambled on me and lost, but his faith in my potential persisted. One of the last times I saw him, he said to me, "Some day, Mary, you are going to do something—I don't know what it will be, but *something*—that will have the publishers dancing around you and bringing you your breakfast in bed!" That will be the day.

3

During the first decade following my return to Vancouver I visited New York every year, sometimes on my way to or from Europe, other years for a stay of one or two months. I found that I could get a single room with bath and kitchenette at the Roger Williams Hotel for as little as thirty-five dollars a week. There were no frills, but it was decent, and I liked the location because it was within walking distance of the New York Public Library, where I continued to spend much of my time until *The Mythmakers* was finally published. During these weeks in New York I made up for lost time, seeing as many people as possible.

I saw Williams for the last time in the summer of 1959, when I was on my way home from Europe. The weather was at once hot and wet, steamy and clammy; I had a bad summer cold; Bill was pathetically frail, and had trouble finding the words he wanted. Nevertheless, I felt that we had a rather satisfactory little visit, although it was overshadowed, on my part at least, by nostalgia and a strong presentiment that this would be our last meeting, as it proved to be. When I left, he presented me with a shakily signed copy of *Yes, Mrs. Williams*, just off the press. He had told me years before that he hoped to live long enough to write that book.

In December of that year I had a fifth letter from Bill about the *Sappho*. An adverse review that had appeared in *Poetry* caused an outburst that began:

> The son of a bitch is the only epithet I can apply to the
> individual who wrote the review of your Sappho that appeared

in the current *Poetry*. Nothing so unfair has greeted my eyes since I have become a reader. It hasn't a word of truth connected with it either in the spirit of its presentation or the details of it.

This was in December of 1959. The last letter I had from him, concerning one of his own poems in *Poetry*, was written four months later, three years before his death.

I paid my last visit to Rutherford in November of 1965, when I went out to see Flossie. I rather expected to find her sad and perhaps apathetic, but on the contrary, "Flossie seems to be leading quite a busy life, and doing very well. She gave me a nice lunch—chicken broth, crab salad, applesauce and cookies. She did most of the talking, partly because she had more to talk about, partly because she had difficulty understanding me sometimes." She seemed on the whole more cordial than when Bill was alive.

Although Flossie was always gracious, always hospitable, I felt in her a certain reserve which I attributed at least in part to the fact that I had entered their lives as a protégée of Pound, whom she loathed. There could have been other reasons; all the New York poets traipsing over to Rutherford and dining at the doctor's table helped to keep him amused, but were in a sense intruders whom she regarded with varying degrees of disfavor. I am sure I ranked above Joe Gould, who used to descend on 9 Ridge Road now and then. "He tells me all the gossip, and I give him five dollars," said Bill with a chuckle. "What the hell!" Flossie looked as though she had caught a whiff of a very bad smell, snorted, and muttered epithets like "deadbeat," and "dirty bum." I could not possibly repay all their kindness, but I did try to make up a little of my debt with boxes of English holly from our own tree sent at Christmas time, or Medford pears. Despite that slight reserve, Flossie was a well-nigh perfect hostess except in one respect. She made the worst cocktails I ever tried to drink. They were notorious, and I always suspected that she did it on purpose to discourage drinking. I doubt whether anyone ever accepted a second.

When I went out to see Flossie after Bill's death, "young Bill" came in from his office to speak to us, and I nearly jumped out of my skin. He looked so much like his father as *he* was when I first met him, that I could hardly believe my eyes. I performed a rapid calculation, and realized with a sinking heart that this "young" man, as I thought of him, must be almost exactly the same age as that "old" man, his father, had been in 1936. I could not believe it had been so long.

Recently a symposium on Pound and Williams was held at the University of Pennsylvania. I have no idea what was said there, but I feel impelled to set down a few remarks on my own view of their relationship, at the risk of repeating what someone else has said better—at the risk, too, of being totally wrong.

No doubt Pound's name cropped up in Bill's conversations with me more often than it would have if I had not written to him in the first place at Pound's suggestion. As it was, he was constantly referring to Ezra, and almost always in order to emphasize their differences. At the party in Brooklyn, he announced that he had decided Ezra Pound was wrong: "One should publish everything—*everything.*" When he read his poems to us the first time I went to Rutherford, he explained that he tried to read in a manner as unlike Pound as possible. The stand he took on the side of American culture as opposed to European seemed to me suspiciously like an extension of the same theme. It was not only that he was first-generation American on both sides (as was Flossie), but he had spent a year or two of his boyhood in Europe, and attended school in Switzerland. He spent another year studying medicine in Germany. After his marriage, when he and Flossie traveled, they traveled to Europe, and he sent his sons to the same Swiss school he had attended. Did he ever travel west of the Mississippi except in later years when he went on reading-and-lecture tours to the West Coast? America is not coterminous with the Jersey marshes, which seemed as alien to me as, say, Dordogne. I often wonder what line Williams would have taken if he had not felt the necessity of struggling against Pound's powerful influence, which forced him, in self-defence, to take a stand opposed at all points except one. He, too, belonged to the avant-garde.

Pound's position, on the other hand, could never be defined as primarily opposed to Williams's position, but simply as opposed to the literary establishment, whatever and wherever it might be. Once he wrote to me: "Yes, like Picards." This perplexed me until I realized that by Picards he meant heretics. How much of Pound's opposition to conformity came from conviction, and how much from pure cussedness is anybody's guess, but none at all, surely, was assumed in order to differentiate himself from Bill Williams. Thus, Pound looms large, but chiefly as a figure to be pilloried, in books about Williams, and Williams receives scant attention in Pound biographies.

That Sunday afternoon in 1942 when I was sorting little magazines in the Williams attic, and Bill was reading letters to me, he said: "Here's the first letter I ever had from Ezra." It was an introduction to Viola Baxter, later Viola Jordan. I was especially interested because I had just met Viola for the first time; when he finished reading it to me, I said, "Why don't you give us that letter? You don't love Ezra any more. You don't want to keep it." Whereupon he burst out, "But I *do* love Ezra! How could I *not* love Ezra?" and he went on to talk about all Ezra had meant to him. While he reminisced, I was thinking that if Flossie hadn't been two floors below, he would not have let himself go like that.

Flossie, too, may have mentioned Pound more often because of my association with him; she seemed to me to seize every opportunity to bring him into the conversation in order to disparage him. The first time I visited 9 Ridge Road, I was looking at the Demuth paintings and another watercolor which Flossie pointed out as the work of Dorothy Pound. "It was in the attic," she said, "but when she left him we brought it down and hung it in the living room." Since I knew nothing at all of Pound's private life, I was left with the curious impression that the Pounds were divorced. If Bill bewailed his fate as a neglected poet living on the wrong side of the Hudson (as he sometimes did), Flossie was quick to point out that Ezra Pound could afford to devote himself to literature because he married money. Occasionally Bill flew into a rage about something and wrote a nasty letter that Flossie dissuaded him from sending (as, for instance, a blast at the editors of *Poetry*, who had confused him with Oscar Williams). But Flossie would never have urged him to stay his hand when he wrote the article for *Decision* that triggered the indictment against Pound for treason. I could not blame Williams for wanting to dissociate himself from Pound after his name was used in a broadcast from Rome, but he himself was dismayed at the consequences. Charles Abbott remarked to me one morning soon after the courts handed down the indictment that he had had a letter from Dr. Williams. "His conscience is hurting him," he said. "He wants to know whether there isn't something we can *do?*" Obviously, there was nothing to be done, now.

I seldom feel the impulse to interfere in any way whatever in the relations between two of my friends, and if I do feel the impulse, I almost always curb it; but once when I was at St. Elizabeth's, and Pound made a glancing reference to Bill's animosity, I said, "You know it isn't Bill, really. It's Flossie. She hates you." Pound smiled his most cat-like smile, and said, "I've known *that* for years." I have been told that after Bill's death, she became much more friendly towards Pound, which rather confirms my hunch that her animosity was founded in large part on jealousy—jealousy of Bill's continued affection for Pound, and jealousy *for* Bill, because Pound's fame as a poet, blighted as it was, exceeded Bill's.

To repeat, I could understand how Williams could have written and published his Lord Ga-Ga article. I knew how quickly he reacted with either enthusiasm or fury, and how little likely he was to think of the possible consequences of what he wrote unless Flossie pointed them out to him. What I could not understand was how he could complain—*complain*, mind you—that he never did get paid for that article.

4

My correspondence with Pound drifted to a halt during his last years at St. Elizabeth's. He was exasperated with me, apparently, for giving up on the fresco book, and he was even more exasperated that I was absorbed in the study of mythology instead of translating Callimachus. Considering the kind of muck I was wading through, I could not much blame him, though I thought if he knew what I was doing with the material, he might change his mind. His scrawls became increasingly cantankerous and infrequent, and my letters were perhaps even more infrequent. After his return to Italy I had no further correspondence with him, but I saw him three times, in 1959, 1961, and 1964.

I have read Donald Hall's account of his interviews with Pound in Rome in 1960. The Pound that Hall describes in *Remembering Poets* was mid-way between the Pound of my two visits in 1959 and 1961, when he changed so much that I should never have recognized him. In only two years he made a descent so steep that any resurrection (because it almost amounted to that) seemed impossible. The third time I saw him, in Rapallo in 1964, he was like another Lazarus, and as silent.

In late May of 1959 I was on my way from the gypsy festival at Les Saintes-Maries-de-la-Mer to Brunnenburg when I stopped at Genoa and went down to Rapallo for the day on the off-chance that I might see Pound. I had nothing special to discuss with him, but I wanted to see him again with the free air around him. I had no address, but I knew the hotel where he and Dorothy had dinner every night. I went there and asked for directions. The desk clerk professed ignorance, but the proprietor, overhearing our conversation, said that it would be all right—he should give me the address. The desk clerk then handed over a slip of paper with an address written on it, but I found, when I got to the street indicated, that there was no such number.

I saw no point in going back to the hotel, but I knew the café on the seafront that Pound had frequented before the war. On the chance that he still came there, I sat at a table in front of the café and wrote letters for an hour or so. Finally I looked up and saw him sitting at a table near me. As I approached he crouched ready to spring, his eyes warning me off. I hurriedly introduced myself, whereupon he relaxed and welcomed me happily, saying that he hadn't known of the "transformation." He was referring, of course, to the added thirty-five pounds. He introduced me to Marcella Spann, who was with him, ordered tea for me, and I told him about the mis-direction given me by the hotel clerk. He nodded, and said they were under strict orders not to give out his address, but he told me I should have gone to the stationery shop and asked for "il Poeta." They might not know his name, but they would know where "il Poeta" lived. Marcella left, and, after some discussion of my travels in France, recent and to come, he took me up to the flat to see Dorothy. I wrote briefly, while waiting between trains, about this visit:

> I found them both very frail-looking, and he is not very well—
> bothered much by a deposit of calcium on vertebrae of his
> neck—has had trouble with that spot for years, but couldn't
> persuade anybody that anything was wrong, but now has X-
> rays, which he showed me, and the trouble seems pretty clear—
> arthritis, I should think, the accretion pressing on a nerve in the
> spinal column. He has been bathing in the sea, and sunning, and
> feels better, but can't sit up for long. I rather expected he might
> be very busy, and surrounded by disciples, and look upon my
> visit as an unwelcome interruption, but I think they were both
> very pleased. He mentioned that Viola had not written since he
> got out [of St. Elizabeth's], and I quickly said that she was in a
> pretty bad way, I thought, and that seemed to upset him worse
> than her not writing. I imagine that she would be surprised that
> he even noticed that she hadn't written.

He saw me to the bus when I left, and I took a snapshot of him standing beside it; he was leaning slightly on a cane, making an effort to stand as erect as possible, and scowling as usual at the camera.

Two years later I was at Brunnenburg in October. By that time Pound was in the nursing home at Martinsbrunn on the outskirts of Merano. He was seeing no one except Mary and Dorothy, who was also at the castle. He refused to see even his grandchildren because he did not want them to remember him as he looked then. I had no expectation of seeing him, but someone, probably Dorothy, who went down to Martinsbrunn every day, told him I was there. Then, the evening before I left, Mary and I came home from somewhere or other to find Boris in a great state of excitement. The nursing home had telephoned to say that Signor Pound wanted to see the American signorina. Dorothy had just come back from her daily visit with no word of any such request. It was all very curious. Apparently he had something he especially wanted to say to me, but no one could imagine what it might be.

The next morning I stopped off at Martinsbrunn on my way to the train. Mary warned me several times that I would find her father much changed; she was afraid that I might register shock when I saw him. I dutifully tried to imagine Pound as a very old man, and thought I had succeeded; but she had not conveyed to me that he looked, not like an old man, but like a dead man, with a fleshless head such as one might see on a slab in a morgue. I am afraid my dismay must have been obvious, after all.

Mary had a word with him, his voice barely audible, and then left me alone with him. I had no idea what to do. I waited to see whether he had something of special importance to say to me, talked a little, and waited again. It seemed that he had had a blood-transfusion that morning, and was extremely fatigued. I thought he was also confused, and doubted whether he knew who I was. When he finally spoke, he surprised me by saying, "H. D.'s death was a great loss." H. D. had died in Zurich two weeks before, on September 27th. I was still more surprised when he added, "You never met her, did you?" No, I had not. Although he had given me her address more than once, I had never made the attempt; apparently he remembered that. By now it was clear that even if the thing he had wanted to say to me had escaped him, his mind and memory were still alive. I stayed with him for perhaps half an hour, but never found out why he had sent word for me to come.

I was sure at the time that Pound was on his death-bed; I never expected to see him again. But when, three years later, I was once more in Italy, he was living with Olga in her house at Sant' Ambrogio on the hill above Rapallo. I was traveling from Pisa to Genoa, and decided to stop off to see them. This time I stayed over four nights, and also I wrote ahead to tell them I was coming, so that when I arrived there was a message from Olga waiting for me. We made an appointment to meet next day after lunch at the Café Castello. I knew that Pound had entered his "silent period," and might not speak at all, but I thought that it would not be difficult because Olga and I could do the talking.

I was there before them. To my consternation, as soon as they arrived Olga said, "Now you can have a little visit with

Ezra while I go do some shopping." She then departed. All I could do was to plunge in with a little aimless chatter, to which he made no response. Again, I was not at all sure what his mental state was. He was not looking at me; was he listening? could he hear? could he understand? did he even know who I was? As Sister Bernetta Quinn once said about him: "It is really very difficult to carry on a conversation with someone who doesn't speak unless he has something to say!" Idle chatter seemed a kind of desecration of his silence, and I fell silent. Then I thought, "This won't do," and tried again, saying the first thing that came into my head, not sure whether there was a mind there to reach. I said something about American dependence on the private automobile, which made life very difficult for elderly people. When they could no longer drive, they were isolated from friends, markets, and activities of all kinds. He looked up in surprise, and said, "But then what do your parents do when you are gone?" I explained that my father at eighty-two was still a competent driver and they got along very well. After that I knew I was talking to someone, and went on with more assurance.

Presently Olga returned and we went by taxi up to her villa. She had a new tape-recorder that she was using to record Ezra's reading of his poems. She played one or two tapes, we had tea, and they both walked part way down the hill with me when I left. By that time it seemed to me perfectly clear that his mind was functioning. He could and did speak, but seldom. For the most part he simply chose not to talk.

The next day, I wrote,

if the weather had been good we were going to meet, same time, same place; but it was bad and I was not surprised when she didn't call. Later—about 5 p.m.—I was walking past the Café Castello when I saw them sitting back under the awning. It turned out she had called just a few minutes after I left the hotel, half an hour before. So I sat with them, and with him while she did errands, until 7:30. He speaks *very* little, an occasional question or comment, but seems to enjoy company and listening to us talk, whether he talks or not. He gets around well, and looks very thin, but not bad, except very old. Hard to realize he actually isn't as old as you are. Loss of considerable weight I dare say has something to do with it. They have surprised me no end by their cordiality and hospitality—I say "their" because I'm sure her actions reflect his wishes, too. I understand they are going to Venice on Sunday—whether this is a move for the winter, I'm not sure, but I rather think so.

The following day I met them for lunch. Olga had with her a copy of the Paris *Herald Tribune*, which contained the news that T. S. Eliot had been awarded the Presidential Medal of Freedom. President Johnson had conferred the honor in ceremonies held in the Blue Room of the White House on September 14th. The news article even referred to Eliot by Pound's nickname for him, "Possum."

The strangest thing Pound ever told me was a story about himself and Eliot. He very likely told other people the same story, and it may be recorded somewhere, but I have not found it. He said that when they first met in London in 1914, Eliot was attracting attention by his bizarre behavior. Pound, by his own account, said to him: Look, I'm playing the wild man; why don't you do the other thing? Why don't you play the ultra-respectable, polite and precise young man? So he did. This immediately brought to my mind (with a shiver) Max Beerbohm's story of the man who wore a mask for so long that his face took on the contours of the mask, and he was able to discard it. I have no idea whether the incident as Pound told it is historical or fanciful, but if it is historical, perhaps the end of the story was in its beginning, when they first assumed the contrasting personae.★

After lunch we went up to the villa again, this time riding the bus part way, and then climbing the *salita*. Olga offered to play more of the taped poems for me, and asked if there was anything I would especially like to hear. When I asked whether Ezra had recorded the "Homage to Sextus Propertius," she said

★According to Basil Bunting, Eliot's mask occasionally slipped. See his description of Eliot at a London party (*not* fancy-dress), wearing an enormous cape lined with red, his eyebrows painted green. Eliot's explanation was that he "thought the party needed hotting up a bit." This was in 1926. In *Basil Bunting: Man and Poet* (Orono, Me., 1981), p. 45.

that he had not, and asked him if he would like to "read the Propertius to Mary," while she recorded it. He agreed, and read from the beginning until he broke off suddenly—I believe towards the end of number VI—saying that his throat bothered him. Shortly afterwards, unexpected visitors appeared, and we all went down to the town again in a taxi. I told Olga and Ezra a hasty good-bye in front of my hotel, and left Rapallo, no doubt for the last time, the next morning.

By now the reader is probably wondering, "But when is she going to get to his anti-Semitism?" In fact, the reader may have been suspicious for some time that ugly, anti-Semitic remarks are lurking behind all those dotted lines in the letters I have quoted. The truth is, that the only word in all our correspondence that could be construed as anti-Semitic was a reference in an early letter, the one concerning my application for a Guggenheim, to "the heberew eye." The letter appears in the English edition of the *Letters of Ezra Pound*, but was omitted by the publishers from the American edition. My intention has been to give a picture of the man as I knew him, and I knew him as a master-poet, not a propagandist. For the full portrait the reader must look elsewhere, and there are any number of places to look. I never, in my dozen meetings with him, distributed over a period of twenty-five years, encountered the buffoon that Williams and others have described. I never encountered the crazed megalomaniac the journalists have depicted. His eccentricity was apparent chiefly in the spelling and phrasing of his letters. The manifestations that *are* Pound to those acquainted with him only by report were not the masks he put on when I was with him. It may be that the face he showed me was a mask, and the other faces were the real Pound. I cannot say; but he *seemed* real.

I am not enough of an alienist to debate the question of his sanity, or perhaps I should say the degree of his insanity; and not well enough versed in the law to say whether broadcasting on the enemy radio (from Rome, but not Hanoi) should be considered a capital crime. In the cage at Pisa, during the twelve years in the ward at St. Elizabeth's, and in the long silence of his last years I think he paid enough. And as he might have said, *Basta!*

5

The 1880's were a great decade for the hatching of griffons: Williams born in 1883, Pound in 1885, Marianne in 1887. Add Eliot, 1888; H. D., 1886. There must have been some conjunction of planets presaging the birth of American poets. When Marianne died in February of 1972, Pound was the last survivor of that clutch. He died in Venice nine months later, in November of the same year, at the age of eighty-seven.

Between my move back to Vancouver in 1957 and her death in 1972, I saw Marianne several times, the first time in 1958 in Portland when she spoke at Reed College. She was in fine fettle then, and delighted the students. She told me she "doted" on my *Sappho*, published earlier that year, and asked whether she had written to me about it once, twice, or not at all. I had to say "Not at all," but I was glad to learn that at least she thought she had written.

The next year, a few days after I saw Bill Williams for the last time, I paid my last visit to Marianne's Brooklyn apartment. She was by that time increasingly unhappy about her noisy neighbors and the rundown condition of the building. "But I won't move," she said firmly. "I *won't* move." The thing I chiefly remember about this visit was that she had just finished reading a dissertation on her life and work, written, I believe, by a nun. I had never seen Marianne so indignant. She said that it was full of errors and misinterpretations. The author had said, for instance, that Marianne had originally chosen to major in biology because her mother wanted her to, whereas, she insisted, her mother had nothing to do with it; she chose to major in biology because she liked the subject. The typescript was lying on the table beside her as she talked, and she kept darting glances at it as thought it might be coiled and perhaps ready to strike her. "And the worst of it is," she exclaimed, "that one is supposed to be flattered by this kind of thing!" Her remarks on the dissertation led us to talk more or less about college experiences, and she described the acute homesickness which had made her physically ill during her first year in college. When I said that I had never been homesick, she stared at me in disbelief and repeated, "Never been homesick!" as though she had never heard anything so strange.

Later, I attended a New York poetry reading in which she participated, but I reported that she looked so frail and tired that I thought I would not attempt to see her. After she finally did move, or was moved by her family, to an apartment on West 9th Street near them, I received several brief notes asking me to come to see her. In 1968 I finally had a chance to go, and saw her for the last time. I took with me some color prints of the pond and garden at our new place on the Evergreen Highway. These seemed to please her, and when the fifteen minutes, to which my stay was supposed to be limited, were up, she insisted on my staying on until her niece came. She would have been about eighty-two at the time of this visit, and showed the effect of the strokes she had suffered. She was diminished in stature, stooped, and trembly in her movements, but still with a mind of her own, and that mind very much Marianne's.

There is another glimpse I had of her in her late years that I prefer to remember. I have no idea what year it was, but she was still active, and going about New York alone. I had just stepped on the long, long escalator in the Independent Subway station at 53rd and Madison, on my way up to street level, when I looked up and saw Marianne at the very top on her way down. She was wearing the tricorne hat that had by now become famous. Two young people with rumba drums on their backs had stepped on the escalator immediately ahead of me, and when Marianne's glance fell on those drums, her eyes lit up with excitement. All the long slow way down the escalator, she gazed in fascination, turning to look back when she passed them. I waved to her, but she had no eyes for anything but those drums. I suppose they were the first she had ever seen, and by the time they disappeared from view she must have absorbed every detail. It was not for nothing that her first book of poems was called *Observations*.

But observation and decade after decade of giving to one's mother—what kind of life is that?

When the historian, the biographer, or the autobiographer nears the conclusion of his narrative and looks back over the road traveled, whether by a nation or an individual (including himself), he may see the road as tending inevitably to one destination, without forks or intersections; or he may see in the past all kinds of possible choices of different and better routes (he thinks). The important point to remember when we talk of what would have happened *if,* is that we don't know and can never know whether a different turn would have led to greater happiness or disaster. When you change one factor, you change all of them.

We could assume that if Ezra Pound had remained in the United States all his life, he would not have been guilty of those broadcasts from Rome, but I can only imagine his somehow reaching St. Elizabeth's or its equivalent in an even shorter time if he had remained at Wabash. And we also have to ask ourselves whether twentieth-century American literature would not have been poorer if he had not been manning an outpost in Europe all those years, and keeping communications open. Bill Williams would have said No, because he viewed any European influence as pollution, while Ezra viewed it as pollenization—an extension of his emphasis on interaction between individual artists. However, we must admit that we shall never know the answer to this question, either.

Perhaps I tend too much to see the road traveled as inevitable, given the point of departure and the character of the traveler. When I consider the limitations of Marianne's life and remember a line from one of her early letters ("I have often thought how much better it would be for me if circumstances were different"), I devoutly wish they had been different. On the other hand, when I find Bill Williams lamenting that Marianne's brother disapproved of the literary types she might have "married among," I wish he would talk sense.

In the first place, she could not have married "among" them. She would have had to marry one of them. When I try to think which one, I draw a blank. I seriously doubt that Marianne failed to marry because her brother disapproved of literary types. If she ever said No to a man she wanted because she thought she should take care of her mother, we might, perhaps, call that a wrong turning, although it was one she would not have made unless it was thoroughly in character for her; but it would be a mistake to assume that for Marianne any marriage at all would have been preferable to spinsterhood. The really important thing is that besides the observations she was making and the years she was giving to her mother, she was producing the most important body of work of any American woman poet up to her own day. I know that statement will be disputed by most critics, and—all right—I am willing to make room for Emily, whose life was even more restricted. I suggest that we should not waste our time feeling sorry for either of them.

And this brings us to the question of women poets in general, and what is wrong with us. James Stephens began a famous poem with the line: "Do not let any woman read this verse." Gentlemen, you may close the book.

Perhaps the first thing to consider is the attitude of the two male poets who were my mentors, both of them comrades-in-arms of Marianne in the modernist literary movement. Bill's attitude towards women generally was something I could never quite fathom. He was continuously harping on the importance of the female principle, but he reminded me of a nimble faun in pursuit of a quarry he had no intention of catching. Pound, so far as I could see, set some kind of record for fidelity in diversity. They both liked women, but whether either of them thought that any woman had it in her to be a really first rate poet I doubt; I also can't blame them when I consider our record. Pound at least took as much trouble over a number of young women as if he thought they could perform adequately given proper training, and while it is true that his interest was more than poetic in some cases, it was not so in all—certainly not in my case. And then Pound read Greek and knew Sappho's poetry in the original, so that he knew it had been done once, at least; but Bill was interested in Sappho not because of her poetry, but because she was a lesbian, and lesbians, like prostitutes, fascinated him. Both Pound and Williams respected Marianne's work, but found it lacking, just as they found each other's work not so good as it would have been *if*, and so on.

I never discussed the situation of women in the literary world and the dearth of good women poets with Marianne herself. I wish I had, now, but the subject never came up, probably because neither of us gave much thought to it. I think she would have said, like Eudora Welty, that the important thing is to get on with the job. For what it is worth, here is a brief résumé of my own experience and observation:

First, I grew up thinking that women were already liberated. We had the vote; we wore clothing that allowed freedom of movement; we were welcomed at co-educational colleges and universities; we could travel alone, and pursue our careers in whatever city we chose; instead of being pressured into marriage, we could choose to marry or not to marry. Occasionally I met a man who said that women never had, and therefore manifestly could not do so-and-so—write great poetry, paint great pictures, compose great symphonies—but my view was that we were now about to show them.

I never at any time needed my "consciousness raised." My ego was in good shape, and still is. I was in co-educational classes all the way through school; I did as well as any of the boys in math, and better in English. When, in college, I first began to sense that some (but not all) the professors regarded the education of a female as of secondary importance, I became a little sensitive on the subject, but when I read Virginia Woolf's *A Room of One's Own*, which was published during my second or third year in college, I thought it a wonderful book and took to heart her advice to women writers: do not, like Charlotte Brontë, mount the soap-box and harangue your audience on women's rights when you should be getting on with the story; do not waste time and energy railing against men; abandon any consciousness of your sex when you write, and write simply as a human being.

Nevertheless, I reacted sharply to certain assumptions on the part of my correspondents. When Pound wrote to me about the "likely lad" who needed "something better than average to look after him," my first thought was: "Wait a minute! Who's looking after whom?" When Laughlin wrote, asking me for four copies of twelve of my best poems, because the four men who were to appear in *Five Young American Poets 1940* wanted to pass on the woman to be included, I complied, but not without letting him know how I felt about that. He replied, reasonably, that you couldn't have "a dog-fight in a shoebox." He had not

313

even thought to tell me the names of the four men. I realized, eventually, that I had got in on the quota. Oh well. At least I was in.

Once I forgot myself so far as to write a feminist fable, directed against the kind of man who persists in saying that women are silly, helpless creatures, and then, when he encounters an intelligent and competent woman complains that she is "unfeminine." From here that kind of man seems too ridiculous to waste powder and shot on. Almost every man I have mentioned in this narrative, as well as others unmentioned, have at the very least cheered me on, and some did everything in their power to help me find my next foothold on the sheer cliffs of Helicon. Diarmuid Russell, in particular, could not have done more for any male writer than he did for Eudora Welty and tried to do for me.

I know very well that there has been flagrant discrimination in the academic world, and in the professions of law and medicine, not to mention business. I realize that women in the other arts have a much rougher time of it, but so far as fiction and poetry are concerned, we have to face the facts, and the facts (as I see them) are these:

For the last two hundred years women have been writing and publishing novels. Although they published at first anonymously or under male pseudonyms, their work has been gathered into the mainstream of the English novel. I cannot imagine anyone writing a history of English fiction without mentioning Fanny Burney, Jane Austen, the Brontës, and George Eliot. Besides these well-known names there were many women novelists who were extremely popular in their own time, but are now forgotten. To give only one example: Mrs. Humphry Ward, who was a friend of Henry James, wrote a best-selling novel called *Eleanora*. At the peak of its popularity it was selling one thousand copies a day in the United States, whereas the *entire printing* of James's *The Awkward Age* was limited to one thousand copies. If Mrs. Humphry Ward is forgotten now, it is not because she was a woman, but because she was a bad writer. James tried for years to explain to her about the art of fiction, but complained that he never seemed able to *communicate*.

In poetry we have a different picture. One might easily write a history of English verse without mentioning even one woman, and a history of American verse without mentioning more than two. This, I submit, is not because of male prejudice, but because the English women poets have not been good enough. I want to stress the fact that women were writing and publishing poetry as well as novels, but most of the poetry has disappeared into limbo along with Mrs. Humphry Ward's *Eleanora*. Felicia Hemans was an enormously popular woman poet whose works were published by Byron's publisher, John Murray. Murray sent copies of her books to Byron as they came off the press. Of one, Byron said, "It is a very good poem—very." A later book pleased him less: "Mrs. Hemans is a poet also, but too stiltified and apostrophic, and quite wrong. . . ." She *was* stiltified and apostrophic, and so into limbo with her. Note, however, that Byron (and I am tempted to say—even Byron) did not dismiss her as no good because she was a woman. Jean Ingelow's poems also ran through edition after edition and are now forgotten. The question I should like to have answered is not why more women weren't writing poetry, but why the women who were writing it produced such popular and forgettable stuff.

If the problem is psychological, I can think of only one possible answer, and that lies in a woman's desire to please, whether that desire be learned or innate—a question I won't try to discuss. When a woman is functioning as a woman, in other words as a wife and mother (and I trust we don't want to do away with that), she is oriented towards fulfilling the wishes and needs of her family. If she has a professional attitude towards her role, she is probably a bad wife and mother. (I imagine such a woman serving up crêpes every night for two months, making them fifty different ways, in order to produce eventually the perfect crêpe. Her family, meanwhile, is ready to throw up at the sight of one.) If a woman is a poet, or painter, or sculptor, and is motivated first of all by a desire to please, she is imitative, and produces work that may be extremely popular for a short time, but has no staying power. The novel, as primarily a form of entertainment (at least from Fanny Burney's day through George Eliot's) has lent itself more readily to feminine handling, especially when it is concerned with the things women spend their lives talking about. In the performing arts women train rigorously and a few of them become first rate artists. Encouragement helps to build confidence, which is necessary to any artist, but discipline and self-criticism are equally essential. I have long believed that the thing a young woman artist has most to fear from the male is not the heel of his boot, but the pat on the head and the chuck under the chin. They encourage one to relax and repeat oneself.

Whatever the problem, I doubt very much that women have been thwarted by editorial prejudice. In my day, at least, I cannot remember any feeling that we were being excluded from the feast.

Beginning about 1912, and for fifty years to come, some of the most powerful editors on the American literary scene, on all fronts, were women. Harriet Monroe and Alice Corbin Henderson were editing *Poetry*; Margaret Anderson and Jane Heap edited *The Little Review*; Marianne Moore edited *The Dial*. Henry Seidel Canby was titular editor of the *Saturday Review of Literature*, but everyone seems to have been aware that Amy Loveman was running the show. Katharine White was fiction editor of the *New Yorker* and Louise Bogan was poetry editor. Helen MacAfee edited the *Yale Review*, and Carmel Snow, *Harper's Bazaar*. Irita Van Doren was for many years editor of the *Herald Tribune Books*, the most influential of the weekly review sheets. The men were even complaining that the literary scene was ruled by a matriarchy. Surely none of these women turned down good material simply because it was written by women.

Women are fairly well represented in anthologies of contemporary poetry, but then, alas, they usually have been well represented in their own time. I still think that their work disappears from view after fifty years or so, not because male editors pass over it, but because it does not stand up. In other words, I think we still have to prove ourselves, and I think we can, but we shall do it only by writing better poetry, not by exaggerating the worth of the few famous women poets to whom we can point with pride, and not by lowering our standards so that we can admire women poets better forgotten. Recently I found in one periodical whose women editors should hide their heads in shame, the statement that Sappho was considered the greatest

Greek poet. Nobody in his (or even her) right mind ever said such a thing. She was always, I believe, considered the greatest Greek woman poet; and some have called her the greatest Greek lyric poet; but no one ever suggested she was a greater poet than Homer or Sophocles. About the same time, I found a feminist article stating that Emily Dickinson had been called the greatest poet in the English language. By whom, I should like to know? Someone may have called her the greatest *woman* poet in the English language; someone *might* have called her the greatest American poet; but nobody can conceivably have called her a greater poet than Shakespeare or Chaucer, to name two. This kind of thing simply makes us ridiculous. Let's stop it. And let us not try to recall Felicia Hemans from her well-deserved limbo, but get on with the job of writing better poetry ourselves.

One final word of caution: before we complain that women cannot create great art because "society expects" them to keep house for their husbands and children, let us pause and ask ourselves what society expects of a man? It expects him to earn a living for a wife and children. It looks askance at a man who sits in an upper room year after year writing unpublishable poetry or novels while his wife earns the living or the family endures deprivation. And if he works from nine to five, comes home, pats the kiddies on the head, grabs a bite to eat, and disappears into that upper room to write until midnight or after, he is likely to find himself one day without a wife or children. Unless she is a Flossie Williams, she will have found a man who has more time for her and taken the children with her. And a man's servitude, if he fulfills his role as provider, continues until the children are through college.

I have known a number of talented and ambitious young women whose artistic careers faded out after they took on the responsibilities of family life; but I have known equally ambitious and talented young men who also disappeared from view after the children came. Others have persisted, but under a burden of guilt that must equal that of any woman. In Coleridge's "Dejection: A Letter" he wrote:

Those little Angel Children (woe is me!)
There have been hours when feeling how they bind
And pluck out the Wing-feathers of my Mind,

317

> Turning my Error to Necessity,
>   I half-wish'd they never had been born!

Frost let his family suffer want while he went on and on writing poems he could not publish; when his wife was on her death-bed, and he asked her to forgive him for it, she refused. I am not arguing that a young writer should abstain from marriage, or avoid having children, one or more. I am only pointing out that family life takes its toll from both male and female, I should think about equally.

That being said, it must also be said that many hopeful young writers who have no families to take the blame, also fail and fall by the wayside. The greatest impediment to success in poetry is not the struggle to find the time and a place to write, and not the struggle to publish, bitter as these can be, but the difficulty of the art itself. If you overcome the first two obstacles, the third may still defeat you. To scale the heights, one must be born with eagle wings and lion haunches, but genuine griffons are as rare as unicorns.

Brunnenburg, June 1980
Vancouver USA, July 1981

Index

unpub.), 266, 271–72, 275, 302; "Rapids, The," 135; *Sappho: A New Translation*, 289–91, 292–93, 298–99, 309; "Sheltered Flower, The" (unpub.), 63; "Shoreline," 63, 64, 70, 75, 128; "Suggested Miracle," 122; *Swamp Lake* (unpub.), 242; "Three Fables," 239, 244–45; "Trefoil," 63

Barnard, Mary Melissa, MB's grandmother, 1–2, 8, 27

Barnard, Samuel M. and Bertha H., MB's parents, 2–10, 13–15, 26, 31–32, 45, 49–50, 129–30, 293–94; MB's letters to, quoted: from New York (1936), 83, 86, 87, 88, 92, 95, 97, 99–100; from Yaddo, 106, 122–26; from New York (1938–39), 130–31, 133, 134–35, 138, 145–46, 148, 149–50, 151, 153–54; from Norfolk, 138–43; from Buffalo, 172, 180, 181–82, 183–84, 186–87, 188, 190, 194–97, 198; from New York (1940s), 203–206, 207–209, 211–12, 215–16, 219–21, 224–25, 227–28, 230–35, 236–42, 245, 246, 252–57, 265, 268–70, 275–77; from Italy, 304, 306–307

Barr, Alfred H., Jr., Director, Museum of Modern Art, 162

Barry, Iris (Mrs. John E. Abbott), Curator, Film Library, Museum of Modern Art, 161–63, 165–67, 176, 181, 218, 220–21

Beerbohm, Sir Max, 252, 307; in Rapallo, 259–60

Benchley, Robert, humorist, 208

Benét, Elinor (Mrs. William Rose Benét). *See* Wylie, Elinor

Benét, Stephen Vincent, poet, 30, 36, 188

Benét, William Rose, poet and editor, 30, 36, 94, 211

Berryman, John (1914–72), poet, 181

Betjeman, John, English poet laureate, 218, 222

Biala, Janice, 153

Bill, service man otherwise unidentified (probably William Meredith), 212

Bion: mentioned by EP, 293

Bishop, Elizabeth (1911–70), poet, 68, 98, 123

Blackmur, R. P., critic and poet, 90, 123, 200

Bodenheim, Maxwell, poet, 155–56

Bogan, Louise, poet, 316

Bollingen Award: given to EP, 253, 254, 292

Brecht, Berthold, 218

Breitenbush Books: publishes MB's *Collected Poems*, 285

Brontë, Charlotte, 313, 314

Brooke, Rupert, 29

Browne, Anita: employs MB, 174–75, 219

Brunnenburg Castle, home of Mary de Rachewiltz, 3, 38, 99, 257; MB visits, 258, 262–63, 304

Bryher, English novelist, friend of H. D., 230

Bullock Foundation, 75

Bunting, Basil, English poet, friend of EP, 276, 307n

Burney, Fanny, 314, 315

Byron, Lord, 315

Cage, John, composer, 82, 110

Cage, Xenia Kashavaroff (Mrs. John Cage), 50, 82, 110

Callimachus: mentioned by EP, 293, 301

Call It Sleep (Roth), 126

Canby, Henry Seidel, editor, 316

Cantos (Pound), 251, 290

Cantwell, Robert, author and journalist, 141

Capen, Thomas, Chancellor of the University of Buffalo, 182

Carlisle, Mr. and Mrs., 134, 140–43

Carnegie Foundation, 166, 170, 176

Carousel (Rodgers and Hammerstein), 208

Carpaccio, 265

Catullus, 74; mentioned by EP, 54, 58, 117, 118

Cavalcanti, Guido: mentioned by EP, 54

Designer:	Sandy Drooker
Compositor:	G & S Typesetters, Inc.
Printer:	Vail-Ballou Press
Binder:	Vail-Ballou Press
Text:	11/13 Bembo
Display:	Bembo Italic

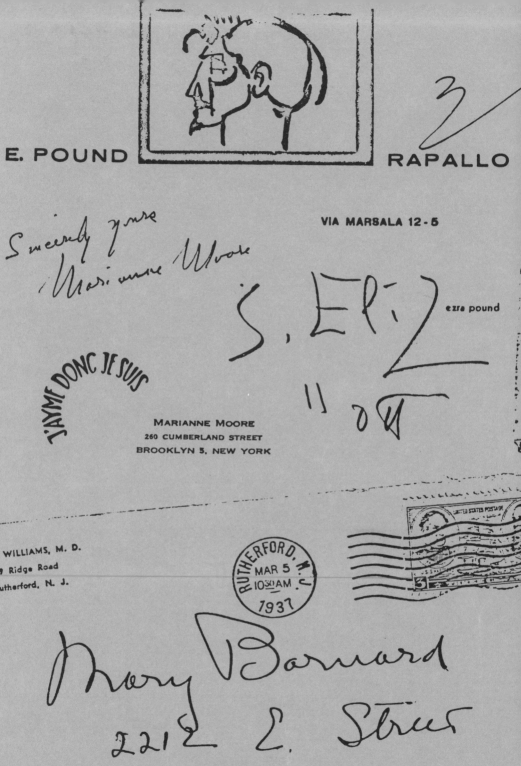

E. POUND RAPALLO

3

VIA MARSALA 12-5

Sincerely yours
Marianne Moore

J'AYME DONC JE SUIS

S. El-2 ezra pound

|| oU

Marianne Moore
260 Cumberland Street
Brooklyn 5, New York

W. C. Williams, M. D.
9 Ridge Road
Rutherford, N. J.

RUTHERFORD, N. J.
MAR 5
10:30 AM
1937

UNITED STATES POSTAGE

Mary Barnard
2212 E. Street
Vancouver,
Washing-